DUKE PAUL OF WUERTTEMBERG ON THE MISSOURI FRONTIER
1823, 1830 and 1851

Hans von Sachsen-Altenburg
Robert L. Dyer

Pekitanoui Publications
Boonville, Missouri

FIRST EDITION
Copyright ©1998 by Hans von Sachsen-Altenburg and Robert L. Dyer
All rights reserved

Manufactured in the United States of America.
Printed by Walsworth Publishing Co., Marceline, Mo.

Typesetting and Book Design by Robert L. Dyer
Pekitanoui Publications, 513 High Street, Boonville, Missouri 65233

Library of Congress Catalog Card Number:
97-78027

ISBN (hdbk) 0-9661902-0-3
ISBN (pbk)   0-9661902-1-1

Excerpt from **Paul Wilhelm, Duke of Wuerttemberg, Travels in North America, 1822-1824**, Translated by W. Robert Nitske and edited by Savoie Lottinville (University of Oklahoma Press, 1973) used by permission.
   Excerpt from the memoirs of C.F. Aehle used by permission of Dr. Mike Aehle, St. Louis, Mo.
   Reproduction of ads from **Missouri Intelligencer** newspaper courtesy of State Historical Society of Missouri, Colubia, Mo.
   Reproduction of William Clark letter courtesy of Western Historical Manuscripts Collection, State Historical Society of Missouri, Columbia, Mo.

Illustrations: Cover and pp. 36-37 used by permission of Schlossmuseum, Bad Mergentheim; pp. 92-94 used by permission of the British Museum, London, England.; top of p. 126 and pp. 132-133 used by permission of the Friends of Historic Boonville; p. 145 used by permission of the Missouri Historical Society, St. Louis, Mo.; p. 155 used by permission of Dr. Mike Aehle, St. Louis, Mo.

All maps prepared by Robert L. Dyer

COVER: Charcoal portrait of Duke Paul of Wuerttemberg ca. 1830 Courtesy of the Schlossmuseum, Bad Mergentheim, Germany.

Table of Contents

Illustrations	4
Acknowledgements	5
Preface	9
Introduction	25
Chapter 1: Paul Wilhelm, Duke of Wuerttemberg	31
Chapter 2: Duke Paul's First Journey to the Missouri Frontier, 1823	43
Travels in North America (excerpt)	59
Chapter 3: The Return of Duke Paul to the Missouri River Country, 1830	81
Chapter 4: Duke Paul's Third Visit, 1851	95
From the Diary of Duke Paul, 1851	100
From the Memoirs of Carl Franz Aehle	153
Chapter 5: Letter from Boonville, 1851	171
Epilogue:	
The Later Years	213
The Flora and Fauna of Duke Paul's Missouri	218
Chronology	236
Bibliography	245
Index	253

ILLUSTRATIONS

Inner courtyard, Mergentheim Castle	36
Duke Paul ca. 1830s	36
Mergentheim Castle, main entrance	37
Map of Germany as it was in 1810	41
From Duke Paul's 1828 preprint edition of **Erste Reise** of 1823	42
Map of the Boone's Lick Country	45
Plats of Franklin and Boonville, Missouri	46
Missouri Intelligencer articles (1823)	57
Map of 1823 Journey	58
William Clark Letter	80
Missouri Intelligencer article (1830)	83
Missouri Intelligencer article (1831)	85
Map of 1830 Journey	86
Duke Paul artifacts in British Museum	92-94
Map of 1851 Journey	99
Duke Paul ca. 1850s	101
Cooper County Courthouse (1840)	114
House of Dr. Augustus Kueckelhan and ad for Kueckelhan's business	116
House of Carl Franz Aehle, ad for Aehle's business and Mike Aehle with portrait of Mrs. Aehle	117
City Hotel and Mansion House Hotel	126
Boonville Map and ad for Pierce's Hotel	127
Joshua Tracy's "Boonville Female Institute" and Rev. William G. Bell's "Boonville Female Seminary"	132
Boonville Wine Company and Central Brewery	133
Page from City Hotel Register (1851)	140
Detail from City Hotel Register	141
St. Ange steamboat and newspaper article about its sinking	141
Episcopal Church, Boonville (exterior and interior)	145
Mr. and Mrs. Carl Franz Aehle and Aehle Coat of Arms	155
Page from the memoirs of C.F. Aehle	156
Plieninger Letter	173
Page from original German edition of the **Letter from Boonville**	179
Page from Duke Paul's original handwritten **Letter from Boonville** with drawing by Duke Paul	185
Drawings of Scotts Bluff and Chimney Rock by Duke Paul	204

ACKNOWLEDGEMENTS

This book is a tribute to a great number of extraordinary people, most of whom remain unnamed:

    The Big Canoe People and other native Americans who lived along the river Pekitanoui.
    The trappers, traders and explorers who followed their own visions of a better life into the Far West.
    The white settlers who decided to make a life for themselves at the beginning of the prairies.
    Captains of riverboats braving snags, sandbars, rapids, floods, ice, and cholera.
    Drivers of coaches on barely passable roads.
    Librarians, historians, and archivists.

This book is also a tribute to a few individuals, all of whom were well-known at one time, but some of whom were forgotten later:

    Pomp, the son of Sacagawea, a child of many worlds.
    Duke Paul, the pioneer Prince, the first royal visitor to Boonville.
    Mr. and Mrs. Carl Franz Aehle, who made a home fit for a prince.
    Dr. and Mrs. Augustus Kueckelhan, who helped when needed.
    Peter Pierce, Prince of Providers, whose Mansion House hotel in Boonville sheltered and helped revive the spirits of an exhausted royal traveller.
    Edward McPherson, whose City Hotel Register in Boonville recorded the presence of a royal visitor.
    And all the other innkeepers along the way.

This book is also in memory of all the beautiful, eternal and yet transitory things:

The butterflies which covered Duke Paul as he made his way upriver to Boonville in 1823.
The eagles which nearly disappeared, but now are coming back.
The forests which are disappearing like the Native Americans they once shaded.
The petroglyphs on the bluffs which were dynamited to make way for railroads.

And, finally, this book is a thank you to those who understand that the future is but a dynamic consequence of past experiences:

Anna Lee Waldo, author of **Sacajawea**.
Martha Clevenger, Missouri Historical Society, St. Louis.
Heinrich Springer, Archivist, Bad Mergentheim, Germany.
Louisa Bowen, Head Archivist, and Leslie M. Bednar, Assistant Archivist, Research and Special Collections, Lovejoy Library, Southern Illinois University, Edwardsville, Illinois. The Betty Alderton Spahn and Raymond Juergen Spahn Collection of Duke Paul von Wuerttemberg Materials.
William Barnaby Faherty, S.J., Archivist, and Nancy Merz, Associate Archivist, Jesuit Missouri Province Archives, St. Louis, Missouri.
Betty Alderton Spahn and Dr. Raymond J. Spahn, Tucson, Arizona.
Dr. Adolf E. Schroeder, Professor Emeritus of

German, University of Missouri, Columbia, Missouri
    Nancy Lankford, Western Historical Manuscript Collection, University of Missouri-Columbia.
    Dr. James Goodrich, Director, State Historical Society of Missouri, Columbia, Missouri.
    Charles E. Hoffhaus, President, The Chouteau Society, Kansas City, Missouri.
    Suzanne Drummond, Boonslick Regional Library, Boonville, Missouri.
    Anita J. von Battaszek, Hannover, Germany, "Mrs. Go-do-it."
    Christy R. Grieff, New York City, consultant in moments of doubt.
    Corina I. Albrecht
    Ron and Jody Lenz, Rivercene Bed and Breakfast, Franklin, Missouri.
    Lela, Paul's pride, had he lived to meet her.
    Jason Fridley, who holds the key.
    The snowplow driver, who let me survive.
    Kirk M. Anderson, Police Officer, St. Charles, Missouri, who did not scold or laugh.
    Dr. David Miller, Dean, School of Liberal Arts, Cameron University, Lawton, Oklahoma.
    Mr. J.C.H. King, British Museum, Department of Ethnography, Museum of Mankind, London, England, who recognizes the Prince Paul Collection as an "invaluable collection."
    Wayne Lammers, Video Memories, Boonville.
    Dr. Andreas Graf, Cologne, Germany, author and specialist on Balduin Moellhausen.
    Dr. Charles Camp, deceased, for having photographed part of Duke Paul's diaries in 1935.
    Dr. Mike Aehle, St. Louis, Missouri, for sharing.
    The Kueckelhan family members in Missouri,

7

Texas, and Germany.

Members of the historical societies of Cooper and Howard counties for their friendship and encouragement.

Laura Gabiger for her close reading, corrections and critique of the manuscript.

Wilma Brengarth Bledsoe for preserving the Boonville hotel register containing the signature of Prince Paul.

Sharon Dyer for indulging an historical obsession.

Note: The spelling of German words reflects the most recent changes recommended by the German speaking countries of Germany, Austria and Switzerland, whereby the so-called *Umlaute* are rendered as *ae, oe, ue.*

PREFACE

Hans von Sachsen-Altenburg

Every book probably contains an element of autobiography. And since this book would not, could not, have come into existence without a certain chain of events, I feel a need to relate some personal notes.

After the fall of the Wall, which had divided East from West Germany from 1961 until 1989, I conducted some research in various archives and libraries previously unreachable for certain "persona non grata" of Communist regimes. While reviewing other documents I found notes about a Paul Wilhelm, Duke von Wuerttemberg, and "an Indian." These notes awakened my interest, and became the basis for later research, which eventually led me to Boonville, Missouri, a small town in the middle of the United States on the Missouri River. But that is jumping ahead.

Who was this enigmatic German Duke who spent more time in other people's castles than his own; this world travelling renaissance man who wanted to know it all, who became the first member of a royal family to journey up the Missouri River and explore the far western trails of the trappers and Indians in America? And who was this "Indian" without a name mentioned in the old papers? To find out, I embarked upon a road of discovery that was at least as unplanned, rocky, and uncharted as any trapper's trail.

In the course of my research, the impatient young duke and the later critic of most establishments became not a task, but a friend to me. As such, I take pleasure in following his steps and thoughts. As he saw the world change from an agricultural, pre-industrial society into a bustling, steam-engine driven world, he realized that major changes were under way that would soon alter the environment forever. As he discovered and recorded with youthful vigor, he realized he was being a witness to a vanishing world.

I have retraced most of Duke Paul's travels, visiting at least the major sites, and found his places of residence and his legacy. Using the meticulous research of others in archives on four continents, I have been able to amass a wealth of evidence that often seems too large to handle. I found that Duke Paul is better known in the United States than in Europe. Unfortunately, much of the information is based on abbreviated and edited transcripts of a German archivist and fraudulent translations by an American professor. Based on the documents now revealed and rediscovered, much of the damage done by that team can now be repaired.

I probably would not have bothered to visit the small, Midwestern river town of Boonville at all if it had not been for Prince Paul's sixth visit in 1851. I wanted to see it, or try to see it, as Paul had seen it and so I planned my visit for December of 1994, almost exactly 143 years to the day that he had made his fateful stop there. My initial guide was Paul's own diary, but I found another guide who would eventually become my collaborator in the writing of this book — a local historian, author and songwriter named Bob Dyer.

How little prepared I was for Boonville! I imagined a tiny, run-down Midwestern village along the river, but what I found was a Sleeping Beauty rich in history of Indian mounds, river captains' mansions, churches, an old opera house, and stories, stories, stories.

Boonville and the adjacent flood plains all the winding way to St. Louis, had still not fully recovered from the flood of 1993. Dirt and debris still blanketed many acres; trees and houses had not been cleansed of the horizontal flood lines. The memory of the awesome power of nature was very much alive there. The river may have shifted a few inches here and there, and the minds of people were adjusted, once again, to respect, to protect, to prepare for next time. As I drove through the Mississippi and Missouri River bottomlands I marveled at the earth moving equipment reestablishing boundaries. Surveyors along the now quiet waters used knowledge developed some five thousand years ago to find imagined lines of ownership washed away or covered with mud. The understanding of this big river had increased one more time, this time recorded by video technology for those who had missed it or would soon forget how bad it really was.

Standing next to Indian mounds on the hills of Boonville, overlooking the northern flats, one could only imagine the checkerboard village of Franklin that had once been home to George Caleb Bingham and Kit Carson and the first newspaper west of St. Louis, the **Missouri Intelligencer and Boon's Lick Advertiser.** Somewhere down there, some twenty or thirty feet below the current cover of silt, are the footprints of a young adventurer from the Swabian hills. Had he fought the drunk assaulters he describes in the journal of his 1823 visit, he could have easily been wiped out. Somewhere in those dusty streets, I thought, Mr. "Benouai" from Bordeaux spoke French with Prince Paul and saved him from the taunts and jeers of the young Franklinites unused to the manner and language of a German Prince. And I also thought of one of the things Paul missed as he left Franklin—the remarkable Botanical Garden of John Hardeman, once flourishing in the bottomlands just upriver from Franklin in 1823, but washed away by the rising waters of the river in 1826.

Thinking about these things, I wondered if anyone else had noted this and the other visits of Prince Paul to Franklin and Boonville? Had anybody bothered to make a written record? In my historical research, I often use the most naive approach: I ask questions, read newspapers and telephone books, walk the streets. I reenact what my character-under-research did or might have done or could or should have done. It is role playing without the dragons, and I am rarely disappointed. Yes, a newspaperman had noted both Paul's coming and going in 1823 and again in 1830. The microfilm records at the State Historical Society of Missouri in Columbia and at the Missouri Historical Society in St. Louis still contain these trivialities. People often say that "Nothing is as old as yesterday's newspaper," but to a historian it is the mythical entry into the talk of the day of a time now beyond reach.

A few people in Boonville, including Bob Dyer, had actually read Prince Paul's diary of the first trip in 1822/24, published in 1835 as **Erste Reise nach dem noerdlichen Amerika in den Jahren 1822 bis 24**. But little knowledge about Prince Paul beyond this diary seemed to have reached Boonville. I felt like I had something to offer.

I walked the steep cobblestone road of the old river landing and told Bob about Duke Paul's and Pomp's return in 1829. The son of Sacagawea had just spent seven years in Europe, returning as Mr. Baptiste, hunter, citizen of Germany. 165 years before my visit, probably to the day, they must have walked these stones, reminiscing of vanished Franklin and restoring both strength and supplies.

Bob introduced me to the beautiful paintings of

George Caleb Bingham. I found one most mesmerizing—**Fur Traders Descending the Missouri**. Had Bingham seen Prince Paul and "Pomp" in their pirogue in 1830, and could this painting have been inspired by what he saw? Paul's diary of this voyage was either lost or destroyed sometime later. However, in his 1851 diary Paul recalls his descent in a pirogue from the "falls" to St. Louis, accompanied by a tame eagle. It is not certain whether Baptiste accompanied him on this trip, but there is reason to assume that he did. And that is what I saw in Bingham's painting—a memory of that visit.

On Duke Paul's 1830 trip he had ascended the Missouri further than before, hunted, collected and bought a boatload of valuables; and on his way downstream to St. Louis, Paul undoubtedly rested in Boonville. Some of the items collected on that trip, securely packed and moored at the Boonville landing for a short time, are still the pride of museums in Berlin and Stuttgart, and of the British Museum in London.

Bob and I walked and drove through Boonville, following the streets laid out many generations ago. This is where thousands left civilization behind and prepared to enter the prairies. This is where thousands had breathed in deep, exhaled the past and drew strength for what lay ahead of them.

Bob knows his hometown history as if he had written the book, which, in fact, he did. We discussed the likely and unlikely sites of the Mansion House hotel, mentioned in Duke Paul's diary. The local historical records are not clear and point to three possibilities. One was now a neglected ruin, the other a private residence, the third a parking lot.

How about the Kueckelhans? An advertisement for Dr. Kueckelhan's drug store was soon located in old newspapers and his home still stands in Boonville. Descendants were located nearby, others in Texas. I later visited their original home and town near Braunschweig in Germany, where people with the same name still live, telling of ancient immigration from Switzerland.

The Aehle house, another residence where Duke Paul felt at home in Boonville, was demolished about the turn of the century (though a photograph of it survived), and the lot where it once stood is now home to a convenience store. The family originated from a small town in the Duchy of Altenburg; descendants still reside near Boonville and in St. Louis. Prince Paul had immortalized Kueckelhans and Aehles in his writings. Were there any traces of his visit in this town?

"Well, there are the memoirs of Carl Franz Aehle," Bob said, "he writes something about Duke Paul's visit." I must have looked like the incredulous, blind chicken that found a piece of corn! Mike Aehle is a professor at Meramec College in St. Louis teaching technical drawing. Like many other family members, he has inherited C.F. Aehle's musical talent. He had recently made available to Bob a photocopy of his great-great-grandfather's handwritten diary written nearly fifty years after Duke Paul's visit.

Just as incredible was the next discovery. "You know, I have a partial copy of an 1851 guest register from one of Boonville's hotels," Bob said, "but I'm not sure what months the register covers." Miraculously the guest register began in the very week of December 1851 that Duke Paul arrived in Boonville. And there it was in the nearly illegible scrawl of a very ill, very exhausted man—"Prince Paul Wurttg, Germany."

My own visit to Boonville was marked by many smaller miracles relating to Duke Paul's visit here in

1851. Bob took me on a tour of the town, pointing out houses and buildings that would have been here in 1851: the clapboarded log cabin of the Swiss emigrant, George Hain; the old Turner Hall—a Baptist church when Paul came to town, but later the home of the Boonville Gesangsverein, and presently being renovated by David Oswald; the stone jail built in 1847; and the Episcopal Church where Paul attended Lutheran services with the Aehles. In January of 1995, this honorable structure was the auditorium where I had the honor of addressing members of the Boonslick, Cooper County, and South Howard County historical associations and descendants of Dr. Kueckelhan, speaking on the subject of Duke Paul's visit.

I was also invited by the Boonslick Historical Society to stay at Rivercene, the gracious home of the riverboat captain, Joseph Kinney, built in 1869, which had been damaged by the recent flood but expertly restored by Ron and Jody Lenz, who had purchased it to operate as a bed and breakfast.

Yet, there seemed to be something missing: How to describe Prince Paul's feelings after or during a snowstorm? As if by doctor's orders, the snow arrived. "It'll be a bad one!" they said on the eve of my presentation at the University of Missouri in Columbia. "Don't talk too long or we'll get snowed in," they admonished in Boonville. Living in more temperate climate zones, I knew not how to heed such advice.

The snowstorm struck through the night and the next morning, keeping us inside for many more hours than planned. So we delighted in the comfort of a well-heated mansion, a delicious breakfast and hot coffee. Quite unlike Paul's experience.

In 1851, Duke Paul was caught in a blizzard that

was later remembered by others as well. He was on the superhighway of that time, the Oregon Trail, not far west of Kansas City, heading for St. Louis. His horses died, and he had to leave his travelling companion to his own fate; emaciated and ill, Paul arrived in Boonville. Great story.

After the white fury had abated, we continued to review ideas at Bob's home, the radio reports telling of I-70 being closed to traffic. When the situation had come under control of man, so they thought, I braved the adventure.

I left my more sensible companion, a descendant of Duke Paul, with relatives in Columbia and headed toward St. Louis. Headed is, in fact, the right term, as it actually implies no movement. As this book will probably be read by people having experienced more blizzards than I would ever care for, I will not bore you more than necessary. Suffice it to summarize. With the renewed onslaught of another snowstorm, I cannot say which vanished faster, my visibility or my courage. Stuck between trucks, crawling at ten miles an hour, I was in the middle of what I had wanted so badly to experience while in the comfort of a reclining armchair. I had a radio, a portable telephone, a tank full of gas, crackers to last until the next fast food place, plenty of books to read in case of a little delay. Frankly, I started to take delight in the knowledge that travelling today was a lot easier than for Paul in 1851.

One or two miles east of the city limits of Columbia my adventuresome spirit surrendered to common sense. But how could I justify such cowardice? What would Paul have said? I didn't care. Maybe this was not the optimal time for literary research or historical role playing. So I took the next exit and returned to Columbia.

On the phone, Dr. Adolf Schroeder gave me precise directions to his home, advising me not to go down one certain road but to leave the car up on the hill and to walk the rest of the way. A ten minute ride took nearly one hour, and my car slid down the very road I was not to take. Immovable in a ditch, it served as an ideal warning to others. Goodbye airplane to the sunny South as I had planned.

After a delightful evening in the book-filled house of the history and language professor, my idea of a wigwam, we spent the better part of the following day trying to free my car. This proved to be as successful as waiting for a stage coach to pass by in 1851. During the early afternoon, as the news programs were full of the record breaking blizzard, I was able to resume the trail. In short, I spent twenty minutes driving, six hours standing, then three hours driving, and arrived in St. Charles close to midnight. Too tired to see straight, I managed to get my car stuck on a curb with the rear tires dangling in the air. After some two hours, during which the friendly St. Charles police officer Kirk M. Anderson tried to help me, I finally got some sleep. My very own blizzard was over.

Before I end this introduction I want to address a few final words to young people in particular and historians in general: This book is but a fragmentary result of methodical and personal research. As such it may at times be a little dry; after all, the subject matter is some 144 to 172 years old at the time of this writing. To understand everything one would have to review the Zeitgeist, the entire understanding, of the people at that time: how they looked at life, politics, problems and challenges. There is plenty of good material for school and college papers.

17

There is another message. Historical research is the study of a dynamic process of people's activities. The people mentioned in this book lived and laughed, ate and drank, thought and traveled, slept and cried. And their history can be researched, told, retold, interpreted. Each time somebody touches it, it may change a little, due to newfound facts. The elements described in this book are, not were, part of the history of Franklin, Boonville, and Missouri. Reviving that history can enrich all of us.

Perhaps this book may encourage some readers in their own search for historical facts, for ancestral roots, and ultimately, of course, for themselves. Life continues through heirs; land gets re-used; buildings rarely disappear without a trace; important papers and messages often were copied and stored elsewhere. Historical research is a living activity—as dynamic and exciting as every day of our lives.

So let this book be a new "Letter from Boonville."

Robert L. Dyer

I would like to acknowledge the fact that the inspiration for this book and the preponderance of the research that lies behind it are solely due to the indefatigable Hans von Sachsen-Altenburg. He has spent many years gathering and analyzing the materials presented here. I, on the other hand, have merely supplemented his work with a few missing, albeit important, pieces of the puzzle.

A work of the sort presented here lies at the very heart and soul of my interest in history, and perhaps it would not be too out of place to explain how my own particular interests led me to a crossing of paths with Hans and Duke Paul. It is a story that begins with the place where I was born and raised and where I have lived the greater part of my life.

    Boonville, my home town and the place that provides the focal point for this book, is the oldest surviving town on the Missouri River west of St. Charles. It is the county seat of Cooper County and lies in the center of the historically significant Boone's Lick country of central Missouri where the first permanent white settlers arrived about 1810. Its ghostly twin, the long vanished town of Franklin that once perched precariously on the opposite bank of the river in the vulnerable bottom lands, actually preceded it in time by a few years and eclipsed it in fame for nearly a decade until the flooding river washed it away. Boonville, wisely platted on the hills along the south bank of the river, has survived and has managed to maintain a slow but steady growth without sacrificing some of the more significant aspects of its 19th century origins. Many of the older homes and buildings remain intact and continue to be cared for. A goodly portion of the townspeople as well as the families in the nearby rural areas can trace their families back to the early settlers and builders of the town.

    When I was a young lad growing up here fifty years ago my interest in the town's history was sparked by the tales of various colorful older citizens who had taken it upon themselves to study and perpetuate the local heritage. Many of the stories they told related in one way or another to the great river that swirled its muddy way along the northern edge of the town beneath the watchful though invisible gaze of the nameless Native Americans buried in the mysterious mounds in the city park where I often played with my friends.

    My nascent interest in the town's and the river's history eventually grew into a full-fledged passion after

I entered the nearby University of Missouri and discovered the rich resources of the university library, which included the endlessly fascinating research materials maintained by the State Historical Society of Missouri. I also found myself being slowly but inevitably drawn under the influence of several remarkable teachers, the most important of whom was probably John G. Neihardt, a spry, elfish poet with a thick mane of white hair, a voice that could raise the hair on the back of your neck and a tangible spiritual aura. Neihardt had studied, lived with and written about the plains Indians for much of his life producing a number of fascinating works including two masterpieces—**Black Elk Speaks,** which contains a spiritual and narrative history of the Lakota people as well as the awesome personal vision of the Lakota holy man, Black Elk; and **Cycle of the West**, a sweeping Homeric-style epic poem about the tragic but inevitable clash between white settlers pushing their way west across the continent and the Plains Indians who futilely tried to maintain a lifestyle incompatible with the demands of the encroaching white man.

Neihardt's personal vision was intimately related to the landscape of his subject matter, and particularly to the extensive watershed of the Missouri River valley. Under his mentoring influence my localized passion for history, folklore and legend expanded and found a connection to a larger pattern that I had been only dimly aware of until then. I also found myself becoming increasingly drawn to the medium of literature and, specifically, poetry as the means of expressing my interest in history.

I obtained a master's degree in English, taking a job as an English instructor at the University of Missouri, writing poetry, playing the guitar, singing folk songs, writing my own folk-influenced ballads, and voraciously reading every thing I could get my hands on related to Indians, the Missouri River and the history of the West. A chance to participate in the historical survey of Boonville and Cooper County drew me back to my hometown where I took a job teaching English at Kemper Military School and College, a pioneering local educational institution that dated back to 1844, where my grandfather served as vice-president and treasurer for fifty years prior to his death in 1955.

My immersion in the history of the town and the surrounding countryside as a result of the historic survey soon led me into the long neglected files of the military school and the preparation of a book length manuscript on its history. At the same time, my accumulation of a number of folk-style ballads about various aspects of local as well as Missouri River history resulted in the production of a recording called **River of the Big Canoes** (the Missouri Indians, for whom the river and the state were named, were the "Big Canoe People") and another called **Treasure in the River**. I was also developing an irresistible itch to put my voluminous files on local history into a book that would celebrate the town's heritage. I formed my own publishing company, Pekitanoui Publications and eventually published the book in 1986 as **Boonville: An Illustrated History**.

My research into the history of the river and the town led me at one point to a very interesting book based on the journals of Duke Paul of Wuerttemberg, the first member of a European royal family to travel up the Missouri River in the first decades of the 19th century. His journey up the river in 1823-24 brought him to the very doorstep of Boonville, though at that particular point in time Franklin, on the opposite bank of the river, was the only town of consequence in the area, and it was there he paused briefly, trading his means of conveyance from keelboat to horse and wagon. Duke Paul's colorful description of the Boone's Lick country as he passed through it provided me with my first detailed view of the area at this very early and highly significant period of time—a time when the Santa Fe trail (which originated in Franklin in 1821) was in its infancy, as was the town of Boonville.

Later, while searching through the extensive files of old Boonville newspapers at the State Historical Society, I ran across another interesting and surprising mention of Duke Paul. He had passed through Boonville at least one other time in 1851. A turn of the century newspaper item mentioned that a log house on the northeast corner of Spring and 6th Streets, which had once belonged to an old German immigrant citizen named Carl Franz Aehle, was being torn down, and that it once had the distinction of housing Duke Paul of Wuerttemberg for several weeks as he recuperated during difficult winter weather on his return from a trip to the West.

And then in 1991 as I was working to save a beautiful old brick mansion on Boonville's Main Street from the wrecker's ball, I discovered that it, too, had once belonged to Carl Franz Aehle. He had, in fact, built the house in the mid-1850s to accommodate a family that had outgrown the smaller log house on the northeast corner of Spring and 6th Streets. My attempt to save the house from destruction proved futile, but in the process I made a contact with one of Aehle's descendants, Mike Aehle, in St. Louis and he came to town, not only with photographs and a painting of his great great grandfather, but also with a long, hand-written reminiscence that Carl Franz Aehle had completed in 1898, not too many years before his death. One of the many fascinating parts of this reminiscence was a two page description of his encounter with Duke Paul of Wuerttemberg during the winter of 1851 and his memory of the Duke's amazing account of surviving a nearly fatal encounter with a blizzard on the Great Plains.

At the time I came across these pieces of information about Duke Paul's visits to Boonville, they were only part of a much larger mosaic of the town's history, and they disappeared into my voluminous local history files; but they would eventually take on an importance of their own that I could not have foreseen when I first discovered them.

In the fall of 1994, Suzanne Drummond, one of our local librarians, gave a letter from Hans-Werner, Prince of Sachsen-Altenburg to another local historian, Florence Friedrichs, who then forwarded me a copy. The letter was a request for any information we might have about a royal visitor named Duke Paul of Wuerttemberg to Boonville in late 1851.

As soon as I read the letter, I remembered those various bits of information I had discovered about Duke Paul in my own researches, and I dug them out of my files and sent them to Hans. I also told him I would very much like to meet him if he came to the area for further research, and I invited him to speak to a gathering of the Boonslick Historical Society, of which I was then the president.

In January 1995 Prince Hans arrived in Boonville anxious to delve deeper into Duke Paul's visit to the town in 1851. Since he has already described what happened next, I will end my own account here at this fortuitous crossing of many paths. Suffice it to say that it is this crossing of paths that continues to keep me interested in studying the past, for it has been my experience that an

23

exploration of the past almost inevitably leads me to the very doorstep of the present and it is this conjunction of past and present that somehow lends a greater significance to our otherwise often mundane, hurried, and distracted lives.

INTRODUCTION

Several important explorations of the Missouri River valley, resulting in published accounts, were made in the early 19th century. The best known of these was, of course, that of Lewis and Clark in 1804/06; but the accounts of Brackenridge and Bradbury in 1811, and of Major Stephen Long in 1819/20 were also important.

Yet another exploratory trip, not nearly as well known as these others, however, was the one made by Duke Paul von Wuerttemberg in 1822/24. He was the first member of the German aristocracy to travel the region, make precise scientific observations and publish his journals (1835). His trip, in fact, came ten years before the 1832/33 trip of the German aristocrat, Prince Maximilian von Wied-Neuwied, whose published account is more widely known, probably largely due to the excellent illustrations executed by his travelling companion, the Swiss artist Karl Bodmer.

Duke Paul, however, had a more thorough scientific education than Prince Maximilian and the journal of his 1822/24 trip is not only highly readable but is also filled with precise environmental, socio-economic and historical information. Duke Paul was, in fact, a prolific writer, who kept diaries containing thousands of pages of notes on twenty years of travelling over five continents (North and South America, Australia, Asia, Europe and Africa) including two more trips in the Missouri River valley in 1830 and 1851. Unfortunately, these later diaries and notes were bequeathed to a friend who was unable (or unwilling) to cope with their sheer mass and thus put them in storage where they were forgotten for over seventy years. Indeed, many of these papers were thought to have been destroyed sometime near the end of

World War II, but recently major portions of the journals, together with many drawings and other papers, have been rediscovered.

In his time, Duke Paul was recognized as an eminent scientist, of equal rank with Humboldt, Catesby, Audubon and Nuttall. He amassed the largest-ever natural science collection, which included more than 100,000 articles ranging from seeds to stuffed giraffes, many of which were exhibited in his 11th century castle. A few years after his death, however, the collection was dispersed. Some remnants have recently been found and documented in Berlin, Stuttgart, and in various private collections. In 1997-98, the bicentennial of Duke Paul's birth, the British Museum in London will show for the first time selected pieces collected on Paul's first trip up the Missouri River in 1823.

In addition to Duke Paul and Prince Maximilian, other royal German travelers in America during the 19th century have included: Alexander Baron von Humboldt, who travelled through Latin America and the eastern United States between 1797 and 1810; Bernhard Duke von Sachsen-Weimar-Eisenach, who travelled through the eastern U.S. between 1825 and 1826, and published a little-known account of the trip in 1828; Wilhelm Eugen, Duke von Wuerttemberg, who travelled through the eastern U.S. and in the West Indies in 1868, later publishing an account of the trip entitled "Six Months in America," no copies of which are presently known to exist; and Ernst Baron von Hesse-Wartegg, who travelled on the Mississippi River between 1879 and 1880 and published a frequently quoted account of the trip that was partially copied by Mark Twain.

In 1823, on his first journey to America, a youthful and inexperienced Prince Paul found a rough river town,

Franklin, about two hundred miles up the Missouri River from St. Louis situated in the bottomlands and defying the voices of riparian experience. In the hills on the opposite side of the river from Franklin were a few straggling log houses and stores where another town, Boonville, had been platted some four years earlier, but Boonville would not come into its own until some five or six years after Paul's 1823 visit to Franklin.

Here, at the dangerous but exciting edge of civilization, the young royal exchanged the planks of a keelboat for a horse and cart, eager to discover whatever life would offer. On his return four months later, he was accompanied by a young half-breed named Jean Baptiste "Pomp" Charbonneau, half Shoshone Indian and half French trapper. Pomp was the son of Sacagawea—the "Bird Woman" who had helped those famous American explorers of the West, Meriwether Lewis and William Clark, reach the western ocean beyond the Shining Mountains. Following the expedition he became the foster child of William Clark, explorer and later governor of Missouri, who saw to his early education in the city of St. Louis. When Duke Paul came to the Missouri River in 1823, Pomp was working at one of Chouteau's trading posts at the mouth of the Kansas River. Paul had heard about Pomp from Clark when he consulted with him in St. Louis before leaving on his upriver journey. After actually meeting the boy he decided he would take him back to Germany with him.

Seven years later, when Paul and Pomp returned to the Missouri River they were no longer the inexperienced, innocent and naive young men they had been in 1823. Duke Paul was on the rebound from a disastrous marriage and Baptiste had seen the nations and systems of the White Man across the sea; there was little room left

27

for illusions. The youthful exuberance of the frontier town of Franklin had also disappeared, for Franklin had vanished in the muddy waters of the Spring of 1826 and now Boonville on the opposite bank of the river was the new queen city of central Missouri, overlooking the flooded and forsaken ruin of Franklin in the bottomlands.

Duke Paul returned to the Missouri River for the third and last time in 1851. Following a frustrating journey to Fort Laramie in the upper Platte River country, Paul and his travelling companion, Balduin Moellhausen, set out on their return trip to St. Louis across the plains and were caught in a blizzard that nearly killed them both. Miraculously rescued, Paul made his way back to Independence leaving Moellhausen to be rescued later. As he journeyed by coach from Independence to St. Louis he stopped in Boonville and decided to stay there for awhile to recover from his fatigue, illness, and the weather. Never before had he been as close to visions of death, but when he reached Boonville he discovered friendship and human warmth. The town and its inhabitants accommodated a desperate, depressed traveller; and so the lonely stranger rested and enjoyed the warmth of Boonville as the temperatures plummeted to record lows.

As he recuperated he composed the longest letter he ever wrote — a letter describing his adventures and his observations about the country and people he had passed through. Until a few weeks before the writing of this book, it had not been known to whom Duke Paul had actually addressed this **Letter from Boonville**, which was published by the leading newspaper in Germany not long after it was written, and which set all of central Europe talking about the town upon the hills of the

Missouri River where civilization meets the wilderness and where a German Prince recuperated from Indian attacks and blizzards. A recent discovery in the archives of a cover letter from Professor Plieninger, a contemporary and highly respected environmental scientist, solved the mystery. The professor had asked for regal permission to publish an edited version of the letter he had received from Paul.

Boonville had found a place on German maps. In the four published installments of the article one could read of adventure, of freedom, of self-determination, of strength gained from overcoming adversity. This was not a real estate salesman's prospectus. This was real life.

We don't know how many people followed the call they heard from Boonville in Duke Paul's letter, but record numbers of German immigrants, including many from Duke Paul's home country of Wuerttemberg, settled on the shores of the lower Missouri River in the years following its publication.

The royal visitor was never granted an opportunity to return to Boonville. After several other travels, including South America and Australia, he suddenly died amidst his huge collection of scientific treasures in his castle. There is evidence he planned to leave Germany forever but was unable to complete his plans.

Unbeknownst to his own family, and to historians, Paul had discreetly prepared his family's escape from the Old Country. In the hundreds of documents I have read in his handwriting, I have come to understand the thoughts of this restless man who had no steadier home than his diaries and scientific observations. Caught and shaken in a post-Napoleonic era that screamed for more democracy and individual freedom, he was a prisoner of his dynastic environment. Ruthlessly suppressing the hopes of more freedom, the Bourbons were restored to the throne of France, and European kings — both those who were kings because of Napoleon and those who still were kings in spite of him — assured their own survival. Paul's escape was to the world at large, the sciences, the unknown. His happiness was in America; and in his little girl, Pauline, not found on any genealogical table of the Royal House of Wuerttemberg, yet cheerfully sitting on a swing attached to the family tree. But that is the subject for another book.

    The focal point of this book is Duke Paul's 1851 trip up the Missouri River from St. Louis and then up the Platte River Road to Fort Laramie and back again (with a few glimpses at his earlier journeys of 1823 and 1830 up the Missouri River, as well as some necessary biographical material). More specifically, the book focuses on Duke Paul's passage through the historically important Boone's Lick country of central Missouri, and especially on his stop at Boonville on the return from the arduous and nearly fatal journey across the Great Plains in the midst of a terrible blizzard. As Paul recuperated in Boonville he wrote his famous "Letter from Boonville," never before published in translation. More about Duke Paul's life and journeys is presently being prepared for publication. For now, however, here is a description of Duke Paul's three journeys through the Missouri frontier and his "Letter from Boonville" to whet your appetite.

CHAPTER 1
PAUL WILHELM, DUKE OF WUERTTEMBERG
1797-1860

Hans von Sachsen-Altenburg

Gypsy Prince they called him, derisively, in German courtly circles. His never ending quest for adventure became the table talk of noble dinners. Is he not the crazy duke who styles himself sometimes Baron, sometimes Count, sometimes General? Is he not the one who forsakes gold-studded halls, endless banquets, beautiful women, in exchange for mosquitoes, bad horses, frost bite, and Indian attacks? Is he not the one who fills his medieval castle with stuffed animals, skeletons, insects, roots, plants, and snakes, rather than with gold, marble, pictures, guests, and laughter? And then all those tall stories he tells; were they true, they would be incredible. And that Indian boy he brought home from the Wild West, a good looking lad, a true noble savage, just like Rousseau had written about. But does one invite a savage, even if he is noble, to dinner?

Very few facts about Paul Wilhelm, Duke of Wuerttemberg, are publicly known. Virtually none of the archived documents dealing with his life have ever been published. In fact, most of them have probably not been read by anyone for many decades because they were misfiled or sealed in various inaccessible vaults.

Paul's personal history is firmly embedded within the circumstances of his family's powerful position in central Europe. Even though the unruly young man often tried to break the mold he was expected to assume as a young student and military officer, he never actually escaped the dynastic shackles. He found true personal freedom only in the woods and prairies. But such freedom was, either by design or by intent, short lived. His name, his aura, his fame would precede him; his knowledge and scientific quest would betray him; his past would always determine his future. The man could not become a great man because he was one already.

The family of the Dukes of Wuerttemberg had amassed territories and wealth for some six hundred years. There was no question in the minds of subjects about their ruling "by the grace of God." These dukes were militarily and economically successful, owning lands and people in regions now belonging to France, Switzerland, Poland, and, of course, Germany.

Paul's early life was basically determined by three men: Uncle Friedrich, reigning Duke of Wuerttemberg, a ruthless and self-serving man who was to become King by collusion with, and by the grace of, a French usurper; brother Eugene, an eminently successful military leader, whose family resided in the castle of Carlsruhe, Silesia, the seat assigned for younger branches of the family; and Napoleon Bonaparte, a ruthless soldier who was to shake and realign the world.

King Friedrich, the oldest brother of Paul's father, was both politically and physically ambitious. In a time when girth told of wealth, Friedrich's girth led Napoleon to gasp: "King Friedrich is God's experiment in how far the human skin can possibly stretch." The King's self-serving and military nature forced Paul into a disciplined and military career, but he frequently rebelled against the role assigned to him. The files are full of royal reprimands and Paul's respectful but schematic devotion.

Paul's brother, Eugene, had followed a military career with significant intricacies. He had accompanied his aunt, a princess of Wuerttemberg, to St. Petersburg where she married Czar Paul, son of Catherine the Great. Eugene had been made a Russian general at age ten. There is evidence, little known in the Western World, of Czar Paul trying to circumvent the succession of his own children in favor of Eugene. After the murder of Czar Paul, Eugene moved back to Germany and joined the anti-Napoleonic forces of Prussia and, later again, Russia. His extraordinary military skills, proven in numerous battles between Crimea and Germany, came to a climax when he attacked the retreating army of the French emperor, giving him the honorary distinction of being called the Victor of Kulm. The most notable statement about Eugene's private life may be that Caroline, daughter of the German poet Friedrich von Schiller, became the governess of his children at the same time Paul and Pomp were in Carlsruhe.

Paul was born Friedrich Paul Wilhelm in the castle of Carlsruhe, a month after King Friedrich had married Charlotte, daughter of King George III of England and Hannover. This union probably kept Wuerttemberg within the confines of today's Germany rather than France. (Both George's mother and his mother-in-law were leaves of the Sachsen-Altenburg tree, which may have been the family's most significant contribution to American independence.)

During his childhood he was called Prince Friedrich Paul. In later years, after Prince Heir Wilhelm had ascended the throne, a politically correct and adulatory shift from Friedrich Paul to Paul Wilhelm occurred. Bestowed with many names and titles, Prince Paul would later travel under the names of Baron or Count von Hohenberg (High Mountain) or Count Heidenheim (Heathen Settlement), both after actual places in the mountains between Wuerttemberg and Bavaria. In America he was forever Prince Paul, both in address and signature, but in Germany he was Paul Wilhelm, Herzog von Wuerttemberg.

The third person to influence Paul's life was Napoleon Bonaparte—the stranger, the usurper, the admired, the detested—even though the two probably never met. Napoleon had taken over the leadership of France and ended the anarchy that developed following the French Revolution. But the "little man's" assumption of power was not enough to satisfy his ambitions. He wanted to dominate all of Europe. Since such costly plans could not be financed by taxes and levies alone, Napoleon acted no differently from any president of a large corporation in that he sold assets for cash, and traded and bartered for revenues and support. And since buying and selling leads to faster profits than manufacturing, Napoleon acquired lands by treaty or military might, to be sold or granted to others for instant or future profit. The huge territory of Louisiana, useless in European eyes, was just another asset to be used. The problem was that Napoleon did not own it. But there were potential buyers, eager and rich, namely George III of England, seeking ways to eclipse the American revolutionaries. Or the Americans themselves, still fearing the might of the King they had humiliated in their Declaration of Independence.

In a masterpiece of diplomacy, not unlike some of the practices of modern business management, Napoleon's diplomats created anxieties in the Americans by closing the Mississippi, thus suggesting to them the need for immediate action. Concurrently, reasons to transfer the territories from Spain back to France were created on dynastic levels, involving the royal house of

Spain and the duke of Parma, Italy. Assuming this trade in real estate futures would eventually take place, a sale was negotiated and concluded between France and the United States. The Lewis and Clark expedition and the fame of Sacagawea were thus a consequence of Napoleon's greed. Similarly, the well-connected duchies of Wuerttemberg and Bavaria made real estate deals, giving up baronies and counties west of the Rhine river in exchange for other promised territorial and political gains. During the months when Sacagawea carried her son, Pomp, across the Continental Divide, significant dynastic links were negotiated, along with secret promises for the future, between the Bonapartes and the Dukes. During the very days when Lewis and Clark established camp at the Pacific Ocean, the Kingship of Wuerttemberg was a Christmas present for Friedrich, later sealed through the bond of marriage between the two families: Friedrich's 24 year-old-daughter Katharine was to wed Hieronymus Bonaparte, King of Westphalia. The Dukes of Bavaria were not a day behind in the official proclamation of the kingdom. The dynastic unification, the wedding between beautiful Auguste Amalie and Eugene Beauharnais, took place two weeks thereafter.

    The transfers of land ownership took many years, often involving protest, massive military suppression and the death of civilians. Most eminent was the region and city of Mergentheim. For centuries, this medieval town had enjoyed complete political sovereignty under the leadership of the Knights of the Teutonic Order, who were now being expelled from all German territories. The ancient water castle of Mergentheim, which for centuries had served as headquarters for the knights, was to become the assigned residence of Duke Paul and

Inner courtyard of Mergentheim Castle (Paul and Pomp lived on the top floor in the left wing of this castle)

Duke Paul Wilhelm von Wuerttemberg ca. 1830s

Mergentheim Castle, main entrance

Pomp in 1827.
   In the aftermath of an ill-fated strategic decision to invade Russia, Napoleon was defeated in October 1813. It took very little time for King Friedrich to change over to the side of the winners.
   Prince Paul had to follow a career that was common for men of his standing and rank within the family. Paul was the fourth son, the second surviving infancy, of the second younger brother of the king. Not yet ten years old, he became commander a la suite, and by the age of seventeen he was officially declared a commander in the cavalry.
   For Paul, there was no room anywhere but in the military. He was too close to the king for meaningful diplomatic functions, such proximity not allowing for mistakes or political reprimands should a mission ever fail. And he was too high in rank to be a page or servant in another sovereign's court, which would be reserved for younger sons of barons and counts. He was also too unruly and independent to enter a religious career, which, in post-Napoleonic times and in a Protestant ruling family, was neither opportune nor available. The military served a meaningful function for sons like Paul. Should they ever rise to shine with success in battle, they might then rule newly conquered lands; should they be killed in action, it would be an honorable exit from an otherwise useless existence.
   The beginning of the nineteenth century was a period of change. Napoleon's soldiers, conscripts of all nations, had spread knowledge, and Rousseau had talked about the freedom of the mind. Renaissance men embarked upon the systematic cataloging of the universe, and some deduced the existence of distant lands before they were discovered; others sought gold in alchemistic

experiments. For Paul, the secrets of life itself—flora, fauna, geology, anthropology—held the greatest mysteries to be understood. The *ancien regime*, foremost King Friedrich, wished for Paul to pursue a military career and once admonished Paul's teachers to put more emphasis on mathematics, Latin and French rather than wasting time with side issues like botany.

In his early twenties, Prince Paul was expected to take a seat in the newly established House of Lords of the Kingdom of Wuerttemberg. Paul attended a few sessions but was usually represented, under power of attorney, by a close relative, Prince Heinrich von Wuerttemberg. Paul preferred to travel, and soon prepared for an important mission: his first voyage to America.

On October 17, 1822, Paul embarked upon an old-fashioned sailboat for New Orleans. His original desire was to visit Mexico, but the political uncertainties there caused him to change his plans. Instead, he spent two months visiting Cuba and then returned to New Orleans again. As the Mexican situation had turned even worse, Prince Paul decided he would ascend the Mississippi and Ohio rivers, then proceed to St. Louis. From there he would go up the Missouri River, cross the Rocky Mountains and visit the British Territories on the shores of the Pacific. Unlike any other traveller at that time, he carried with him books describing earlier western travels, scientific instruments, and European guns that rarely missed their mark.

Prince Paul met the right people and used the network. Bishop DuBourg, aboard the same steamship, *Cincinnati*, on the Ohio River, wrote letters of introduction to the most influential people of St. Louis, the gateway to the west and a city now numbering five-thousand

39

residents.

The doors were thus opened to the office and home of William Clark, who issued Paul the necessary passport to ascend the Missouri and who almost certainly told the royal visitor about his young protegé Pomp, Sacagawea's son, whom he had educated in St. Louis, and who, at the time of Paul's arrival, was working at a small fur trading post at the mouth of the Kansas River.

The doors were also opened to the offices of the Chouteau empire and to the estate of the grandseigneur, Monsieur Chouteau himself, residing not far from Florissant. Berthold, Pratte & Chouteau, the company under the leadership of Chouteau, had successfully obtained a license to trade with the Kansas and Osage Indians, thus expanding and establishing their network throughout the wilderness. Other traders established posts and fierce trade wars developed. Takeovers, mergers, acquisitions and divestitures became a routine as the fur trade grew. Paul received a list of posts, names, hints, also a boat and a crew to take and supposedly protect him on his perilous journey into the West. Equipped with introductions to all trading posts and important people along the river, Paul left St. Louis.

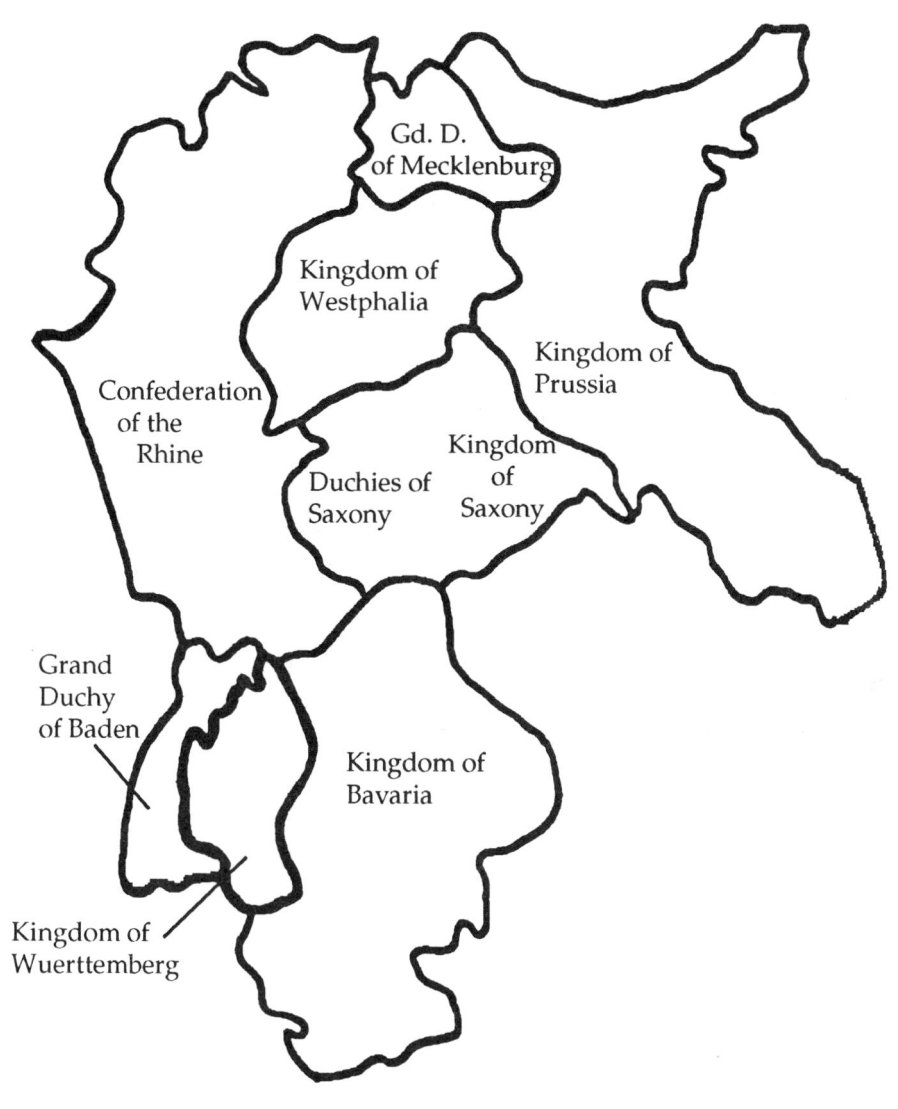

Germany as it was in 1810

From Duke Paul's 1828 pre-print edition of **Erste Reise** of 1823 (page 161) in which he tells of his adventures in Franklin and Boonville. Note Duke Paul's 1833 handwritten revisions in the margin of the manuscript page.
Courtesy Huntington Library, San Marino California.

CHAPTER 2
DUKE PAUL'S FIRST JOURNEY TO THE MISSOURI FRONTIER, 1823

Robert L. Dyer

At the time of Duke Paul's first journey up the Missouri River in the summer of 1823 Missouri had only been a state for two years and was, for all practical purposes, the far western frontier. With the exception of Texas and California, Missouri would remain the farthest western state in the Union until the admission of Kansas to the Union in 1860, and the lower Missouri River would be the launching point for most of the major western exploratory trips from the time of the Lewis and Clark expedition down to the time of the Civil War.

Although a few small towns were scattered up the Missouri River between St. Charles (just west of St. Louis) and the Chouteau trading post at the mouth of the Kansas River (site of present day Kansas City), the only significant settlement in the interior of the state in 1823 was the Boone's Lick country (sometimes rendered as "Boon's Lick" or Boonslick"), a somewhat vaguely defined region bisected by the Missouri River in the center of the state. The region got its name from a salt spring (or "lick") worked by Nathan and Daniel Morgan Boone (sons of the legendary Daniel Boone) between about 1805 and 1812. Daniel Boone had come to the lower Missouri River county in 1799 with his family and settled on land granted to him by the Spanish in the Femme Osage River valley just west of St. Charles. He and his sons roamed up and down the Missouri River in the years before his death in 1820 and often stopped at the salt spring that would come to be known as "Boone's Lick."

The countryside in the vicinity of the spring was recognized as a highly desirable area for settlement and this, along with the legendary appeal of the Boone name, attracted a group of immigrants from Kentucky in 1810 and an even larger group of immigrants who arrived in the years following the War of 1812. The first group of Kentucky immigrants was led by Col. Benjamin Cooper and included Hannah Cole, the widow of William Temple Cole (who had been killed by Indians not long after they arrived in Missouri Territory), her nine children, and her brother-in-law, Stephen Cole. The Coopers settled in the bottomlands north of the river not far from Boone's Lick itself, while the Coles chose to settle on the hills south of the river where Boonville is now located. A number of other Kentuckians trickled into the area over the next year, including Lindsay Carson, who came with his wife and family, including their two-year-old son, Christopher. At the age of 16 Christopher would join one of the early Santa Fe Trail caravans headed west and would eventually achieve fame (or infamy, depending on your point of view) as the frontier guide and Indian fighter, "Kit" Carson.

Following a three year period of difficulties with the Indians during the agitation connected with the War of 1812, these original settlers were joined by a huge influx of immigrants, principally from the southern states of Virginia, Kentucky, and Tennessee. Timothy Flint, a Presbyterian missionary living in St. Charles from 1816 to 1818 vividly described this migration in his **Recollections of the Last Ten Years in the Valley of the Mississippi** (Southern Illinois University Press, Carbondale and Edwardsville, 1968, pp. 146-148; originally published 1826):

Between the second and third years of my residence in

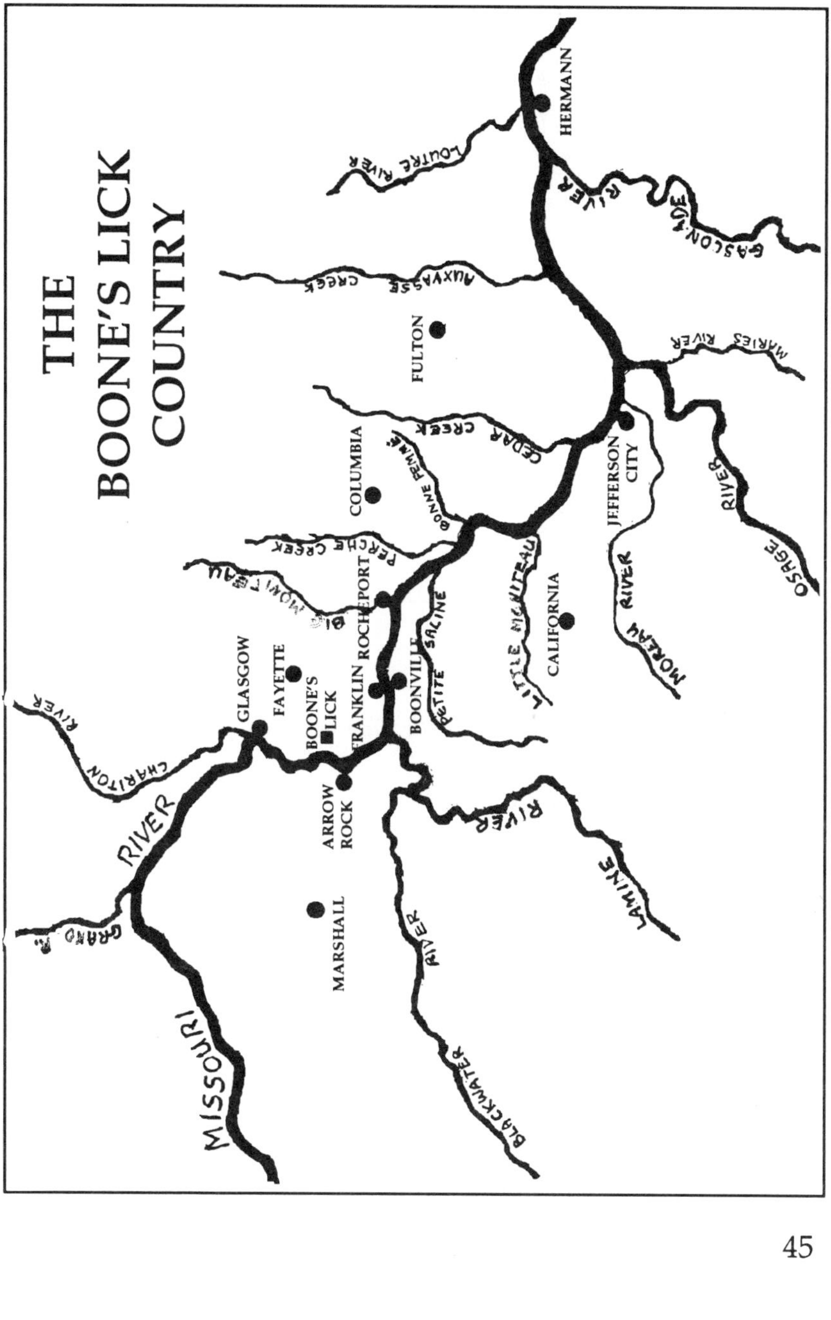
THE
BOONE'S LICK
COUNTRY
HERMANN
LOUTRE RIVER
RIVER
GASCONADE
AUXVASSE CREEK
FULTON
MARIES RIVER
CEDAR CREEK
JEFFERSON CITY
COLUMBIA
BONNE FEMME
RIVER
OSAGE
PERCHE CREEK
ROCHEPORT
SALINE
LITTLE MONITEAU
CALIFORNIA
MOREAU RIVER
GLASGOW
FAYETTE
BOONE'S LICK
FRANKLIN
BOONVILLE
PETITE
CHARITON RIVER
RIVER
ARROW ROCK
RIVER
LAMINE
GRAND R.
MARSHALL
RIVER
BLACKWATER
MISSOURI

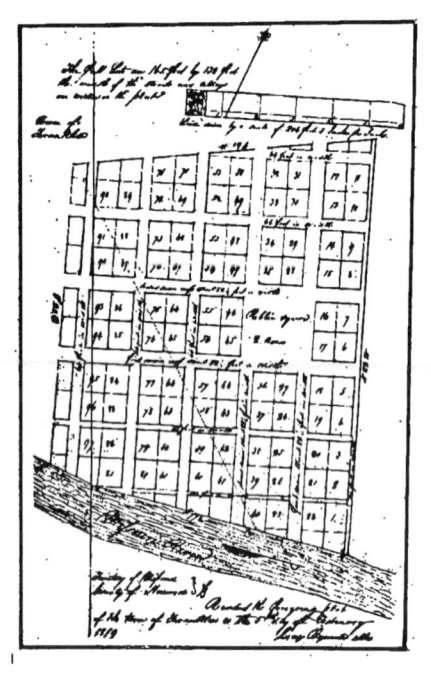

Plat of Franklin, Missouri, 1819

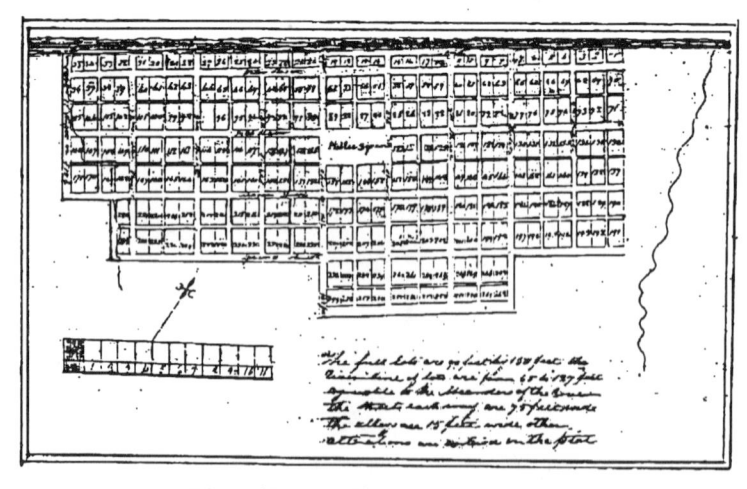

Plat of Boonville, Missouri, 1818

the country, the immigration from the western and southern states to this country poured in a flood, the power and strength of which could only be adequately conceived by persons on the spot. We have numbered a hundred persons passing through the village of St. Charles in one day. The number was said to have equalled that for many days together.... From some cause, it happens that in the western and southern states, a tract of country gets a name, as being more desirable than any other. The imaginations of the multitudes that converse upon the subject, get kindled, and the plains of Mamre in old time, or the hills of the land of promise, were not more fertile in milk and honey, than are the fashionable points of immigration. During the first, second and third years of my residence here, the whole current of immigration set towards this country, Boon's Lick, so called, from Boon's having discovered and worked the salines in that tract. Boon's Lick was the common centre of hopes, and the common point of union for the people. Ask one of them whither he was moving, and the answer was "To Boon's Lick, to be sure." I conversed with great numbers of these people, affording just samples of the great class of frontier or backwoods people, who begin upon the retirement of the Indians, and in their turn yield to a more industrious and permanent race who succeed them, and they in turn push on still farther, with their face ever toward the western sea. And thus wave propels wave.... Nothing can or will limit the immigration westward, but the Western Ocean. Alas! for the moving generation of the day, when the tide of advancing backwoodsmen shall have met the surge of the Pacific. They may then set them down and weep for other worlds.

    Various early travelers, prior to Prince Paul, made note of the Boone's Lick region as they passed through it, including John Bradbury, an English botanist, who made a trip up the Missouri River with the St. Louis fur trader, Manuel Lisa, in 1811. Bradbury's description of the

Boone's Lick region (he, like other early commentators, spells Boone without the final "e"), published in 1817 in his book **Travels in the Interior of America in the Years 1809, 1810, 1811,** is the only contemporary description that gives a specific size for the area:

We encamped this night a little above the mouth of the Bonne Femme, where the tract of land, called Boon's Lick settlement, commences, supposed to be the best land in Western America for so great an area: it extends 150 miles up the Missouri, and is near 50 miles in breadth.

Bradbury's western boundary for the area would, according to this description, be some sixty or seventy miles beyond the mouth of the Grand River. Most contemporary descriptions of the western boundary are somewhat vague, though occasionally it is mentioned that the area extended to the territorial boundary on the west. In terms of the actual area of early settlement, however, it is probably more realistic to place the western boundary at about where the Grand River enters the Missouri, or perhaps even closer to where the Chariton River enters the Missouri just above present day Glasgow, Missouri.

The northern and southern boundaries of the area are also often only vaguely delineated, though several observers place the southern limits of the area at the Osage River. Bradbury described the area as being some fifty miles in breadth (about 25 miles on either side of the Missouri River), a description that most accurately reflects the actual early settlement area.

John Mason Peck, a Baptist missionary who came to Missouri Territory in 1817 and remained until 1821, describes the Boone's Lick region (he includes the final "e" in his spelling) in a journal entry dated January 1819 in a book of his reminiscences edited by Rufus Babcock and published in 1864 under the title, **Forty Years of Pioneer Life.** His description places the beginning point of the area on the north bank of the river at Cedar Creek (the present eastern boundary of Boone County, Missouri) about 20 miles downstream from Bradbury's beginning point of the Bonne Femme Creek:

The country on the north side of the Missouri above the Cedar, a small stream on the western border of the present county of Callaway, was known as Boone's Lick from an early period. Also under the same cognomen was the country on the south side and west of the Osage River.

Nicholas Patterson, a Presbyterian missionary who was sent to Missouri Territory in 1818 and traveled through the settlements along the Missouri River, echoes Peck's description in a letter he wrote on December 28, 1818, describing the Boone's Lick country as "one extensive range of rich land" encompassing all the region above Cedar Creek.

The center of activity in the Boone's Lick country at the time Paul passed through in 1823 was Franklin, a frontier boom-town, established on the north bank of the river in 1816. Within a year or two of being platted Franklin became a bustling mecca for trappers, traders, merchants, land speculators, frontier lawyers, and others with their eyes on the far western lands. By 1823 the town had nearly two hundred buildings and a thousand inhabitants, though Paul estimates there were only about 500 residents—"mostly Anglo Americans and Irish"— and he says there were "only two well-built houses" in the town, "all the rest were merely wooden shacks." The larger estimate comes from a local writer in the **Missouri Intelligencer and Boon's Lick Advertiser** on January 7, 1823, and may have been somewhat exaggerated since one of the purposes of the newspaper was to lure people into the region. This newspaper, the first to be established west of St. Louis, published its first issue in 1819. This was also the year in which the **Independence**, the first steamboat to ascend the treacherous Missouri River, reached Franklin, as well as the year Major Stephen Long's ill-fated "Yellowstone Expedition," passed up the river.

1819 was also the year the first lots in the newly platted town of Boonville, just across the river from Franklin, were sold, and a young Virginian named Henry Bingham arrived in Franklin with his wife and family, including their eight-year old son, the soon-to-be famous frontier artist, George Caleb Bingham. Henry Bingham established a popular hostelry, **The Square and Compass**, in Franklin, and got involved in an unsuccessful venture in the tobacco business before his death from malaria in December 1823. In later years, George Caleb Bingham would remember that his first exposure to art came in the year 1820 when an itinerant artist named Chester Harding came to Franklin and stayed for a time at his father's inn sketching and painting. Prince Paul mentions the attempt of some of the locals to lure him to a tavern in Franklin during his stay there, but he is advised not to accept the invitation and he declines. One wonders if the tavern might have been Bingham's.

One of the most significant events in the Boone's Lick country occurred in 1821, just two years before Paul's arrival, when William Becknell and several other opportunists living in and around Franklin, set off for the west on a trapping and trading expedition. They had the good fortune to encounter a group of Mexicans who informed them of the recent overthrow of Spanish rule in Mexico and the fact that they would now be welcome in Santa Fe, a market American traders had been trying unsuccessfully to enter for many years. Initiation of the Santa Fe trade by Becknell and his men would resonate economically throughout the Missouri country for many years to come.

Jonas Viles, a University of Missouri historian in the 1920s, gathered together all the known information about Franklin for a paper he presented at the fifteenth annual meeting of the Mississippi Valley Historical Association at Iowa City in 1922. In this paper, published in the **Mississippi Valley Historical Review**, Vol. IX, No. 4, March 1923, under the title "Old Franklin: A Frontier Town of the Twenties," Viles describes the town as follows:

The ground plan of Franklin as it took final form in 1819 covered about two-thirds of a square mile. It was the familiar checkerboard pattern, divided into fifteen blocks along the river and ten blocks deep by streets from sixty-six to one hundred feet wide.... The heart of the town was the "first Main Street," leading from the river to the public square.... On the west side of the square was the two-story jail, built in 1817 at a cost of $1,199; on the southwest corner was the brick market house; out in the square was the public well and, probably, the temporary three-hundred-dollar courthouse. The square and Main street must have been built up nearly solidly, as the lots were subdivided into frontages of forty or even twenty feet. The buildings were, for the most part, one-story, one- or two-room log cabins, with occasional two-story frame buildings.... The square and Main street were given over chiefly to the stores and shops, which were usually single rooms with frequently a storehouse in the rear. The lawyers, the doctors, the taverns, and the printing house were within a block or two. Along the water front were two ferries and the warehouses. Scattered around this nucleus were the dwellings....

There was a brickyard somewhere on the outskirts of

town and there was also a wool-carding machine to prepare the rolls for the spinning wheel. The cheapness of furs explains the presence of hat manufactories. Shoemakers, saddlers, cabinet-makers, and potters all supplied local needs. The blacksmiths were also makers of hoes and the like and of nails, and they used considerable quantities of the more easily transported bar and scrap iron. There was usually a tinware and copper "factory" in town, largely interested in mash kettles and stills. Distilling seems to have been almost a household industry. The tobacco manufactory, with its varieties of chewing tobacco and cigars, and the ropewalk, both established in 1823, were the two industries which clearly looked beyond a local market....

Skilled labor, as ever on the frontier, was scarce, irresponsible, and hard to hold off the land. Most of the local industries advertised at one time or another for apprentices; the court regularly bound out needy orphans and dependents. Even the apprentices ran away—among them Kit Carson, [who had been apprenticed to the saddlemaker, David Workman, sometime after his father died in 1818, but] who found the saddler's trade too tame for his adventurous spirit [and left town with a group of Santa Fe traders in 1826]. There were negro slaves in the Boonslick as early as 1814; slaves figure frequently in inventories of estates and in the advertising columns of the paper.... [Slave] holdings were [,however,] small, rarely more than three or four [per owner]. As fourteen and three-fifths per cent of the population of all Howard county in the census of 1820 were slaves, it seems conservative to estimate that they comprised twenty percent of the population of Franklin....

By origin of its population and social customs, Old Franklin was a bit of the Kentucky river valley transplanted to the far west. There were individual Irish, French, and Pennsylvania Dutch; the editor [of the newspaper] was born in Roxbury, Massachusetts, and was always somewhat of a

52

Yankee; piedmont Virginia and Tennessee were well represented; but the mass of the population were Kentuckians. Many of them were substantial persons of some means who brought slaves, blooded stock, and considerable cash with them....
    Many men later prominent in Missouri history tarried a longer or shorter time in our town. Four of the lawyers were later judges of the supreme court and one of them was Missouri's war-time governor [Hamilton Gamble]. Two other future governors [Lilburn W. Boggs and Claiborne F. Jackson] kept store there for a time and a fourth [John Miller] was register in the land office. Both [Thomas Hart] Benton and [David] Barton [Missouri's first two senators] visited Franklin on their campaign tours. William H. Ashley was a familiar figure on his trips to and from his rendezvous with his Rocky mountain hunters. Occasionally an army officer at Council Bluffs left his family in Franklin. The Santa Fe trade brought at least one Mexicon don....
    Franklin, then, was throughout its brief career rather a transplanted, exotic growth, the product of temporary advantages—in many ways in the far west rather than of it. Its ending, too, had in it some element of romance. Just as Independence was beginning to supplant it in the Santa Fe trade, Franklin's one remaining special asset, the erratic Missouri, swept the town out of existence. The encroachments began apparently in the unusually high waters of 1826.... By 1828 the situation was so serious that the community decided to move bodily two miles or so to the present town of New Franklin. In 1828-1829 as buildings were completed there the transfer was made and the old town fell into the river. But later the Missouri shifted back to the southward and rebuilt the original site of the town. Barring the timber and the railroad, the bottom lands opposite Boonville are to-day substantially as they were in 1816....

53

Prince Paul's journey through the Boone's Lick, as described in his 1823 journals, commenced when he passed Cedar Island, at the mouth of Cedar Creek, on the morning of June 4. Shortly thereafter he stopped briefly "at a so-called town, consisting of three wretched cabins, named Jefferson." This, of course, was the town that would eventually become the Missouri state capital in 1826, but at this time it was in its infancy and Paul spent an uncomfortable night there during which most of his crew got drunk and rowdy. For the next seven days they continued up river and Paul described each stream entering the river as well as the numerous islands that were once an integral part of the river corridor.

Finally, the keelboat arrived at Franklin on Wednesday, June 11, 1823. His arrival was noted in the weekly issue of the **Missouri Intelligencer**, which appeared on Tuesday, June 17. After receiving a less than pleasant welcome from a group of locals, Paul was saved from further indignities by a Frenchman, "Mr. Benouai from Bordeaux." The next day Paul purchased a "frail one-horse cart" and a "weak, worn out" horse and began his journey overland to the Kansas River, accompanied by his Creole traveling companion Caillou and "a small boy of fourteen" who agreed to drive the cart and act as a guide of sorts on the next leg of the journey. It is unfortunate that Paul does not mention the name of this boy. Is it, for instance, at all possible that this fourteen-year-old boy could have been Christopher "Kit" Carson, who was just a few months shy of his fourteenth birthday when Paul arrived in Franklin, and who would eventually achieve lasting fame for the part he would play in the exploration and settlement of the western lands?

It is also unfortunate that Paul seems to have been unaware of the existence of John Hardeman's amazing early botanical garden just a few miles up river from Franklin in the bottomlands along the Missouri River. Paul would have passed within less than a mile of this experimental garden on the road between Franklin and Arrow Rock when he continued his journey, and it is strange that no one in the area mentioned this to him given his obvious interest in things botanical. John Hardeman had come to Franklin in 1817 from Tennessee with his father, Thomas, and had established two large farming operations, one near Franklin that he called "Fruitage Farm" and another he called "Penultima" near what would eventually become Jefferson City.

At "Fruitage Farm" John Hardeman established a ten-acre experimental garden in the form of a square where he planted various kinds of grapes, berries, fruit trees, and ornamental flowers and plants. The square was criss-crossed with walkways, and in its center was a formal one-acre labyrinth flanked on either side by ponds. A letter from John Hardeman to Missouri's famous senator Thomas Hart Benton in 1822 (which appeared in the **Missouri Intelligencer and Boon's Lick Advertiser** in November of that year) described some of the remarkable results of his botanical and agricultural experiments.

John O'Fallon, an early St. Louis botanist, corresponded with Hardeman frequently about his experiments and may even have visited the garden. Prominent St. Louis botanist Henry Shaw may also have visited Hardeman's famous garden, though no certain evidence has yet been located to verify this. It is known, however, that Shaw got many of his early gardening ideas from John O'Fallon and thus was at least indirectly influenced by Hardeman's experiments. Given the obvious significance of Hardeman's early botanical experiments in the Boone's Lick region, it is indeed a shame that Duke Paul was not able to visit "Fruitage Farm" and converse with Hardeman, especially since within three years of Paul's visit to the area most of the garden (along with most of the town of Franklin) would be wiped out by Missouri River flooding, and by 1828 Hardeman, himself, would be dead.

It is also unfortunate that Paul has so little to say on his 1823 journey about the town of Boonville located on the bluffs opposite Franklin, especially given the significance the town takes on during his 1851 journey. Admittedly the first lots in the town had only been sold in 1819 and the town was in its infancy at the time of Paul's arrival in the area, but there was more to the town than he indicated in his brief mention of it as a place with "a few scattered cabins, whose inhabitants have a competitive attitude toward Franklin, [and] hold their settlement to be a town." According to an article describing Cooper County and Boonville in the **Missouri Intelligencer and Boon's Lick Advertiser,** December 31, 1822, Boonville was then a town with four streets running parallel to the river, eight streets crossing them at right angles, a public square containing two acres, an "elegant" two-story court house, a log jail, and "forty-one neat dwelling houses, inhabited by about 116 souls." It is too bad that Paul did not have the opportunity or motivation to take a closer look at Boonville in 1823 since there are very few detailed descriptions of the town at this period of time.

There is, however, much to be thankful for in what Paul does see and describe for us. His 1823 description is especially interesting in light of his 1851 trip through the same region, since it provides a basis for understanding what changes occurred (and did not occur) during this highly significant 28-year period of time.

Here then is the account of the 1823 journey beginning on the afternoon of June 9th as he passes the mouth of the Petite Saline, which presently empties into the Missouri River just below the Cooper County river town of Wooldridge, and ending on June 16th when he reaches the town of Liberty just down river from present day Kansas City, Missouri.

Franklin,
TUESDAY, JUNE 17, 1823.

F. PAUL WILLIAM, *Prince of Wirtemberg*, arrived here on Wednesday last, and proceeded on his tour the next day. It is his intention to ascend the Missouri to the mouth of the Yellow Stone River.

Articles from the **Missouri Intelligencer and Boon's Lick Advertiser**, June 17, 1823, and October 7, 1823, Franklin, Mo. (State Historical Society of Missouri)

FRANKLIN,
OCTOBER 7, 1823.

The Prince of Wurtemberg, who ascended the Missouri early in the summer, had got no further than Fort Atkinson—where it was supposed he would remain for a while, before he proceeded higher, in consequence of the Indian disturbances.

DUKE PAUL'S 1823 JOURNEY

Duke Paul left St. Charles by keelboat on May 15, 1823, and went up river, passing the newly established town of Jefferson (the state capital) and arriving in Franklin on June 11. He continued his journey by land to Liberty and then the mouth of the Kansas (Kaw) River, arriving there on June 17 and remaining about a week during which time he met Jean Baptiste Charbonneau ("Pomp").

Then he again boarded his keel boat and continued up river, passing Roubidoux's trading post (present St. Joseph) on July 13 and reaching Ft. Atkinson at the Council Bluffs in early August. From there he continued overland, crossing the Niobrara River on August 16 and reaching the White River and Joshua Pilcher's factory (Ft. Recovery) on August 23. He remained there about a week, during which time he also visited nearby Ft. Kiowa, then returned to St. Louis by boat, picking up Pomp at the mouth of the Kansas (Kaw) River on October 9, passing Franklin and Boonville on October 19, and arriving in St. Louis on October 24.

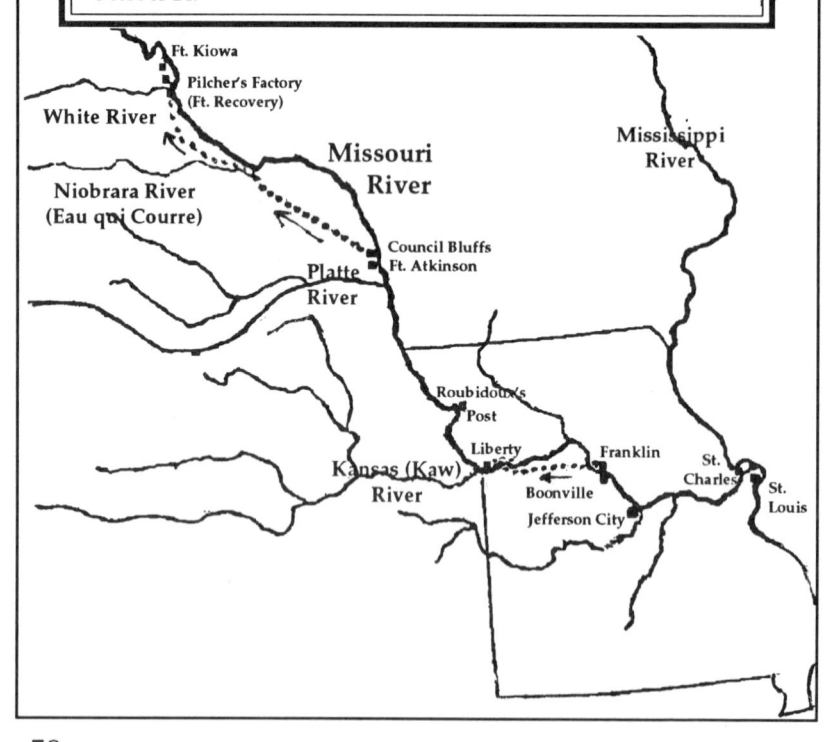

Travels in North America
1823

Paul Wilhelm, Duke of Wuerttemberg

[*The original account was written by Paul in 1823, but was not typeset until 1828 when a few copies containing 180 pages were printed. In 1833 Paul hand-corrected the manuscript and added passages to include experiences gathered during his second trip in 1831. The book was then printed by another publisher in 1835. The following is from Paul Wilhelm, Duke of Wurttemberg, Travels in North America 1822-1824, University of Oklahoma Press, 1973, translated by W. Robert Nitske, pp. 252-267 and p. 460. It is used here by permission. Page 161 of the 1828 pre-print edition, reproduced here (see page 42) courtesy of the Huntington Library, San Marino, California, Dr. Alan Jutzi, Curator of Rare Books, includes references to Franklin and Boonville. Duke Paul made only a few grammatical corrections on this page.*]

At five o'clock [on the afternoon of June 9] we passed a small saline creek [La Petite Saline] which would not arouse the interest of the traveler except for its large content of salt, which might in time make it quite valuable. From now on the stream was bordered by long, low banks, *battures,* or high, timber covered land, *cotes basses,* alternating with one another. The water in the Missouri had fallen so much that I could notice many places where the bottom of the river bed became visible and even formed sandbars. In many places the water was so shallow that even our flat-bottomed boat could hardly be pushed ahead, and only with the aid of poles. With great difficulty and strenuous work, we succeeded in making two miles beyond the saline creek, and in the

59

night we had to endure a slight rain with a sultriness which attracted an insufferable number of flies and mosquitoes. Despite the utmost weariness we could not sleep.

The morning of the tenth requited us, for the air became cool, and by poling and rowing we had arrived at an island, the Ile du Grand Manitou, whose banks consist of many shelves. It is two miles long but narrow and partially overgrown with cottonwoods. At eleven o'clock we reached the point of this island. I estimated the distance from this point to the saline creek at five English miles. At daybreak the hunters started out and came back with a fallow deer. On the hooks which I had set out a fine fish of the sheat-fish family was caught. I took it to be a *Cataphractus costatus*, one which I had not seen until then. Of the scaly fish, several excellent kinds are found in the waters of the northwest of America. All fish of prey, their scales, often forming an impenetrable armor over the whole body, are so strong that they can resist the effect of firearms.

Our journey continued along the right bank, which remained low from shallow water. The left bank on the other hand rose to high bluffs sloping abruptly into the water. These bluffs contain many caves and clefts. This row of hills, called La Côte du Grand Manitou, extends six English miles along the stream to the mouth of a creek.

By evening we were opposite the end of this chain of hills. Here the Missouri makes a sharp curve to the west, and the already low left bank of the river changes suddenly into shallows, so that our boat touched bottom, although it drew only two feet of water. The yellowish gray color of the water of the Missouri, impregnated with clay, made it impossible to recognize such places, and the sounding lead usually leaves the boatman in the lurch in a swiftly flowing current, with the boat moving slowly upstream. After the boat had been set afloat again, it nevertheless seemed impossible to get directly across the stream to the deep water along the rocky bank. With the greatest difficulty we had passed rapids hard by the bank, and now we had to recross it with the current greatly endangering our lives.

The current carried us swift as an arrow toward a pile of driftwood dominated by a giant sycamore trunk lying in the way of our boat. With a loud roar, the river, running in short, high waves, leaped in a huge surf over all objects barring its course. The only outlet the water could find was among the piled up debris, for in the bed the rapids created many whirlpools. As if by a miracle the boat turned through the most dangerous places without striking the driftwood. Finally, far below the rapids, we reached the deep and quieter channel on the opposite bank of high and rocky leaning cliffs. As a precaution I had caused my best and most necessary things to be taken on land, since Caillou, whose expert knowledge had been shown anew on this occasion, had earlier called my attention to the great danger. My concern was therefore centered only on those men whose services required their presence on the vessel, several of whom could not swim.

Without delay we once more rowed upstream, after the crew had succeeded in turning the boat and steering against the current. With much exertion another mile was made, at which point we halted at a suitable place. I scarcely recall having spent a more magnificent evening in the New World than that which followed this painfully lived-through day. The sun set in a most beautiful purple, and a gentle east wind cooled the air so completely that even the mosquitoes had to give up their restless activity.

Very early on the morning of June 11, a strong favoring wind rose, lasting several hours and bringing us soon to the Big Manitou. Here we could see the end of a chain of hills of the same name. A rock decorated with genuine Indian painting throws a weak light on the crude conceptions of the idolatrous worship of the wild aborigines. Here the Indians occasionally bring sacrifices to an evil being whom they fear, and in outline the idol in symbolic form seems to assume the shape of an animal. Judging from the effect which the weather has had on the coloring material, it clearly pointed to a remote time, a time when this mass of stone served the aborigines for the performance of their mystic worship. It even seemed to me as if the painting had been frequently renewed, and the paint on several other better preserved drawings was especially fresh and bright. With considerable skill and proportion, they quite clearly represent battles and hunting expeditions of the aborigines.

We again crossed the stream at the nearby island called Ile de la Grande Bonne Femme on the right bank of the river. Here we encountered a plague of a new and most peculiar kind. Entire billions of butterflies belonging to the family of *nymphalidae*, closely related to the European *Aegeria* covered the vessel and all objects, hindering almost every activity in that they ceaselessly darkened our eyes and hands, even clinging fast to our nostrils and flying into our mouths while we spoke or breathed.

In the hot belt of the New World this phenomenon seems to occur more frequently. While navigating with difficulty along the south side of the island of Cuba in May, 1494, Christopher Columbus stated that he had met with a like phenomenon. I myself recall having seen huge swarms of migrating butterflies on the swampy coast of Cuba, especially in the region of Battayano. In all probability these insects had but recently escaped from their chrysalis, and since they had metamorphosed as a community they had not yet had time to disperse.

About noon we were opposite the mouth of the small La Bonne Femme River, which should not be confused with the Petite Bonne Femme. The right bank of the Missouri changed here to moderately high rows of bluffs perhaps measuring no more than one hundred feet in height. The sun burned intensely, with no breeze, and the thermometer rose to 88° in the shade. However, with that the air was clearer and the heat more tolerable than on sultry days with lower readings on the thermometer.

The left bank is low, and near it, at the mouth of the Grande Bonne Femme (Big Good Women Creek), are several small islands overgrown with willows.

In the afternoon at five o'clock the boat reached Franklin, a small, but not entirely unimportant, town where I noticed only two well-built houses at the time. All the rest were merely wooden shacks. This town on the left bank of the Missouri counted about five hundred inhabitants, mostly Anglo-Americans and Irish. In the midst of wild aborigines and surrounded by forests, its location was in many respects very much exposed to the attacks of the wild hordes, and the carelessness of the inhabitants showed itself only too plainly by the few measures that have been taken for the security of the place.

The locations of newly built towns, removed from the mouths of the large tributaries of the Missouri, are, in my opinion, poorly chosen, for these towns are usually inhabited by merchants, who sooner or later may leave if the population and trade should increase on the Osage or the Kansas.

On the right bank atop a high cliff opposite Franklin are found a few scattered cabins, whose inhabitants have a competitive attitude toward Franklin, hold their settlement to be a town and have named it Boonville. Hardly an hour had elapsed after our arrival until the effects of the near-by saloons were clearly seen. The entire crew was drunk and created much noise. Under the circumstances it is incomprehensible to me that we had no accident because gunpowder constituted the main portion of our ship's load, and the indiscriminate use of pipes could have caused an explosion at any moment.

I had decided to go on land the following morning, since neither the town nor the inhabitants appeared very inviting. Soon, however, I received visits from all sorts of stupidly bold and curious people addressing me with all manner of indiscreet questions. Their intention seemed to be to make fun of me as a stranger. When they saw that they did not gain their purpose, they committed other incivilities and even tried to gain possession of my papers and things while they decried me as an adventurer and spy.

In order to rid me of these unpleasant guests, my valet in the meantime interested Caillou and a few boat hands, who were not yet entirely drunk, in my behalf, requesting the obtrusive company, with whom I was engaged in a lively discussion, to return to shore. The Franklinites did not seem inclined to do so good naturedly.

Speaking again in my own behalf, I was finally lucky in persuading both parties to leave the boat and settle their affair on land. A terrible fight resulted. During this time a Frenchman, Mr. Benouai from Bordeaux, a well disposed man, came on board to quiet me. Benouai promised the full protection of the law if I would stop at his house. He urged me not to accept an invitation of the young people who, under the pretext of friendship, would try to take me to their tavern in order to start a quarrel there. He also advised me not to leave the boat unarmed. Soon recognizing the sincerity of his intentions, I promised the obliging Frenchman a visit on the following day.

Under the pretext of reconciliation, two persons came to me and, after offering some awkward apologies, requested me to accompany them to the boarding house to celebrate a feast of reconciliation. At first I excused myself in a polite manner, but when they became more and more insistent and laid hands on me, I chased them from the boat amid the uproarious laughter of their comrades. As this decisive manner seemed genuinely popular with the Franklinites, they let the affair stop there.

[*Note: On Paul's return trip through the area in October he received a considerably better welcome and a more favorable impression of Franklin. In his journal entry for October 19 (p. 406) he says that this time he "was received much more courteously than at the time of my other visit, for the good citizens of Franklin may have become convinced that they had been mistaken in me."*]

Since the journey by water went extremely slowly, I resolved to travel by land to the Kansas and await the arrival of the boat there. From Franklin a passable road leads to the mouth of this great river, where all further white population ceases and only a few wild people live. There the traveler can view nature in her virgin state, unchanged. I longed very much for these wildernesses because of the chances of better hunting and the abundance of animals of all kinds.

Even though the habitations of civilized people are few and far apart, all freedom loving animals retreat from them to the completely uninhabited regions, especially in the western part of North America, where such regions are still so numerous. In the populated countries of our civilized Europe, the wild animals find but little real solitude and for this reason they stay in uninhabited and lonely forests. There their survival is even protected and no hindrance is placed in their way, but some die out entirely, as many beasts of prey have done when existence is incompatible with the nearness of man and such creatures as are useful to him.

To prepare for my land journey I went to town early on June 12, accompanied by Caillou, and made my way to the house of Mr. Benouai. Even on the day before, he had endeavored to procure a few horses for me. Saddle horses could not be provided here, as was the case in St. Louis, and only weak, worn-out animals were available. I had to be content to take an extremely wretched and frail one-horse cart (which on the morning of my departure was hastily repaired with nails) to make a journey of over sixty hours along a very poorly kept road, or more correctly stated, to walk this distance.

There was just room enough in the cart for the driver and my very scant baggage. A small boy of fourteen dared to drive this conveyance through an unknown wilderness, where dwellings are often many miles apart. I had left my servant on board the boat to watch my property and my collections, which caused me great worry.

At half past ten we finally started to move out, despite intense heat and a hot southeast wind. The rough trail, dignified with the name of road, was so poorly defined that the traveler often lost it from sight altogether, and it contained so many trees broken off by the wind and so many swampy places that I often spent hours in overcoming these obstacles in our path.

Before one reaches the Kansas River, the Missouri must be crossed twice, the first time at Pierre de la Flèche [*Arrow Rock*], and the second in the neighborhood of Tabeau Creek. The road to Pierre de la Flèche by way of the river, a distance of twelve English miles from Franklin, led through a sparsely inhabited region. For the first two miles the way was passable. The forests consisted of beautiful trees spaced apart and a dense composite undergrowth of herb-like plants. Magnificent groups of trees were created by the numerous sycamores mixed with luxuriant gleditsia, locust, ashes, and oaks.

A swamp hard by the road bordered the latter for more than an English mile. This stagnant water was covered with aquatic plants of the genus *Typha*, *Potamogeton*, and *Rumex*. A beautiful flowering Nymphaea also delighted my eye. Countless water fowls took wing in fright and a huge flock of *Anas sponsa* [wood ducks] passed over my head. From a botanical and ornithological point of view this region seemed engrossing, and I regretted very much that I did not have the opportunity to remain a longer time.

At the end of the swamp the adjoining hills flattened out and a lowland, for the most part inundated by the river, took its place. Our cart broke down for the first time in a deep hole, but after a stay of two hours was temporarily repaired by Caillou, who fortunately had provided himself with an ax. During this time, countless blood-thirsty mosquitoes stung me. They seemed to like the interior of the forest even better than the region close to the river bank.

We made seven more miles through the swampy

primeval forests, during which time I had ample occasion to make unpleasant observations concerning the lack of skill of our young American driver. About four o'clock in the afternoon we reached an isolated house on the Missouri opposite Pierre de la Flèche.

Here lived the owner of the ferry on which one crosses the river. The inhabitants of the wretched hut were poor but good-hearted people, and we stayed an hour to rest. [*Note: The inhabitants were probably members of the Ferrill family. John, the father, and his son Henry, were long-time trappers on the Missouri and operators of the ferry at Arrow Rock, according to Louis Houck,* **History of Missouri**, *III, 115.*] In Franklin I had provided myself with a few necessary provisions, but in the haste of departure Caillou had forgotten them. This loss was to me very unpleasant, for the package contained several bottles of rum. In this great heat, drinking water unmixed with some kind of spirituous drink is very harmful and may produce fever. In the house we could get nothing at all to eat except some old milk which had almost turned to cheese and some dried-out cornbread. This constituted dinner.

The bank forming the Pierre de la Flèche is high and composed of beautiful rocks. This chain of hills on the right bank of the Missouri is hardly twelve English miles long and it gradually runs over to the lowland which extends as far as Franklin. A small stream, called Riviere à la Mine, empties into the Missouri four English miles from Franklin. There, near its mouth, lies a large island, two English miles long and overgrown with high cottonwoods, with a narrow channel between it and the bank. [*Note: Hardeman's Garden was located across the Missouri River from the mouth of the Lamine. The island mentioned is Hardeman's Island.*]

Nothing remarkable occurred during my crossing of the river on a raft. Requiring almost an entire hour to get across, the raft had to be pulled half an English mile up the stream. The current in the neighborhood of the rocks called Pierre de la Flèche is extremely swift and it was most difficult to make the raft fast on the right bank. We climbed a rather high, steep hill on which nut trees and sassafras grew. On the ridge of these hills the timber become thinner. Forest and prairie alternate with one another. The vegetation becomes more luxuriant, the dense underbrush gives way to grasscovered spaces, and more and more the region takes on a lighter aspect clearly indicating the transition from the forest region to the prairie.

Half a mile farther to the west, one begins to see larger stretches overgrown with herbaceous plants and scattered clumps of brush such as sumac, walnut, and sassafras *(Rhus glabrum, copallinum, Juglans procina, Quercus ruba, echinata, Populus angulata,* etc.) and also scattered oaks and poplars of most slender shapes bearing the stamp of unhindered growth. Tall plants, among which I observed as yet undetermined *Aquilegia* with very small light blue blossoms, also *Acnida cannabina* and *ruscocarpa* which attained a height of five to six feet forming an edge around the forest, at last gave way to the short prairie grasses whose light green carpet, yet unbleached by the rays of the sun, reached to the blue horizon among hills of soft, wave-like elevations. [*Duke Paul notes that this prairie is called Prairie à la Mine, after the river that originates on it and flows through it. It is connected uninterruptedly with the great prairie region of North America and is bounded in the west by the Cordilleras of New Spain.*]

This sight I enjoyed for the first time after I had climbed a slight rise, on whose summit was one of the last of the above-described clusters of trees. It appeared picturesquely beautiful when it presented itself to the eye for the first time, but loses much of its interest, for its monotony wearies the senses. Illumined by the golden rays of the nearly setting sun, the charming picture in its simple beauty was still more captivating and reminded me of the sea in still majesty touching the sapphire blue of the darker vault of the wonderful heavens—happy evenings I had spent in the midst of the great ocean under a tropical sky. There the emotions of man are deeply touched, and the soul of man is filled with devout praise of the Creator.

After traveling on for a short distance over the prairie, we stopped at a cabin of a kind-hearted family of settlers. At first sight this dwelling appeared very poor, but presently we observed the inhabitants and saw signs of considerable well-being, which in this blessed region cannot fail to come as a result of diligence and industry. Entirely unacquainted with luxury, these people lacked the most necessary conveniences inside their cabin. They had considerable wealth in livestock and farm implements, yet I could not find a table on which to enter the necessary remarks in my diary. I had to use a turned-up butter churn for this purpose.

The woman of the house busied herself at once, making preparations for supper. In comparison with the meager dinner at the ferryman's house, it was quite ample.

During the night we were threatened by a severe storm from the north-east, whereupon it became so cool for this season that the effect was felt in the interior of the cabin. In the morning the wind subsided and we could start in good time. To the first and nearest dwelling in the prairie, which was to be near the Missouri, the distance was twenty-eight English miles, a stretch which one could cover perhaps in one day during the dry season in the summer.

We followed the tracks of a wagon which must have preceded us for some time, but the tracks were still recognizable to the trained eye of my companion. In this manner we traveled in intense heat until noon, through a grassy plain apparently extending unendingly to the west and to the south, interrupted only occassionally by scattered wooded spots. Such brush, with trees rarely attaining a considerable height, when seen from a distance, looks like groups of islands rising from the lap of a calm ocean. The sea-green color of the prairie, the peculiar wave-like movement of the tall grasses as they are stirred by the breezes, that peculiar appearance of the air, the mirage playing on the horizon and resembling a body of moving water (which the Arabs call "the thirst of the Gazelle") misleads men and animals famishing from thirst. This synthesis contributes much to the deception. The searing heat, intensified by a dry and burning southwest wind, had wearied our thirsty horse to the extent that it could go no farther after having made a distance of eighteen miles.

Going ahead and off to a side, I was finally fortunate in finding a spring among a few stunted trees, but the water was warm and muddy. Despite my yearning for a drink I could not make up my mind to taste it. At that time I was still a novice and not sufficiently acquainted with the hardships of a journey through the wilderness. Later I had to accustom myself to drink water much worse than this merely to stay alive. At that time I was also of the opinion that tepid and turbid water was enervating and, because of the repugnance which one felt on drinking it, must be unhealthy. This is, however, by no means the case, for, on the contrary, consuming cold, refreshing spring water is said to be extremely harmful, and even the Indians never drink it as cold as it comes from the spring.

My little driver, afraid to spend the night on the prairie, allowed the exhausted horse scarcely the necessary noon rest and after half an hour drove on. On the prairie the unskilled traveler must make use of the compass in order not to lose his way, since he misses every landmark, which is visible only to the keen and experienced eye of the native. I therefore took refuge in the magnetic needle. My companion would pay no heed to it and soon lost the right direction. We found it again only after taking a far, roundabout way.

With the setting of the sun the scorching heat lessened, and at eleven o'clock at night we reached a lonely cabin. However, it was impossible to stay because of the number of insects and the stifling heat. The inhabitants, too, seemed little pleased by our late visit. During the night a heavy dew formed, so that I was thoroughly drenched and in this condition found the coolness of the morning quite unbearable.

The house where we had spent the night was not far from the Missouri, separated from this river only by a swamp and a narrow wooded strip. From the nearness of the stagnant water, I could easily explain the excessive number of mosquitoes that during the night had stung me so horribly. My whole skin was inflamed as if from the sting of nettles.

On the fourteenth we continued our journey at eight in the morning. The day's task was smaller and the region might have more inhabitants. On the prairie we passed through the previous day, it was most desolate. Only a few birds enlivened this lonely region, in addition to a few deer and elk, which at a distance of one thousand paces fled shyly from us.

In herbaceous plants this prairie is also poor and very rarely did I observe blossoming plants. Among these I was interested in one of the Syngenesia with large but not yet fully developed flowers, probably a *Rudbeckia*, whose roots have the unpleasant odor of the rattlesnake during its mating season. Moreover, here and there in moist places grew a *Datura*, which differs from *D. stramonium* only by having larger and more lobed leaves, and a *Sambucus*, growing in clumps as low bushes.

Until three o'clock in the afternoon we continued our journey without interruption. As we neared the Missouri, the country assumed a more wooded character, which finally gained the upper hand entirely. The Rivière à la Mine runs almost parallel to the bed of the stream for a distance taking about twenty hours to cover, and with the many tributary creeks this little stream waters a grass-rich area. Its rich fertility would invite cultivation if it were not so poor in timber. For the raising of horses and cattle there is no better location, but for sheep raising the climate does not seem to be conducive, and the wool is poor.

Even before the approach of night we reached the Tabeau River [*modern Tabo Creek*]. Emptying into the Missouri and flowing between high banks, it is swift and deep during the rainy season. Even now its bed had six to eight feet of water, and I found the water strikingly cold. I stopped at a house whose inhabitants were of German origin. They felt an unspeakable pleasure in hearing themselves addressed in their mother tongue. Judging from the hospitable reception I received, I concluded that they were well-to-do. There was nothing lacking to satisfy our hunger. For people who have health and an inclination to work industriously, this fruitful land, properly used, yields all the blessings of a generous nature.

Refreshed by a bath in the cool stream and strengthened by wholesome food and a real bed during the night, I was able to start my journey again the following morning at an early hour. As we had to travel over a poor and stony road on the ridge of a chain of hills sloping to the Missouri, we had the greatest difficulty in making headway with our conveyance. Finally we reached the river, where we proposed crossing near a little, now abandoned, town of Brington.

The right bank, La Côte du Soldat de Duchaine, bounded by low hills, touches upon a swamp, Marais du Sorcier [*modern Hicklin Lake*], which has the worst reputation among the aborigines and immigrants, and gives occasion to all sorts of rumors and stories. It is indeed incongrouous how the Indians, with their pronounced bravery and their contempt for all danger, fear the influence of spooks and wicked spirits. These Indians also share with the ignorant lower classes of Europe the superstitious belief of assigning supernatural beings a definite, limited area within which they are said to manifest their influence.

From Brington to Pierre de la Flèche is considered sixty English miles, a distance we made in two and one-half days. Because of the wretched condition of our wagon and hindered by the bad roads, I had made almost the entire distance on foot. This was especially difficult on the fifteenth because of the hilly and stony ground, and was still more taxing because of the almost unbearable heat, which every noon rose to 92° or 95° in the shade.

My companion, the Creole, a man to endure the utmost hardship, called this a pleasant walk and often ran barefoot over the hot stones with a pack of eighty to one hundred pounds suspended from his long rifle. He it was who procured all necessary things for us, loaded and unloaded our baggage, and cared for the horse, because our driver was only a boy, hardly able to stand the long trips in the sun.

The Creole was the last to go to bed and the first at break of day admonishing us to start. With it all he ate only a little and drank only water. His whole wardrobe consisted of a leather jacket, a pair of linen trousers, and a woolen blanket. Only such race of men, accustomed, almost as if in a play, to endure the gravest dangers and privation, could succeed in discovering and populating the endless regions of the new World.

After calling for a long time and waiting in vain for the ferry people who lived on the opposite bank, Caillou was obliged to cross the Missouri on a rickety boat which he fortunately found on the bank. After an hour he brought the ferrymen, rough and unobliging Irishmen. They first entered into a long spate of bargaining with me, but nevertheless after crossing they demanded twice as much as the price agreed upon.

On the left bank the road is extremely bad and undefined. I had to travel either through a bottomless morass and great stretches of standing water, or over hard, bumpy, sun-baked clay ground. Much of the region was overgrown with impenetrable brush and thorn, and in part also with nettles as tall as a man. Here our wagon broke down completely and our horse became so lame that the suffering of the animal aroused our pity. The large amount of game, especially the great number of turkeys, the sight of countless birds, notably huge flocks of parrots [*Carolina parakeets*], and also the splendid, luxuriant shapes of trees in full bloom, all would have repaid me amply for the strenuous foot journey if my attention had not been diverted in a painful manner by countless insects.

In the evening, burdened with a considerable load of game, we reached a group of houses called Blufftown. Here I found a pretty good tavern and, dissatisfied, I left the wretched wagon and the little driver to their own fate, paying the lad for the entire contemplated journey.

The owner of the tavern agreed to provide me with a horse to carry my baggage, and over these arrangements for the continuance of my journey, by this new means, the whole evening and a great part of the next morning passed by. All types of people from the neighborhood gathered, for the tavern at Blufftown seemed to be the meeting and amusement place of the region. Several women had also come along, and among these there were a few who could lay some claim to beauty, and conscious of this advantage, they showed off before the others.

As a stranger I was especially favored, particularly when the customary diversion of the American, rifle-shooting, was resorted to, and my exceptionally good gun won for me the best prizes. Target shooting is the most passionately pursued form of sport of the inhabitants of the northwestern states. Much money is made and lost. The best shot is preferred here, as he is in the Tyrol and Switzerland, and rarely loses favor with the women. In a country where guns are of as much importance as they are in the wilderness of the New World, this is easily understood.

The people of the upper Missouri travel almost always on horseback, and I believe that I have hardly ever seen anything as bizarre as the pose of the women riding. Too, the entire attire of the women, more comical than their odd carriage, a mixture of the old and the new, was funny. They wear a white linen hood, a cone-shaped pointed cap like a truncated sugar loaf, and twice as high as the head covering of Wendic women in the Lausitz. Earlier I had seen similar costumes among the American women, but never of such an exaggerated form. They wear their hair either in long curls or shorn quite short, and the waist is forced into ill-cut tight jackets, distorting the whole figure.

Finally the next morning, after much fruitless effort, I was presented an old horse, almost blind, on which my belongings and, in case of extreme fatigue, myself were to be transported to the little town of Liberty. This place, twenty-four miles from Blufftown, is situated on a small stream which empties into the Missouri almost opposite the mouth of the Kansas.

At eight o'clock we finally started. The heat began early to be quite unbearable. The way led through the woods and a number of creeks and brooks, whose crude bridges had been washed away, or along steep, bumpy hillsides. My packhorse unendingly stumbled and fell, and I even feared whether I would reach Liberty alive.

After covering twelve miles, I saw the bank of the winding Fish Creek, or Rivière aux Poissons, which is navigable in canoes. Fairly deep and muddy, it has bad-tasting, gray water. We crossed on a raft and stopped for an hour at the house of a settler, the first house we had seen since morning. In the forest one could not rest because of mosquitoes; moreover our poor, tired horse swam in his own blood from the countless bites of gadflies and horseflies.

The country teemed with deer and wild turkeys,

so tame that they sunned themselves and their broods close to the house and were not in the least disturbed. The next dwelling was another six miles away. In its proximity a hot engagement between Osage Indians and settlers had taken place a few years ago. The former had made several thieving raids and stolen many cattle and horses. Despite this, the Osages were not as much feared as the Iowas, whose raids were usually accompanied by murder and plundering. The region of the newly settled land between the Grand River, or Grande Riviere, and the Kansas was severely harassed, and isolated settlers could barely maintain themselves in spite of the greatest vigilance.

To the left, not far from the trail on which I was traveling, was an extensive swampy meadow stretching toward the Missouri, about eighteen miles from the last night's camp. At some points the country is vividly beautiful, and a chain of high hills extends from the north to the southwest toward the banks of the river. Not until it had become dark, about nine o'clock, did we reach Liberty Town after a day's journey of almost twenty-six English miles. This time my Creole was so tired that he could not have gone a step farther. The exceptional heat of some 100° in the shade had produced in us a feverish condition which might have had serious consequences, but fortunately passed with mere fatigue.

Liberty consists of a few poor log cabins put up for temporary use. The tavern where I spent the night was crowded with people who did not make arrangements to retire until about midnight. The resulting noise in the small room of the house and the horrible heat occasioned by the presence of so many people were little suited to accord a weary traveler necessary rest. To give the reader an idea of the innocence and the naturalness of the customs of this land, so far removed from the heart of civilization, I will only remark that the daughters of the house, young girls of fifteen to sixteen years of age, out of the kindness of their hearts and touched by my utter exhaustion, publicly suggested that I share their bed with them since it was the only comfortable sleeping place in the whole house.

As before, I again had a hard time the next day, which was June 17, getting two horses, one to be used by myself and the other for Caillou, who was sick and seemed to be suffering. My intention was to ride to his acquaintance's cabin on the Missouri, three miles from the confluence of the Kansas, in order to rest there a few days, and during the absence of my boat to make several incursions into the interior of the country to the west and along the Kansas River.

[*Note: Prince Paul continued his journey to the mouth of the Kansas River where he met Jean Baptiste Charbonneau. Later, at the Council Bluffs, Paul also met the father, Toussaint Charbonneau, who became the guide to the northernmost point of the Prince's trip, Fort Kiowa. Due to the hostility of the Arikara Indians, Paul decided to abandon plans to further ascend the river. From today's view we wonder why he missed, or decided to forego, the opportunity to join Ashley and Sublette in their expedition to the Rocky Mountains. Paul had met with the retreating group right after their getting attacked and while they finalized plans to follow an alternate route. Instead, Paul returned down river, picked up Pomp, and entered the Franklin/Boonville region again.*

The remaining section of the trip is described with unusual haste and platonic precision. After a quick visit with friends in St. Louis they took the steamboat **Cincinnati** *for New Orleans. The boat sank off Ste. Genevieve, and Paul's party spent many days there before returning to St. Louis to* find another boat. Once in New Orleans, they boarded a ship owned by the famous entrepreneur, Vincente Nolte, and set off for Europe. Paul had paid for the passage by promissory note, and Nolte had to sue for some eighteen months to collect on it.

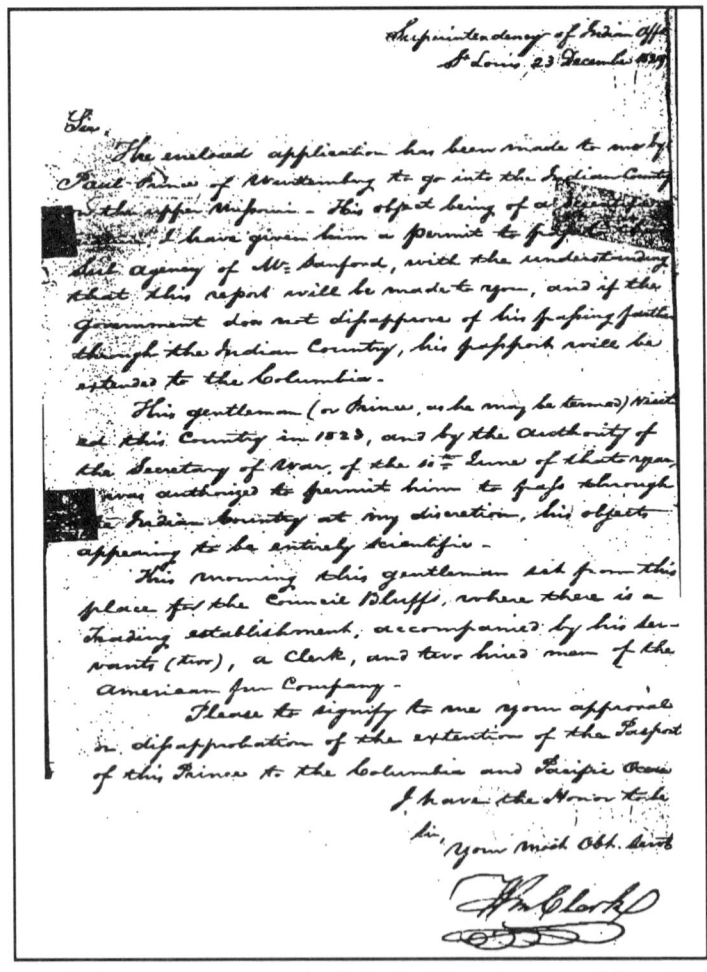

William Clark requests a passport for Duke Paul from Secretary of War, Eaton, December 23, 1829. (Courtesy Western Manuscripts Collection, State Historical Society of Missouri, Columbia, Mo.)

CHAPTER 3
THE RETURN OF DUKE PAUL TO THE MISSOURI RIVER COUNTRY, 1830

Hans von Sachsen-Altenburg

Shortly after the passage quoted from Paul's 1823 journal cited in the previous chapter Paul had his fateful meeting with Pomp at the Kansas River. His decision to take Pomp back to Germany with him in 1823 would have a profound effect on the boy's life. During the next seven years in Germany Pomp witnessed a world that was perhaps as strange and difficult for him to comprehend as it would have been for most other people in America and Europe unacquainted with European courts and their aristocrats trying to outdo each other with architectural splendor, cultural refinements, political intrigue, and interfamily marriages arranged to maintain peace and to increase power. It was, however, a world that was undergoing revolutionary changes. The aristocrats, kings and veterans of the old order and of the Napoleonic wars were gradually being superceded by a younger generation. This younger generation would bring about significant changes in the old concepts of nationalism, changes that would resonate and be the source of strife and bloodshed for the next 175 years.

When Paul arrived in Germany with Pomp, the two young men embarked upon the traditional circuit expected of a prince who wanted to see and to be seen. The long distance between Stuttgart and Carlsruhe allowed visits to many castles. A close friendship developed with the dukes of Altenburg who established Europe's first environmental museum. Of particular delight was the friendship with Ludwig, the young King of Bavaria.

He had married Therese Duchess von Sachsen-Hildburghausen, or Sachsen-Altenburg, and their wedding date has ever since been commemorated as a major festival for the common people. Still today, the same meadow, Theresienwiese, is the site of the annual commemorative Oktoberfest.

For Pomp, this was a time of personal growth and confusing observations. He learned to speak the German language and with his native French, the official language of the European courts at that time, he observed how skeletons were put into closets.

There were cultural aspects, too. Mozart's creations were being performed as had no music ever before, and the mysterious death of the young genius kept people shuddering. During the months before Beethoven's death, couriers carried extensive protocols and drafts of wedding contracts between Stuttgart and the north Bavarian castle of Regensburg. The splendor of a 400 plate seating at the wedding of Duke Paul Wilhelm and Princess Sophie von Turn und Taxis exceeded anything ever seen before in the castle.

Members of a ducal or royal household usually received a so-called apanage, a support payment from the sovereign's coffers, in money and kind. Paul's apanage consisted of money, wood, and hay for the horses. In addition, King Wilhelm had assigned the Castle of Mergentheim, that feisty and rebellious town, to the young couple. A member of the ruling house was to symbolize royal presence in the peripheral region of the kingdom. It took many months to convert the former knightly headquarters, which had recently been a school and a garrison, into a place fit for a member of the royal family. The King provided an additional onetime allowance for renovation and furniture, enough to make do, insufficient to finance the role the young ducal family was expected to fulfill.

Paul was thirty years old when he married, and with stereotypical precision he did what was expected— he planted trees, wrote a book, and begot a son. Those were the happy days.

Then things deteriorated. Paul's marriage failed, and son Maximilian was born in another castle belonging to Sophie's family. The contract of separation was at least as tedious to conclude as the marriage contract before. And there were many creditors demanding payments on yellowing bills.

On a different front, but affecting the minds of the entire family, Paul's brother Eugene was fighting a desperate and seemingly endless war against the Turks, or Moslems, in Bosnia.

This was a good time for Duke Paul and Jean Baptiste to leave. After a quick visit to Paris and Bordeaux in France, a visit to the Basque country and Spain, they departed for the West Indies. In late November of 1829, after several months on various Caribbean islands, they arrived in New Orleans.

Paul's second trip up the Missouri basically traced the path of the first trip back to where Paul had met Pomp, at the mouth of the Kaw. On this second trip, Duke Paul, now 32 years old, but pretending to be 45, was traveling as

> PAUL WILLIAM, of Wurtemburg, nephew of the King of Wurtemburg, arrived at New Orleans the 1st ult. from Europe. About six years since he spent some time in exploring the upper regions of the Missouri; but business requiring his return to Europe, he has revisited the American hemisphere, and will, in the prosecution of his former plan, cross the Rocky Mountains, and visit the continent on the Pacific. He is in his 33d year.
>
> Missouri Intelligencer,
> Fayette, Mo., Jan. 29, 1830

the naturalist Baron von Hohenberg. He was accompanied by two servants, Mr. Zierlein, supposedly 30 and called "Shirly" in America, and by "Mr. John Baptist," 25. The latter, of course, was Jean Baptiste Charbonneau ("Pomp"). As before, Duke Paul also hired additional help in St. Louis.

Between Christmas and New Year's Eve of 1829, the group passed the region of Boonville again, but no record of this visit seems to exist. There is, however, an interesting description of Boonville at this time, which comes from a diary kept by William M. Campbell, a Virginia attorney who moved to St. Charles, Missouri, in 1829 and took a trip up the Missouri River in the spring of 1830. A copy of this diary is in the archives of the Boonslick Historical Society. Campbell approached Boonville on April 30th, about four months after Paul passed through the area:

Boonville is a flourishing little town. It is the county seat of Cooper and has a very good brick court house. The town is built on the top of the high bluff of the Missouri river, which runs close by the base of the hill and affords excellent landing for steamboats. The principal part of the buildings have been put up within the last two or three years. Five stores, brewery, tannery, etc. This promises to become a very respectable town.

From the town the citizens have a fine view of the Missouri river and can look down with pity on the town of Old Franklin, which is situated on the low bottom on the other side of the river and is represented as being a very sickly place and in great danger of being washed away by the falling in of the banks into the river.

This has caused the establishment of a new town, called New Franklin, about 2 miles from the River. A great many of the houses have been removed from the old to the New Town, which last is flourishing on the ruins of the former....

Steamboats make a trip to St. Louis and back in about 10 days and frequently arrive in the summer season. A cabin passage from Boonville to St. Louis amounts to 8 dollars and a return to 12. Deck passage to one-fourth of that amount.

> The Prince of Wurtchiburg arrived at New Orleans on the 29th Nov. after an absence of a year, during which time he has explored the vast regions in the Western World, even beyond the Rocky Mountains. This toilsome and even dangerous voyage, he has performed with the greatest intrepidity, and not without having to encounter the threats and hostilities of the Indians. He was to leave New Orleans in a few days, to make a tour of the Republic of Mexico.

Missouri Intelligencer,
Columbia, Mo., January 29, 1831

Paul spent the entire winter and summer hunting and trading between the Bluffs and Fort Union, a hitherto unheard of region for Europeans. No comprehensive diary has survived from that particular trip, but plenty of evidence and documentation can be found in other primary sources. Of particular importance are Paul's later flash backs, written in his 1851 diary, like this entry dated August 25th (translation by David Miller):

At 7 o'clock we again reached a bad shallow place and the boat ran aground, but there was not a long delay since it presently came loose again. A thickly forested row of hills form the right (southern) bank, with sycamores, linden, ash and small-leaved aspen comprising the principal trees. The region extends thus without noticeable change until before Lexington. There the right bank rises into sizable hills, on whose slopes the lively, flourishing city lies. Twenty years ago when I was coming from the Rocky Mountains in my pirogue and stopped here to buy flour, there had been only a few houses. At that time I had a remarkable tame eagle which had accompanied me

85

DUKE PAUL'S 1830 JOURNEY

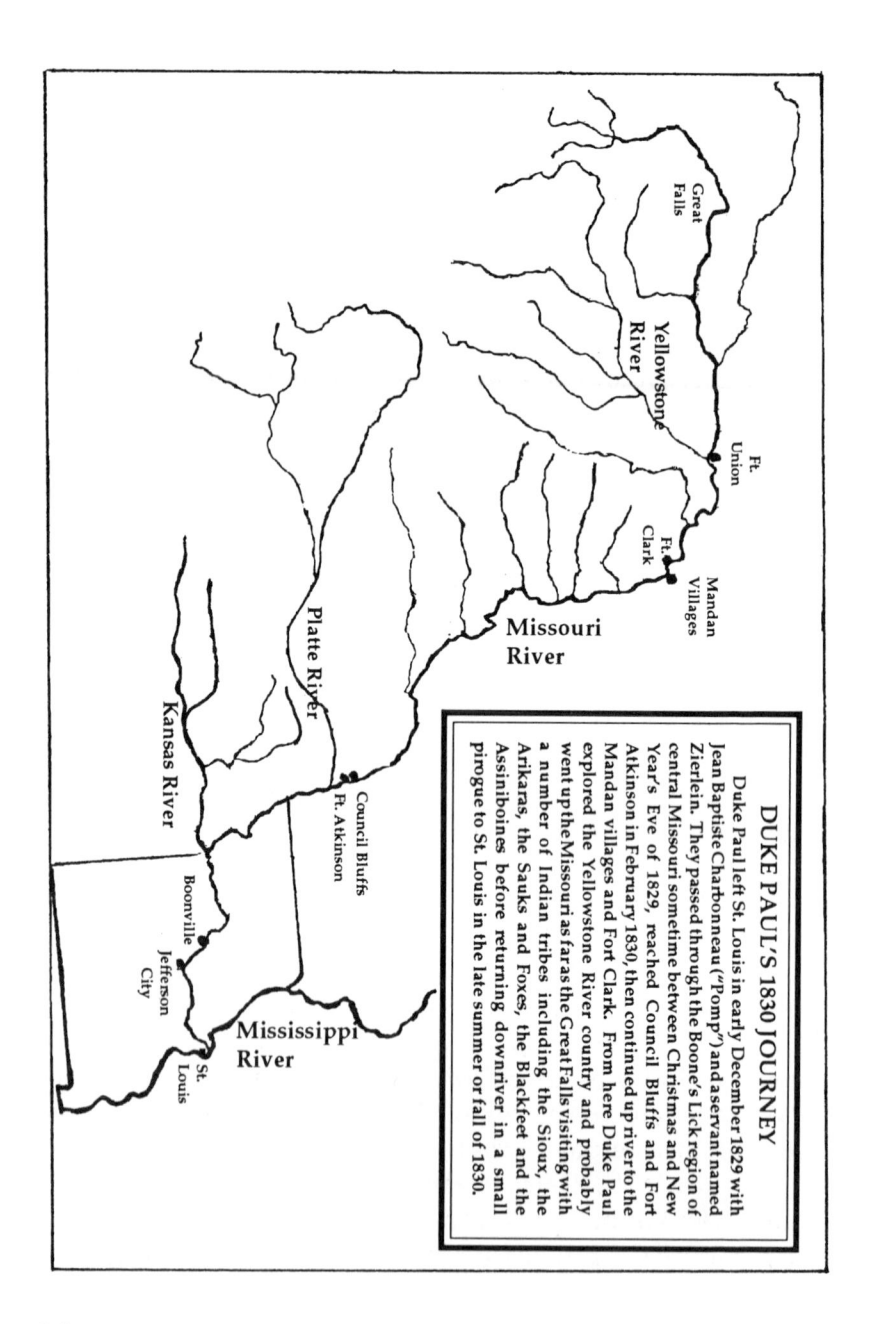

Duke Paul left St. Louis in early December 1829 with Jean Baptiste Charbonneau ("Pomp") and a servant named Zierlein. They passed through the Boone's Lick region of central Missouri sometime between Christmas and New Year's Eve of 1829, reached Council Bluffs and Fort Atkinson in February 1830, then continued up river to the Mandan villages and Fort Clark. From here Duke Paul explored the Yellowstone River country and probably went up the Missouri as far as the Great Falls visiting with a number of Indian tribes including the Sioux, the Arikaras, the Sauks and Foxes, the Blackfeet and the Assiniboines before returning downriver in a small pirogue to St. Louis in the late summer or fall of 1830.

faithfully from the falls. It would perch unfettered on the prow of the pirogue, and then it would fly away, sometimes to the far bank, but it always came back immediately when it saw the boat in motion. The inhabitants would gather to watch it, and it gave us all much pleasure. This marvel of domestication accompanied me as far as New Orleans, where I gave it to a friend. The fact that I was granted the privilege of seeing these regions again in good health and spirits, after so many years and travels, filled me with a sincere feeling of gratitude toward the great master builder of the universe.

On his return to St. Louis, Duke Paul took passage on the steamboat *New Jersey* bound for New Orleans. Amazingly enough the *New Jersey* sank at exactly the same place off Ste. Genevieve as the *Cincinnati* exactly seven years before.

In New Orleans, Paul was severely attacked by some unknown foe as being an agent of European powers. Angrily, Paul left the U.S. and spent the following nine months criss-crossing Mexico.

Upon his return to Mergentheim in Germany, the people greeted him cheerfully and the mayor pronounced him an honorary citizen.

For Paul, the thirties were a period of finishing and working up the past and starting over again. He revised and finally, in 1835, issued the diary of his first trip, incorporating many comments of his second journey. The divorce proceedings were finalized, and a liaison that was to be kept a secret for years to come would result in the birth of a daughter whose identity would also remain a secret for many years.

In 1839, after several short European trips, Paul embarked upon an excursion to Egypt and Nubia, Sudan. Invited by the powerful and ruthless viceroy of Egypt to help in searching for gold, Paul entered territories never before visited by Europeans. For years to come, naturalists and explorers would follow his descriptions and claim for themselves to have discovered new places. As usual, Paul took extensive notes in his diaries and wrote voluminous letters to many people. His whereabouts and some of his letters were published both in Germany and abroad. He returned to Europe via Constantinople (Istanbul), Trieste, and Vienna to Stuttgart. The citizens of Mergentheim gave him a torchlight reception at the time of his arrival in September of 1840.

The years of the 1840's can best be described as being filled with family life, maintaining a small court in Mergentheim and Carlsruhe, and corresponding with numerous savants, the "who's who" in various fields of science. The University of Tuebingen bestowed an honorary doctorate, and Paul was made honorary member and president of several scientific organizations in Europe.

By April 1843, when the Scottish traveller and hunter, Sir William Drummond Stewart of Murthly in Perthshire had returned to St. Louis again, having spent 1834 until 1838 visiting the West and the intermittent years sorting the inheritance of his baronetcy in Scotland, Jean Baptiste Charbonneau had traversed the breadth of Missouri numerous times. His background at Duke Paul's castles had allowed him to become a good cart and carriage driver, his connections to the right people in St. Louis—and his being there at the right time—got him the job of accompanying the Scottish gentleman.

Jean Baptiste had been with Sublette for many years; they had met at several rendezvous of the fur trappers in the thirties and then had joined their expanding operations in today's Colorado. Knowing the Missouri river well, he was in charge, among other things, of transporting furs to St. Louis. It may have been after another successful descent of the South Platte and the Missouri when Jean Baptiste was asked, most probably by William Sublette himself, to join this exciting expedition.

Since each picture is worth a thousand words, earlier travellers are often better known through their painter companions, as for example the Prince von Wied-Neuwied/Bodmer team. Sir William is no exception, for he is perhaps best known for having been accompanied by the artist, Alfred Jacob Miller, who left an invaluable record of the travels during the 1830's. The baronet's writings are virtually unobtainable in America, but his biography makes better reading anyhow.

In contrast to the earlier expeditions, the 1843 excursion lacked all the elements of immortality; there was no true diary, no Sir William novel, and no awesome sequence of pictures by a Miller. Yet, the group was more illustrious than before, including invited guests not only from St. Louis and New Orleans, but also from Maryland and Indiana. Father de Smet went along, too. It may have been the situation where everybody thought the other one would write the journal or take hasty scribbles to be turned into oil at moments of greater comfort. Strangely enough, nothing of this trip would be known had it not been for two separate, fragmentary diaries, one lacking historical substance, being primarily an exercise of bookkeeping, and the other one lacking proximity in time.

The journal of William L. Sublette covers the timespan from 1 May until 10 June 1843. Incidentally, the surviving fragment ends at exactly the location where Duke Paul and his companion nearly met their death, eight years later, on the Oregon Trail.

Sublette's group, only nine days behind Fremont, builds a bridge between Baptiste Charbonneau and Duke Paul, who used the learning experience of the earlier groups and Fremont's maps on his trip to Laramie.

William Sublette's life is so well-known to readers of early Western history that we refer to those tomes of biography. Suffice it to mention that he had been with the Ashley men whom the young Prince Paul encountered after their defeat by Arikara Indians in 1823. Now, twenty years later and tired of the fur trade, he was to honor his Scottish friend by accompanying him into the ever-exciting wilderness. It was to be William's last major trip.

There is evidence that this expedition departed from St. Louis in two separate parties a few days apart, William Sublette leading the first, Sir William the second. As the former lists his six-person team, we may safely assume that Baptiste must have been with the other group which unfortunately kept no records. Taking literary license we might imagine a transfer of his presence into the following quotation from Sublette's journal as even the sparsest comments are more elucidating than none at all. There is no narrative for the days between St. Louis and Westport, on 27 May, the journal being a mere cash book journal of expenses ("Journal of William L. Sublette," **Mississippi Valley Historical Review**, VI, No. 1, June 1919, pp. 99-110).

At Round Grove, also Elm Grove, at the headwaters of Cedar Creek, the Sublette party missed Sir William's party as they took another trail; and both missed an emigrant's train which included Peter Burnett, later to become California's governor. Seven years later, on July 4, 1850, Duke Paul was to ride in the same carriage with this gentleman. The two Williams joined their groups on

May 30, 1843, on the Soldier River. The second record of the very same excursion was recorded sixty-eight years after the fact, in 1911, by the daughter of the participant, William Clark Kennerly. One needs to wonder why there were not more memoirs of this type produced by the early leaders of St. Louis, or if they were, why they have not yet been published. Kennerly was eighteen years old in 1843, and we can only surmise the exactness of his memory when he retold the adventure at the age of 86. Kennerly seemed to have a nearly perfect recall, setting the stage for great imagination. On the return trip the apparent excellence of recall was based on an existing diary, "My Hunting Trip to the Rockies in 1843," written by Kennerly and published in **Colorado Magazine** (XXII, No. 1, January 1945, pp. 23-38).

They spent the Fourth of July at Fort Laramie and continued to the Wind River Mountains, the ancient hunting grounds of the Shoshone, and to today's Yellowstone National Park, returning some six months later.

[*Note: The following photographs are of items from the Duke Paul Wilhelm Collection in the British Museum and are reproduced here courtesy of The Trustees of the British Museum. This collection has been in the possession of the British Museum since 1869 when it was purchased from an antique dealer in Hamburg named Umlauf by Augustus Woolaston Franks, Keeper of the Ethnography Department.*

There is reason to assume that the items belonged to a specially selected core collection the Duke wished to have shipped back to America in connection with his plans to establish a permanent residence in that country. His sudden death thwarted such plans and only through the indiscretion of a former servant did the royal estate learn of the existence of a rented, two room suite in a Bremen hotel filled with trunks, bags and collectibles.]

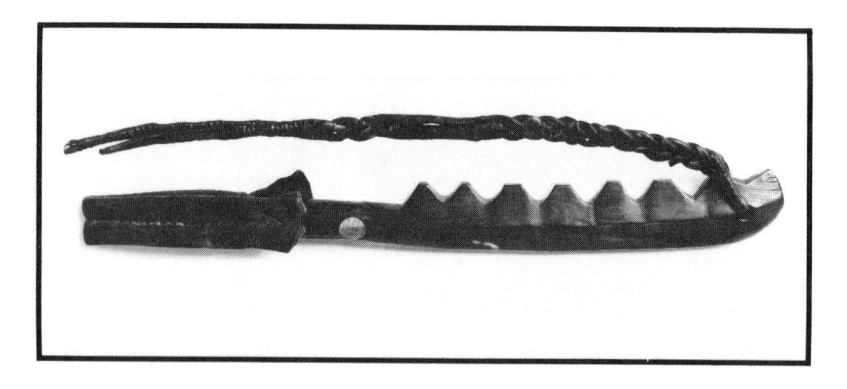

Riding Quirt, possibly Kiowa or Commanche (British Museum Catalogue No. 5213): Probably collected on Duke Paul's third Missouri River trip. Polished pecan (?) wood serrated on one edge, buffalo hide lash. Handle 36.2 cm long, wrist strap 15.9 cm, lash 49.5 cm. This quirt may have been in Duke Paul's possession when he recuperated in Boonville in 1851.

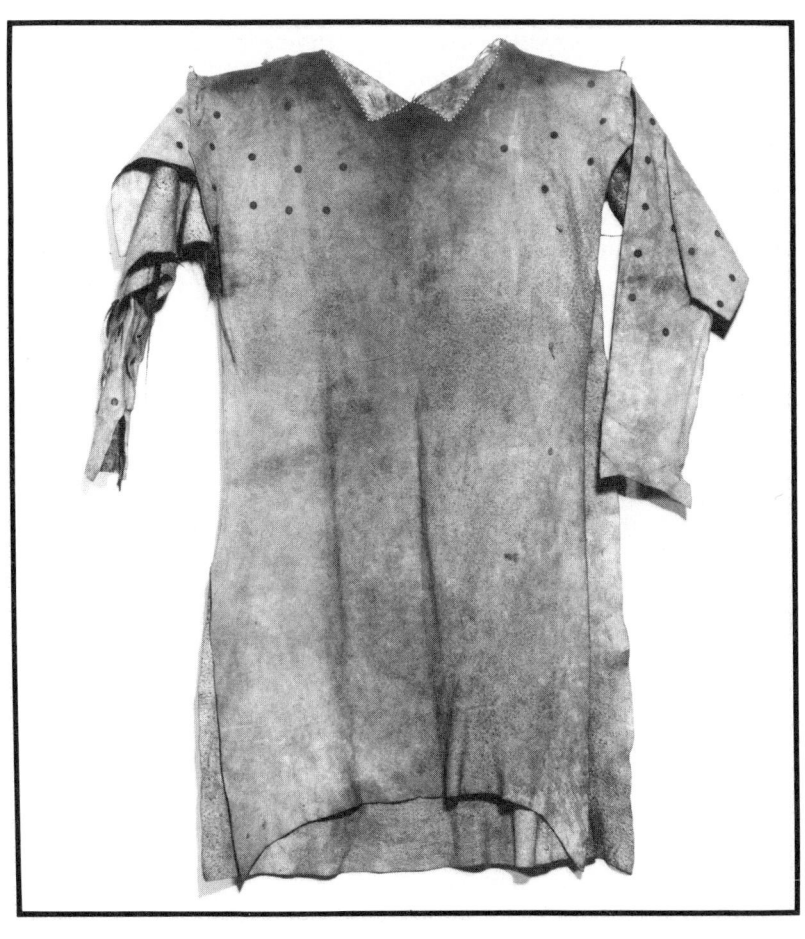

Teton Dakota (Sioux) Shirt (British Museum Catalogue No. 5203): Probably collected on Duke Paul's second Missouri River trip from Mato Tatanka (Bull Bear), head warrior of the Kiyuksa band of the Oglalas. Buckskin with red and black paint, white beads, horsehair locks, a powder measure made from the tip of a buffalo horn and a bear claw (the last two, symbols of the man's name). 106 cm long; sleeve to sleeve 162.6 cm wide; body 54.6 cm wide.

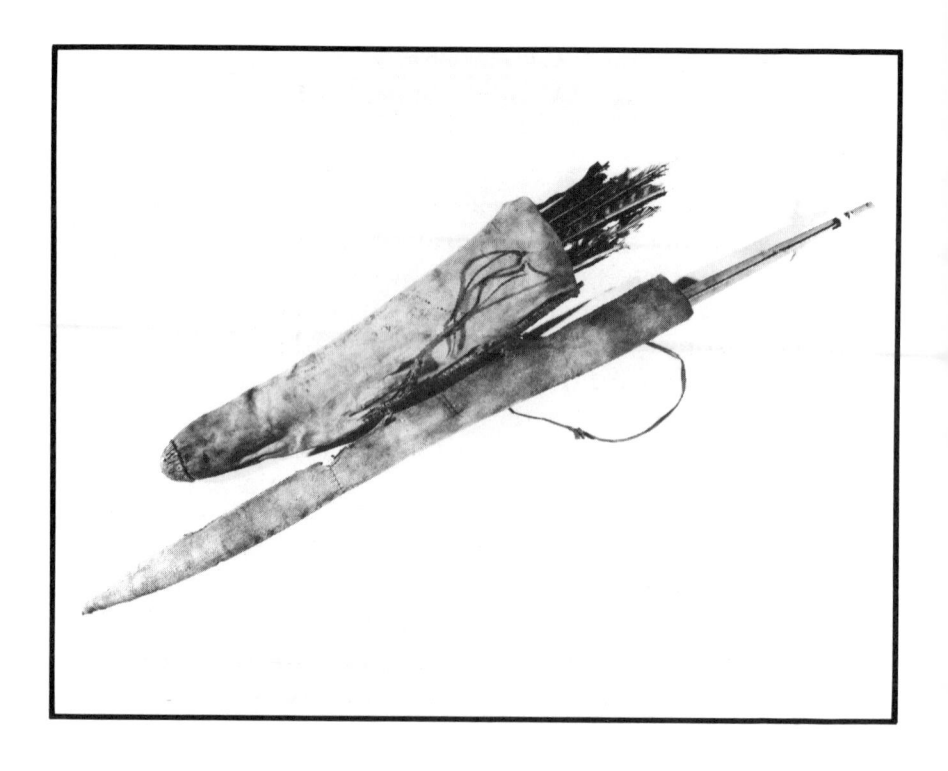

Osage bow, arrows and quiver. (British Museum Catalogue No. 5206): Probably collected on Duke Paul's second Missouri River trip. The Bow may be of Osage Orange wood and the string is twisted sinew. The quiver consists of buckskin fortified with a stick, 12 arrows (six with metal heads) bound to the shafts with sinew, each decorated with 3 flight feathers from hawk, wild turkey and eagle. The upper shafts are painted red with grooves. Bow 120 cm long, bowcase 95.3 cm; quiver 63.5 cm; arrows 61 cm (average).

CHAPTER 4
DUKE PAUL'S THIRD VISIT, 1851

In Germany the 1840s started out as a quiet decade, the quiet before the storm. Paul may have sensed a continuing political unsettledness in the populace of Germany and other countries he visited, but there were other reasons for him to worry. Paul had not paid many bills nor wages for a while. The small apanage simply could not cover the expenses. Miraculously, creditors would carry the debts for as long as seven years. Paul became less and less at ease in Mergentheim and regularly escaped to a small hunting cottage in the mountains, the Swabian Alb, located between the Kingdoms of Wuerttemberg and Bavaria.

Following the popular outbursts in Paris and elsewhere in early 1848, unrest became the fuse to the powderkeg. The House of Representatives cut the apanage rendering Duke Paul even more unable to cover his debts. Finally, the creditors had enough. Some used the legal way of trying to get their money; others took the more direct approach by storming the castle and plundering the rooms. The Duke of Wuerttemberg could not pay his debts. The royal connection did not help. Paul wrote a friend that he was secretly making plans to emigrate to California.

As pressure by creditors mounted, Paul disappeared. His beloved little secret, Pauline, had been spirited away before, staying with friends. After hiding valuables and friends in the mountain cottage, he disappeared.

For the following eight years, Schumacher, a trusted friend and legal counsel, experienced in matters of fighting, negotiating, and staying creditors, acted first under Paul's power of attorney, then under court orders to settle with creditors. He was the only one to know of Paul's whereabouts. Today, we know of the cunning, and successful, double-dealing the clever man managed in squirreling away property and money for Paul, raising money from the royal family, and even getting Paul's divorced wife, Sophie, to sign supportive papers. A true friend in need.

Prince Paul had taken off for Texas to cross the Sierras for the Pacific. He took a boat in Mazatlan and sailed for San Francisco. On the Fourth of July of 1850, partaking in the great parade to the California gold fields, Prince Paul rode in the same carriage with Colonel Sutter and the governor and lieutenant-governor of California. Paul visited the Placer gold fields and, according to his own diary, bought a few choice nuggets.

Paul returned to New Orleans via Panama and Havana and visited Illinois, where a former servant of his, now a Lutheran pastor, had settled to found a new church in a largely German community.

In the summer of 1851, Paul, at the age of 54, decided to attend the widely publicized Indian Treaty Council at Fort Laramie, a region he had not visited before. The trip would take him up the Missouri to the Platte where he would take the Great Platte River Road, also known as the Oregon Trail, to Fort Laramie. He also hoped to pay a visit to the Rocky Mountains while at Fort Laramie. Sensing a great adventure, Paul embarked with a team of two German greenhorns, one of them was a Mr. von Zichlinsky, a young immigrant from Saxony about whose background and future nothing is known, and the other was the famous writer of western stories, Balduin Moellhausen.

Moellhausen was born in Bonn, of Pomeranian parents—a Prussian military officer and a Baroness von Falkenstein. It is still a mystery when Moellhausen entered the U.S. and where he met Duke Paul. The young man's father, having abandoned his baroness-wife and their five children in Germany, once served as a soldier in the Texas army. Through Duke Paul's introduction, Moellhausen became a close friend of Alexander von Humboldt and may even have married the savant's illegitimate daughter. In 1853 Moellhausen accompanied Capt. A.W. Whipple on an expedition to California. On another trip he accompanied Lt. Joseph C. Ives along the Colorado River. In Germany Moelhausen's books, based on his travels and adventures in America, became bestsellers. A street in Berlin is named after this former greenhorn, and a complete reprint of all his works is currently underway in Germany. His descendants live in Germany today.

As always Duke Paul kept a detailed diary of his 1851 trip to America. In the account that follows portions of this diary will be used to tell the story. This is the first-ever publication of parts of the 1851 diary (possibly edited by him in 1852). The diaries were photographed in 1935, and were probably destroyed in 1945. Negatives of the 1935 photographs were obtained from Dr. Charles Camp by Dr. David Miller in 1968. Dr. Miller made prints from the negatives and then transcribed and translated the diaries in 1973. The translation was reviewed for accuracy by Dr. Raymond J. Spahn and Betty Alderton Spahn. For the unusual history of the diary see Hans von Sachsen-Altenburg, "Rewritten History: Embellished Diaries of Duke Paul von Wuerttemberg's Trip to Ft. Laramie in 1851 Unmasked." Suffice it to point out, as a warning to serious readers of Western history, that the publication of a segment of this particular diary by Louis C. Butscher, "An Account of Adventures in the Great American Desert by His Royal Highness, Duke Paul Wilhelm von Wuerttemberg," **New Mexico Historical Review**, XVII, 3, July 1942, pp. 193-225 and 294-344, contains falsified and partially contradictory "facts" which Duke Paul had neither experienced nor noted in his diary. Butscher based his highly creative translation on an already altered transcription of the diary by German archivist, Friedrich Bauser.

The same holds true for the otherwise excellent publication by John Hussey and Michael Harrison, editors, **Early Sacramento, Glimpses of John Augustus Sutter, The Hok Farm and Neighboring Indian Tribes** by Prince Paul, H.R.H. Duke Paul Wilhelm of Wuerttemberg, The Sacramento Book Collector's Club, Sacramento, CA., 1973. In this edition, Butscher even managed to expand Duke Paul's actual experiences by a major trip northward, covering several weeks of time.

Both of these publications, based on incorrect transcriptions and maliciously falsified translations, should be discarded as fraudulent in their entirety as they hold neither scientific nor historical value.

Paul, Zichlinsky and Moelhausen obtained passage on the steamboat *Pocahontas* and left St. Louis after dusk on August 21, headed for Independence. The steamboat soon reached the German colony of Hermann where Paul made some interesting notes about the recent (and, to Paul, unsuccessful) attempts of the German immigrants there to make wine from Catawba grapes. Leaving Hermann, the steamboat *Pocahontas* continued upriver and was soon within sight of Missouri's state capital, Jefferson City.

DUKE PAUL'S 1851 JOURNEY

Duke Paul left St. Louis on the steamboat **Pocahontas** on August 21, 1851, went up the Missouri River and passed through the central Missouri region on August 24 landing at the town of "Kanzas" (present day Kansas City) the next day. He then set out overland on the California Road, passed by the Shawnee Mission and the Potawatomi Mission (Union Town), crossed the Kansas River to St. Mary's Mission and proceeded up the Little Blue River valley to Ft. Kearney on the Platte River. From Ft. Kearney he followed the Platte to Ft. Laramie, passing by Ash Hollow, the Chimney Rock and Scott's Bluff.

He began his return trip in early October, arriving at the forks of the Platte on October 26 and reaching the Little Blue River on November 4. For the next two weeks he was slowed to a standstill by a blizzard, finally making his way to Independence in early December and then to Boonville, arriving there on December 7, 1851. He left Boonville by stage coach on December 24 and arrived back in St. Louis on December 31, 1851.

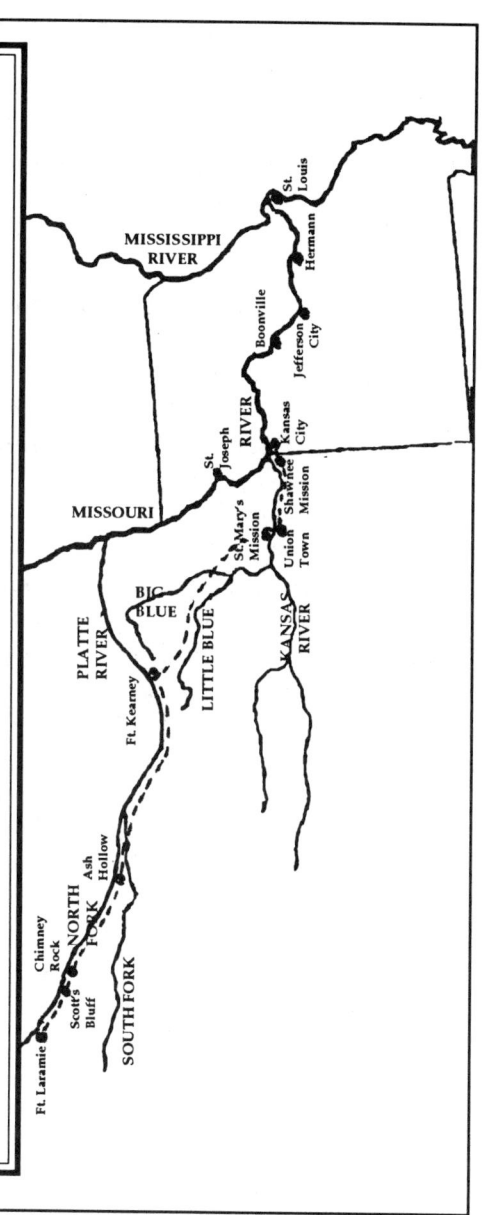

[From the diary of Duke Paul, 1851]

23 August. Saturday — *In the morning thick fog lay on the riverbed. Therefore we remained anchored until the breakfast hour. Then, however, the sun illuminated a remarkably delightful region, and outlines of the well-known Côte sans Dessein became visible. Then the mouth of the Osage (wasa-sehe) — the Rivière des Grands Os of the Creoles — appears camouflaged by timber opposite the large island. The stream here is very wide and full of shoals. Its right bank is dotted with large islands, the N.W. bank of the Missouri with luxuriant stands of virgin forest.*

A butte with protruding rock rises up directly above the river's mouth. At its foot lies a settlement of some houses and a saw or grist mill. They form a picturesque grouping which I sketched in haste. The Missouri's banks with their beautiful clusters of rocks and hills and the virgin forests so exceedingly rich in manifold varieties of timber and shrubs, have lost nothing through the advancement of cultivation and the establishment of cities and farm settlements, for although these appear infrequently up to now and are to some extent shabby, they nevertheless embellish the scenery; the alternation between cultivated places and those that appear touched only by the hand of creation is pleasing to the eye. Since it rained more than usual this summer, the vegetation was still uncommonly vivid and the most lovely green brightened not only the ground covered with weeds and grass, but also colored the branches and crowns of the trees with most delicate adornment of abundant foliage in a hardly believable nuance of hues, which with the advancing summer season turn more and more from the light and deep greens into blue, yellow, red and brown, and the landscape puts on a raiment that not even the tropical zones of our planet can produce.

We then approached another very lovely Missouri landscape namely the city of Jefferson situated on the right bank with its magnificent capitol and government seat, one of the foremost and finest buildings of the Union. The state penitentiary, a square building surrounded by high white walls, is situated on a hill on the western edge of the city, not far from the river. The hill forms a smooth grassy ridge, which terminates in steep limestone bluffs at the river. This hilly little city is most attractively situated, a picture of prosperity, and fairly healthful, a great advantage on the fever-infested Missouri, whose shores are so inviting outwardly, so deadly in general. Orchards flourish here as in Hermann, and the most excellent and delightful peaches are sold for a trifle. This is one of the most healthful and useful fruits of the land, often as large as a Stettin apple and thereby so valuable that it furnishes a choice article of food when dried. The state capitol is in the style of the capitol at Washington and like the latter is laid out on an elevation encircled by lawns and parks. Here as well, the elevation slopes down to the river in a sharp limestone bluff.

Duke Paul von Wuerttemberg during the 1850s

The boat passed the Rivière à Moreau (Morrow Creek) and the Ile aux Cèdres, where I found no great changes in the bank before reaching Jefferson, which at the time of my first journey was a miserable nest of drunkards and is now the seat of state government. During my first journey I had gained the sad impression about it during an unpleasant layover there.

The boat moved at a fast pace, and without further

delay traveled by Joncar, past the Pointe à Ducharme, toward the Petit Manitou with its charming limestone cliffs and high junipers. The influx of the Petite Bonne Femme Osage was almost completely hidden in the forest. The region around the Cap à l'Ail has continually increased in population. Shortly after our meal we reached the Little Manitou whose hilly right bank contrasted with the lowland along the left bank, which was covered with a stand of timber that unfolded into a great display of tall tree trunks. It was a beautiful, clear day, but unbearably hot. My companions visited the bank while wood was cut, but brought back little of value. I noticed that there had been a partial collapse of the left bank of the river at the little town of Nashville. The Little Saline River comes in from the N.W. through low-lying land, terres basses (bottoms), alternating with battures; eventually, however, after a bend in the stream these merge with higher land. A chain of rocky hills rises on the left bank. Everywhere here, the Missouri still retains its earlier character, and my itinerary of 1823 still served me in 1851 as a guide book. An extremely bad place along the left bank which had made my keel boat so hard to manage, was full of snaggers and an angry current. The steamer easily overcame it. The thick growth of the deciduous trees and the dark green of the cedars with the singular shapes they assume when old, as well as the white contrasting coloration of the limestone bluffs enhanced the landscape's picturesque quality. A mass of creeping vines encircled the pillar-like trunks of the smaller-leaved poplars with their dense garlands, and the leaves of the sumacs and the Ampelopsis were already turning red. The picturesque, long, rocky chain of hills visible from the river often assumed the most grotesque shapes, sometimes taking the form of walls riddled with grottos, and the heights were always covered with magnificent woods. This gave the landscape an inexpressibly beautiful character which served to bring back recollections of my youth. A fur company clerk whom I had earlier encountered on my first journey, derived the most heartfelt delight skimming through my diary and recalling the old times.

Rocheport lies at the end of the picturesque chain of hills on an open almost level place, so the location of the little town is not bad. Naturally it was not there 30 years ago. The Missouri becomes very wide before and after Rocheport, full of shoals and difficult to navigate at low water. Upstream, close to the city the rocky hills once again press near and form the 2nd part of the grotesque scenery. The Big Manitou adjoins this rocky chain, but it eludes the eye because of a sandy expanse on the stream bed overgrown with willows and poplars. The evening was beautiful but still oppressively hot, and the sun went down serenely in a purple brilliance. The stream, although very wide, no longer offered so many obstacles as at Hermann. There was not a breath of air. In the night the boat toiled several hours in the shoals in the vicinity of the Prairie [Pierre] de la Fleche (Arrow-Rock) above Boonville, where we only stopped half an hour at 9 o'clock. Boonville has prospered at the expense of Franklin which lies almost directly opposite. The latter is in decline, since its location is unsuitable. The night was uncommonly dark, so that when I got up I saw nothing except the heavens with stars and gloomy river banks disappearing in the nocturnal haze. How one can navigate with a steamer under such conditions with a low water level is a mystery which only the steamboat captains know how to solve.

24 August — Sunday. The bright morning sun illuminated Glasgow town on the left bank. The eastern and Grand Chariton flow into the Missouri at Glasgow. The flourishing town is well situated, has fairly good houses and serves as a market place for a rich countryside. Across the river is flat forest land. A large island lies at the mouth of the

Chariton, and the little stream flows by the hills upon which Glasgow is located. The region produces much tobacco and excellent corn. The river makes several great bends and flows many miles through a broad, level valley, constricted by bottoms and strewn with islands and sandbars, while the lowlands are resplendent with the finest giants of the forest. The newer islands won from the stream bed and the level shores are often covered only with low willows and aspen, often with sandy meadows where turf and sand impede walking. The prairie on the right bank draws near to the Missouri and then extends in a boundless expanse as a grassy plain as far as the foot of the high mountain chain which in western America forms the continental divide. In the west a chain of hills first interrupts the level region, which is settled and where tobacco is grown. After this the land is once again flat for the most part, and the river—in parts very wide and shallow—is filled everywhere with snaggers. Consequently navigation is very difficult. The heat was moderated by some wind; otherwise it would have been unbearable. At midday about 1 o'clock the left bank rose from the bottoms and Brunswick lay on a bare place before us below the Grand River (Grande Riviere). It is a small place of close to 1000 inhabitants, with many warehouses since it is the market place for several counties, and the land is cultivated back from and along the river. Formerly the Iowas lived along its banks, and long years before I had found the population still very sparse. Since it was Sunday, many people were assembled at the landing place. The flat point of land which extends upstream as far as Grande Riviere, is a sort of prairie covered with high brush and weeds, as they often appear along the stream on the Upper Missouri. At the end of the latter a fairly large river flows into the Missouri without being concealed by an island, but its water, which is clear, is dammed up by the force of the great river, and the division of color is very distinct. An extensive lowland adjoins the Missouri bank. The stream is divided into two parts by an island in its center, but the channel is deep enough. On the island, which terminates in sandbars, lay many snaggers which formed rafts, but they were not so enormous here as on the lower Mississippi and Red Rivers. We approached the small town of Miami, situated on a low, pleasant chain of hills between lowlands where the dense forest is overrun with the greatest variety of creeping vines, giving it an extremely peculiar character.

The heat was hardly bearable. The channel led again many miles through lowlands, and the stream bed became more or less difficult because of sandbars, shoals, snaggers, whirlpools, etc. Colossal rafts covered the lowlands or had lodged in the stream bed itself and formed great piles of wood whose fantastic forms were amazing to the eye. Large parts of the bottoms had been undermined by the violent torrent and torn loose from the mainland, sinking into the stream bed and filling up the deep places of the river. The torrent's gigantic forest trophies had either surged downstream with the current or gone under with it so that only their upper branches extended above the niveau of the stream, forming enormous sawyers (chicots). These eboulis (places where banks have caved in) were the most dangerous places in the river.

The immoderately hot day ended in a beautiful sunset, and a cool evening set in. The current was very stong; consequently the trip on the average was slow. Carolina parakeets flew over the river in noisy swarms, and great blue herons rose up awkwardly from the sandbanks. The night was still relatively warm; the journey was continued after dark, naturally very cautiously, as far as Grande Passe, near which we awaited the morning. All in all, the stretch we traversed in the night was of little consequence.

25 August. Monday — It was again very warm in the morning, and an agonizing day was to be expected, all the more so since not the slightest breeze stirred. The sky was very clear and little dew had fallen. The region, mostly forested lowlands, had practically nothing to distinguish it from yesterday's except that there were countless caterpillar nests and webs in the trees along the bank that I had not observed previously in Missouri. The banks of the Missouri are covered with a veritable virgin forest in all stages of growth from sprouts to complete decay. Long years must elapse and a great mass of people emigrate before the country is stripped of its primeval character. The American, driven by the passion to migrate, continually looks into the distance for that which his immediate surroundings could offer him, and new states arise while the old ones still afford so much space. It seems to me that a large concentrated population would be politically more sound than this disunion. Since the American nation has yet little to fear from without, the present system may endure for the time being, but in the presence of an external threat it would be untenable and very inexpedient.

At 7 o'clock we again reached a bad shallow place and the boat ran aground, but there was not a long delay since it presently came loose again. A thickly forested row of hills form the right (southern) bank, with sycamores, linden, ash and small-leaved aspen comprising the principal trees. The region extends thus without noticeable change until before Lexington. There the right bank rises into sizeable hills, on whose slopes the lively, flourishing city lies. Twenty years ago when I was coming from the Rocky Mountains in my pirogue and stopped here to buy flour, there had been only a few houses. At that time I had a remarkable tame eagle which had accompanied me faithfully from the falls. It would perch unfettered on the prow of the pirogue, and then it would fly away, sometimes to the far bank, but it always came back immediately when it saw the boat in motion. The inhabitants would gather to watch it, and it gave us all much pleasure. This marvel of domestication *accompanied me as far as New Orleans, where I gave it to a friend. The fact that I was granted the privilege of seeing these regions again in good health and spirits, after so many years and travels, filled me with a sincere feeling of gratitude toward the great master builder of the universe.*

After Lexington the region became level again, the river wide and dangerous, the air hot and calm. In the afternoon, when wood was taken on at a new settlement situated in the bottoms, this oppressive heat became so intense that one could have suffocated; at the same time a sort of haze darkened the atmosphere (104°F. in the shade).

At 4 o'clock we reached Camden, whose excellent location on the left bank I mentioned before. It had not grown very much. The hills, crowned with tall deciduous trees, served as the domicile of much game, especially countless turkeys. I found little change on the island of Fort Osage, but there was a noticeable change in the settlement itself, which we reached before 7 o'clock in the evening. The old barracks had long since disappeared, and an imposing number of farms enlivened the area. Before evening the sky clouded up and the heat became totally unendurable so that one could not tolerate the clothes on one's body. It appeared that the night would be very dark, naturally impeding navigation. The region around Ft. Osage is still wild forest and the hunting ground good. Before one reaches the island, Fish Creek flows into the Missouri. Fort Osage, where we landed for some time, has some merchants now and some fairly large brick houses and steam mills. The hill on which the fort was situated a good many years before, is a bare place and rests on limestone which crops out on the bank.

Now the sky darkened in the N.W., there was violent lightning accompanied by the distant rumbling of thunder, and a slight wind sprang up, a veritable restorative for all the sweat-soaked people here. The last thunderstorms are likely to occur toward the end of August.

Since the Americans do not pay attention to previous nomenclature and designate every settlement with a name of their own choosing, despite its having been named long before—especially by Creoles—I could not find Fort Osage on the new map nor immediately enter the new name. It is now called Sibley.

A terrible thunderstorm with frightful rain broke out as night approached and we remained anchored for the night.

26 August — *The morning was overcast, but we got underway early and reached the small town of Wayne City* [assumed by Dr. Miller to be the present day town of Richfield] *at 6 o'clock. The sky remained overcast and the atmosphere cooled off only slightly. At last a refreshing N.W. wind sprang up. After 8 o'clock the first bluff landing, a well situated place on the right bank, appeared ahead of us. There were a few houses back upon the parallel rocky bluffs of the multi-sectioned elevation. The Mississippi and the Missouri exhibit identical geological formations over a vast area, and exceedingly remarkable geological phenomenon, when one considers that an expanse larger than all of Germany exhibits only low elevations of limestone formation, generally extending in a parallel direction along the rivers with alternating deposits of sand and clay strata. Blue Mill is the first bluff landing. All guide books and river navigators which appear in the U.S. are grossly incorrect. The maps are comparatively good concerning the mathematical bearing and demarcation; even the statistical surveys of the large lots are excellent; yet the designation of settlements is incomplete. Somewhat further upstream the limestone lies upon gray clay; the latter appears above the water level at low water. Now the sky threatened with renewed rain, but despite the earlier thundershowers the creeks were still dry.*

At 9:30 o'clock we came to Liberty Landing — *with*

which I was previously acquainted — situated on the left bank along rocky bluffs, with its freight depots for the town of Liberty.

[The basic facts of Paul's trip across the plains to Fort Laramie and back again are given in his **Letter from Boonville.** The diaries contain additional important information about the circumstances of this exciting and hazardous journey, but as they are in the process of being published as a whole, and the primary focus of this book is on Duke Paul's various passages through the Boonslick region of Central Missouri, we will simply summarize the trip here and then continue with the conclusion as Paul arrives in Boonville.

This turned out to be the most dangerous trip Paul had ever undertaken, and a series of omens at the beginning of the trip seem to foreshadow its disastrous climax. In Kansas City, Paul injured his back and lost several days recuperating. Finally, on August 30 he left for Westport.

As the Fort Laramie Treaty council began, Paul was hastening westward hoping to arrive before it ended, but his inexperienced companions caused one delay after another. First, von Zichlinsky ran into a tree, breaking parts of the wagon. The next day Paul's wagon got stuck in a mudhole and they spent the better part of the day unpacking before freeing it.

As the Treaty Council moved to Horse Creek to accomodate the huge number of participants and their horses, Paul and his companions descended some dangerous ravines. Paul was thrown out of his wagon and again hurt himself. Farther up the trail, they encountered supply wagons for the Council meeting and Paul began travelling at night, both to escape the insects and to make up for lost time. Later, Paul would write that the insects were so unbearable he only got "eight hours sleep in twelve days." But that was not all.

During the following days, both Moellhausen and von Zichlinsky started feeling increasingly sick, and there is reason to think they suffered from a bout with cholera. As the treaty was being signed, Paul and his two sick companions had barely crossed the Blue River. Here, von Zichlinsky lost control of his reigns, the horses stampeded and the result was a completely demolished wheel. One can almost hear the sequence of shouting and curses as the disgruntled Duke and Moellhausen left the young Saxon to wait for help from the approaching government train. They were never to see von Zichlinsky again.

After several lonely days along the Platte River, and frightening moments at Ash Hollow, the two encountered the Jesuit Father de Smet and other people Paul had known for many years who had attended the Council. Both Father de Smet and the Duke made notes of this meeting. A few days farther along the trail, Paul and Moellhausen passed Chimney and Courthouse Rocks, then arrived at Fort John and the old Robideaux settlement where Paul made a detailed drawing of the site.

Finally, they arrived at Fort Laramie and Paul wrote an excellent description of the fort and the surrounding area, mentioning how a wolf caused one of his horses to break loose, requiring a midnight search. The next day, Paul met Lord Fitzwilliam, another famous traveller, and accompanied him to his camp on the Laramie River. Moellhausen was still suffering badly, and some of their horses escaped.

Before beginning the return trip, Paul had a Sioux

tipi made—for a souvenir—which was later to help save their lives. After another series of mishaps—a broken axle, and a burning prairie—they missed von Zichlinsky, who was supposedly somewhere nearby with another party of travellers, and pushed onward to Ash Hollow. This incline, described with dread by many travellers on the Oregon Trail, caused so much pain that Paul wrote a furious, tongue-in-cheek description of the place.

In a scene worthy of cinematic illumination the Duke got his wagon stuck in quicksand in the middle of the South Platte and had to spend the entire night there to safeguard it from Indians. Barely rescued from this situation, Duke Paul and Moellhausen were accosted by hostile Indians, first by Sioux, then by Kiowa, and a few days later, with Moellhausen still sick, by Pawnees. No sooner had these dangers been overcome than the two men found themselves in the midst of a raging prairie fire and barely escaped with their lives.

During the following week it began to snow, and two of their exhausted horses died one after the other as the fury of the snowstorm increased. Confined to their tiny tipi by the blizzard, Paul partially lost his eyesight either because of the smoke in the tipi or because of snowblindness, while Moellhausen started hallucinating. The two men struggled through the snow to a campsite along the Big Sandy Creek, probably not far from Fremont's 1842 campsite and Jean Baptiste Charbonneau's 1843 campsite on his expedition with Sir William Drummond Stewart. Here, completely snowed in and immobile they tried to stay warm in their Sioux tent and prayed for a miracle.

Somehow their prayers were answered. As the very last horse died, a mail stage miraculously appeared. But it could only take on one additional passenger. Paul was selected as the one to go with the stage, but he told Moellhausen he would send a rescue party back for him. The stage first stopped at the Jesuit Mission, but Paul could not find a rescue party there, so he continued onward to the settlements where he organized a rescue mission. Although this rescue party never reached Moellhausen, he was later rescued from his plight by friendly Indians, though Paul would not learn this until much later.

On the evening of December 3, Paul reached Independence. After a short stay there he took another coach, and on December 7, with badly impaired vision, exhausted and emaciated, he arrived in Boonville where he spent the following two and and half weeks recuperating. We continue now with his diary entry for 7 December.]

7 December — At daybreak we reached Marshall, a small place which is just now being built, crossed the small Saline Creek over a good bridge, and detoured over a wretched road to Arrow Rock. I have long been acquainted with its landing place due to my earlier journey. It is a flourishing little town and like the majority of places on the west bank is growing more rapidly than those on the northeastern bank. The Big La Mine River, which we crossed on a ferry boat, delayed us somewhat. We stopped at noon for only 20 minutes at the comfortably furnished home of a farmer, where we ate a good meal. This friendly man had a large family and handsome children. From here the roads were abominable, especially from the Big Lamine River on, and the passengers had to wade miles in deep mud. American humbug demonstrated itself here in the shabby wagon boxes, which appeared to stem from the reign of Queen Anne, into which 3 more passengers had been admitted than there were seats. The Americans appeared to have invented the art of building the worst post wagons in the world, their construction being totally impractical.

Pitch darkness overtook us before we arrived through deep mud at Boonville on the Missouri. There in the Mansion Hotel owned by P. Pierce I had a very hospitable reception. I forgot the hardships of the day with a good supper and bed, and planned to rest up on Monday. A terrible rain storm raged throughout the entire night.

* * *

Before continuing with the remainder of Paul's diary entries, it seems appropriate to give a description of the setting. Boonville in the 1850s was a town on the rise. Settled originally in 1810 by the families of Hannah Cole and her brother-in-law, Stephen Cole, transplanted Kentuckians who had followed fellow Kentuckian, Benjamin Cooper and his entourage of family and friends to the "Boone's Lick Country," on the Missouri River some 200 miles upriver from St. Louis, the town was not platted until the period between 1816 and 1818, and the first lots were not sold until 1819.

For a variety of reasons, not the least of which was the thriving nature of the rival town of Franklin, founded in 1816 on the opposite bank of the river, Boonville's progress was slow at first, but by 1826 when Missouri River flooding seriously damaged Franklin, Boonville, on the high ground, began to flourish. By 1839 when the town was officially incorporated with the State of Missouri and steamboat trade had been firmly established on the river after two decades of slow development, signs of growth were everywhere apparent, and the initial stock of transplanted Southerners from Kentucky, Virginia and Tennessee had begun to be supplemented by a steadily increasing flow of emigrants from Germany.

The second Cooper County Court House built in Boonville in 1840 on the site of an earlier one built in 1823 (the year of Duke Paul's first trip up the Missouri River). This second court house faced the Missouri River on High Street and was razed in 1912 when the present court house was constructed. (Friends of Historic Boonville)

These German emigrants came in two major waves. The first wave came in the 1830s and included many Germans attracted here by the writings of Gottfried Duden, whose 1829 publication in Germany of his **Report on a Journey to the Western States of North America** was popular in Germany at the time. The second wave was largely made up of Germans fleeing from the abortive 1848 revolution. Many of the German emigrants in both waves settled in and around St. Louis, and in various towns on the lower Missouri River, the best known of which was Hermann.

By the mid-1830s some of the first wave of German emigrants had reached Boonville, among whom was Dr. Augustus Kueckelhan, a well-educated and culturally refined medical doctor, who figures prominently in Paul's diary entries during his stay in Boonville. Dr. Kueckelhan was born in the duchy of Brunswick, in Germany, May 1, 1812. His father, Henry Kueckelhan, was manager of a feudal barony, and his mother, Augusta, came from a French Huguenot family. Augustus, one of three children born to them, received his early education in languages and the sciences while living at his uncle's home near Hannover, completed his classical education at Holzminden, and matriculated as a student of medicine in the university of Goettingen in 1827. At Goettingen he got involved in a student revolutionary movement, and it soon became expedient for him to leave the kingdom of Hannover. He and several of his friends then went to Wuerzburg, kingdom of Bavaria, and it was there that he was awarded a degree of doctor of medicine, surgery and obstetrics in 1832.

In 1833 Dr. Kueckelhan came to America, landing at Baltimore and then assuming control of a company of 240 emigrants who were bound for St. Louis. He re-

House of Dr. Augustus Kueckelhan on the southeast corner of Spring and 3rd Streets, Boonville, ca. 1890

A. KUECKELHAN,
AT THE SIGN OF THE
Big Golden Mortar.

Is now in receipt of a fresh supply of drugs, medicines, chemicals, oils, paints, glass, dyestuffs, liquors, papers, perfumeries &c., keeps always on hand and offers for sale at the lowest cash prices: Quinine, Peruvian barks, calomel, ipecac, rhubarb, aloes, jalap, colocynths, epsom, glauber salts, saltpeter, borax, alum, asafoetida, opium, valerian, snake root, blood root, turpentine, castor oil, quicksilver, seidtzlets and soda powders, blue mass, saleratus, starch, soda, linseed oil, s and w s sperm oil, gas, madeira, old ports wine, cognac brandy, extract of logwood, blue stone, indigo, madder, fustic, camwood, coppal, and japan varnishes, glue, putty, window glass, soaps, pepper, mace, alspice, ginger, mustard, cinnamon, sand paper, pumice, rotten stone, black lead, wrapping paper, inks, pens, pencils, surgical instruments, patent medicines, together with all other articles belonging to that line.

E. A. BENEDICT

Ad from **Boonville Weekly Observer**, June 20, 1850

116

Ad in Boonville Weekly Observor, February 11, 1854

Dr. Mike Aehle, St. Louis, Mo., with a portrait of Mrs. C.F. (Elizabeth) Aehle his great great grandmother.

Log house (here covered with clapboard ca. 1900) on the northeast corner of Spring and 6th Streets, Boonville, where C.F. Aehle lived at the time of Duke Paul's visit in December 1850 (photograph by Truby, Vine Clad City, 1900)

mained in St. Louis for three years and then came to Boonville and established both a medical practice and a drug store, the latter on Boonville's Main Street "at the sign of the Big Golden Mortar." In 1840 he married Mrs. Margaret Quarles, the widowed daughter of Dr. William Mills, and they had four children. Their home in Boonville was on the southeast corner of Third and Spring streets in 1845, which, in somewhat altered form, is still standing and is now an apartment house. In 1854 Dr. Kueckelhan retired from the practice of medicine and bought a 700 acre farm he called "Portum" near the town of Lamine, not far from Boonville. In 1863, due to the chaotic and dangerous conditions in the countryside brought on by the Civil War, he took his family to St. Louis and reestablished a practice there for a period of time before returning to his country estate, "Portum." He died in Boonville on February 28, 1893.

Other Germans who arrived over the next two decades were George Hain, a Swiss blacksmith and horticulturist; Christian Keil, a merchant; Charles W. and Julius Sombart, brothers from Prussia who initially engaged in farming and then established a highly successful milling operation after striking it rich during the 1849 California Gold Rush; Alexander Seultzer, a stone mason; George Vollrath, a potter and miller from the duchy of Saxe-Coburg; Anthony Fuchs, a brewer from the Grand Duchy of Baden; Christian Force, a wagon maker and blacksmith from Prussia; Reinhard Heisrich, a butcher from the country of Hesse; Abraham Hirth, a Bavarian wagonmaker; John Otten, a merchant tailor from Hannover; Louis Bendele, a Bavarian cabinetmaker; the brothers Viet and Joseph Eppstein, dry goods merchants; Frank Stretz, a potter; Leonard Kline, a Bavarian cabinetmaker; Louis Weyland, a wagon maker; William

Haas, a vintner and brewer from Hesse-Darmstadt; Phillip Gross, a cooper; Ernest Roeschel, a druggist and vintner; George Sahm, a Bavarian shoemaker; John Bernard, a manufacturer of cigars and dealer in tobacco from Lorraine; John H. Boller, a farmer and vintner living about three miles west of town, who came from the duchy of Nassau; George Reppley, a vintner from Baden; and Carl Franz (Charles F.) Aehle, who initially formed a partnership with Dr. Kueckelhan, and then became a dealer in groceries, dry goods, and hardware before becoming involved in banking.

Because Aehle is mentioned prominently in Paul's diary during his stay in Boonville, and since Aehle, himself, mentions Paul's visit in his own reminiscences written some forty years after the fact, it seems fitting to take a more in-depth look at Aehle's life, and especially at his German heritage. Some of this information comes from Aehle's own reminiscence and the rest is gleaned from Edwin H. Aehle's **Complete Genealogy and True Original Crest of the Aehle Family**, a copy of which is in the collection of the State Historical Society of Missouri.

Carl Franz Aehle was born August 21, 1818, in Gera, the largest and most important city in the principality of Reuss in Thuringia (central Germany). His father, Ernst August Aehle, born about 1780 in the duchy of Sachsen-Altenburg, graduated from the University of Leipzig, was a practising physician and surgeon, and served in the Prussian army as a surgeon during Napoleon's invasion of Germany from 1806 to 1812. His wife, Amelia Mueller, was born in 1794. The family was descended from the *Aelino* family of noble Italian origin but dropped the ending *-no* after settling in Germany, and retaining their coat of arms.

Gera, Carl Franz's native town, is situated on the

banks of the river Elster, and was, even at that time, an important manufacturing city. It also had an endowed college, free to all boys "to the manor born." Aehle became a student of theology at this college, receiving instructions in music, Greek and Hebrew. But, finding his studies there "not to my taste, nor the prospect of a pastorate...and a parsonage very encouraging," he left college and took a position with Monarch & Co., one of the most important mercantile and banking houses in central Germany. In due time he was promoted to the position of chief correspondent and accountant and began to participate in the aristocratic social life of Gera.

In 1838 or 1839, his mother's brother, who had established a business in St. Louis, Missouri, offered Aehle a partnership in his business, and he decided ("foolishly enough", as he later said) to accept the offer. He left Gera June 13, 1839, after a round of going away parties thrown by "former college chums" who were then pursuing higher studies at the nearby University of Gena. He then travelled to Bremen by way of Weimar ("the so-called Athens of Germany"), Erfurt, Gotha, Cassel, Hameln, and Hannover, and set sail for America on the *Neptune*. Forty two days later, on September 3, 1839, he arrived in Baltimore and travelled by land and water to St. Louis where the anticipated position with his uncle somehow failed to materialize.

In order to learn the English language he took a position as piano tutor for the daughter of a rich planter living some twelve miles south of St. Louis. Following this he secured a job as an accountant at a wholesale house in St. Louis and then worked for a year at a similar job in Cincinnati. Returning to St. Louis he made a fortunate contact with the music company of Balmer and Weber who secured for him, in 1842, chairmanship of the music department in a seminary in Glasgow, Missouri. In 1844 he moved to Boonville (and played the first pipe organ brought to Boonville that year by the Episcopal Church) where he first engaged in the drug business as a partner of Dr. Augustus Kueckelhan and then started a general store in his father-in-law Nathaniel Mack's building (Mack retired in 1848) on the southeast corner of Main and Spring Streets, which he operated until about 1868 when he engaged (at the same location) in a banking business with W. F. Dunnica (an acquaintance from Glasgow) as a member of the firm of Aehle, Dunnica & Co.

On June 14, 1846, about two years after his arrival in Boonville, he married Elizabeth Jane Mack, daughter of Nathaniel Mack, and nine children were born to their union. Living first in a log house (razed at the turn of the century) on the northeast corner of 6th and Spring Streets (where he entertained Paul), the Aehle's built a fine brick house in the mid 1850s between his father-in-law Nathaniel Mack's home and his business partner, W.F. Dunnica's home, at 615 Main Street (this house was razed in 1993 by the Baptist Church of Boonville which erected an educational building on the site). He lived in this home until 1868 and then moved to a house on the southwest corner of 6th and Locust Streets (still standing) where he died September 21, 1901. His wife died at the home of her son, E. F. Aehle, in St. Louis, January 27, 1910.

In 1850 the first census to give specific population figures for Boonville showed that the town had a total population of 2,326, about a 40% increase over her estimated 1840 population. Approximately 70% of this total 1850 population (1,642) were white, and the other

121

30% (684) were black slaves.

Although there is no breakdown of the population of Boonville in terms of nationality in the 1850 census, one can gain some perspective on the number of German immigrants living in the town at this time by examining Cooper County Circuit Court immigration records. These records indicate the names and country of origin of people either making declarations of intention to file for naturalization or naturalizations themselves. Prior to 1838 there are no recorded documents of either kind for German immigrants in the Circuit Court records, but in the period between 1838 and 1853 there are 125 adult male German immigrants listed as either declaring their intentions to be naturalized or actually being naturalized in Cooper County. If we assume that at least 100 of these were heads of families, and we further assume approximately 4 persons per family group, this would mean that there were about 400 Germans living in Cooper County in 1850. If we further assume that about half of this number were living in the rural areas and the other half were living in the town of Boonville, this would mean that about 200 Germans (or about 50 German families) were living in Boonville in 1850. Biographical data in various county histories and genealogies account for about a dozen German families living in Boonville during this time, but these sources obviously only mention the more prominent German families.

A further analysis of the Cooper County immigration records reveals that about 30% of the German immigrants were from Prussia (northern and central Germany), 25% were from various parts of Hesse (central Germany), another 25% were from Bavaria (southeastern Germany), 8% were from Saxony (central Germany), 6% were from Baden (southwestern Germany and one of the centers of the 1848 revolution), and the remaining 6% were about equally divided between Wuerttemberg, Austria, and several neighboring German areas like Lorraine and Switzerland.

Cooper County, of which Boonville had been the county seat since 1818 when the county was formed, had a total population in 1850 of 12,950, about a 25% increase over her 1840 population of 10,484. About 75% of this total population (9,837) were white and the other 25% (3,113) were black slaves. Boonville and Cooper County were not as heavily populated with slaves as were the neighboring counties of Howard, Boone and Saline. Nevertheless, slavery was a pervasive fact of life in the counties bordering the Missouri River during this time and the dominant culture of the area was clearly Southern in its general tone.

Census records also reveal that there were perhaps as many as 1,500 family farms in rural Cooper County in 1850 and that the average acreage of these farms was about 150. Given the $6 per acre average value of farm land with buildings at that time (about a three fold increase over land values in 1820), this would mean that the average farm could have been purchased for about $900 (the same farm today would probably cost somewhere in the neighborhood of $150,000). It might be noted that Paul mentions in his 1851 diary that he asked one of his hosts, C. F. Aehle, about the price of farms in Cooper County and learned that "from 60 to 1,200 acres with sufficient grass, including the dwelling and the necessary buildings," could be had for $8 to $12 per acre. He adds that he "was offered a 200 acre farm situated near to the Missouri [River] with excellent land for $5 per acre and a good frame house for $500 with an assorted inventory for the lowest bid on credit terms." He further notes that "many farms are for rent for from $50-$300 per year."

Another gauge of what the town of Boonville was like at this time can be determined from the "Products of Industry" section of the 1850 census. According to this survey of the town's economic base there were 40 manufacturers in Boonville in 1850 employing 150 men and 12 women (the latter concentrated in two shoemaker's shops and one tailor shop). The total capital investment of these 40 manufacturers amounted to just over $50,000, and the total value of their annual products was just over $113,000.

The manufacturers generating the largest annual product in 1850 were: nine wagon and carriage makers (including blacksmiths) generating nearly $16,000 in annual product; two pottery and brickmaking firms generating $14,000; three saddlers generating just over $13,000; five carpentry and house building firms generating just over $12,000; a pork packer generating $10,000; a tobacconist generating $3,100; and two tinners generating $7,000.

Among the flourishing businesses in Boonville during the 1840s and 50s, were several hotels, the two most notable being the City Hotel and the Mansion House whose histories are so intertwined as to be somewhat confusing. Perhaps the earliest hotel of any substance in Boonville was Judge John Dade's Hotel and Tavern (later known as the "Virginia Hotel") on the south side of High Street about a block west of Main (present location of the **Boonville Daily News** offices), perhaps established as early as 1826. But only a few years later (the date is uncertain) another hotel, apparently known initially as Bailey's Mansion House, was established across the street from Dade's Hotel. Then in 1839/40 a transplanted Virginian named "Colonel" Peter

Pierce built the town's first premier hostelry, the City Hotel, on what Boonville's **Western Emigrant** newspaper (January 17, 1839) called "that beautiful lot, which from its elevated situation, has excited the admiration of those who have seen it, situated at the corner of 4th and Morgan Streets," just one block south of Dade's Hotel and Bailey's Mansion House. By 1843, however, Pierce had gotten himself into some rather complicated money problems and was forced to sell his City Hotel to Edward B. McPherson, who then continued to operate it down to the time of his death in 1869, after which his wife, Mary J. "Auntie" McPherson, operated it down into the 1880s (the hotel, in much altered form, is now a residence in Boonville).

At about the same time Pierce was experiencing financial difficulties, Jonathan Bailey and John Dade also seem to have gotten themselves into problems with debt. As a result, Bailey briefly took over Dade's "Virginia Hotel" and Peter Pierce took over Bailey's "Mansion House." But, by 1845 the "Virginia Hotel" was sold at a Sheriff's sale and Peter Pierce had moved to a new location on the north east corner of 6th and Morgan Streets and had taken the name "Mansion House" with him. He apparently continued at this location down into the early 1850s at which time the proprietor became William P. Speed, and then (in 1854) Allen Hammond. Pierce seems to have moved back to one of the old hotels on High Street (perhaps Dade's old hotel or one that had been erected just down the street from it) and called it simply "Pierce's Hotel". He probably continued to operate this hotel until about the time of his death in 1871.

Thus, at the time Paul arrived in Boonville in December of 1851 and took rooms at what he calls "Pierce's Mansion Hotel", it is not entirely clear which of

City Hotel, built 1839 by Peter Pierce on Morgan Street between Main and Fourth Streets, and sold to Edward McPherson in 1843 (Friends of Historic Boonville).

The Mansion House, built in the early 1830s, still stands on the north side of High Street just west of Main, one block north of the City Hotel. Originally known as "Bailey's Mansion House" then as "Pierce's Mansion House" (ca. 1843-45). By the time this photograph was taken by James C. Macurdy in the 1870s it was the "Ballantine House." During most of the 20th century it has been known as the "Commercial Hotel." (Dyer Collection)

PIERCE'S HOTEL.
BOONVILLE, MO.

THE proprietor of this house respectfully announces to the public, that, with the improvements and additions, which he has had made, he is now prepared to accommodate his guests in a style that cannot be excelled by any other house in the State. Those whom it has been his pleasure to entertain, are aware, that he is always most assiduous in his endeavors to please, and with his increased facilities, he trusts that he will be able to render increased satisfaction.

His prices are as follows:
Single meals, . . . 25 cts.
Lodging, . . . 25 "
Horse feed, . . . 25 "
Man and horse over night . $1 25.
Do. one day, . $1 50,
Regular Boarders per week, $2 00.
His house is the office for the Eastern and Western stages.

☞ Joseph West is my authorized Agent to collect and receipt all accounts in my name.
PETER PIERCE.

Aug 8, 1850.

Left—Ad for Pierce's Hotel [corner of 6th and Morgan Streets], **Boonville Observer,** November 28, 1850. Pierce moved here ca. 1845 after operating the hotel on High Street known as the Mansion House. He seems to have taken the name "Mansion House" with him since the hotel advertised here was also sometimes referred to as the "Mansion House."

Below—Map of downtown Boonville showing the locations of sites associated with Duke Paul's visit. The hotel on High Street was originally known as "Bailey's Mansion House" and then as "Pierce's Mansion House" (1843-45). The hotel at the corner of 6th and Morgan Streets is almost certainly the one Duke Paul stayed in during his 1851 visit. There are no known photographs of it. Aehle's house is shown at the corner of 6th and Spring Streets and Dr. Kueckelhan's house is shown at the corner of 3rd and Spring Streets. The Episcopal ("Anglican") Church is at the corner of 4th and Vine Streets.

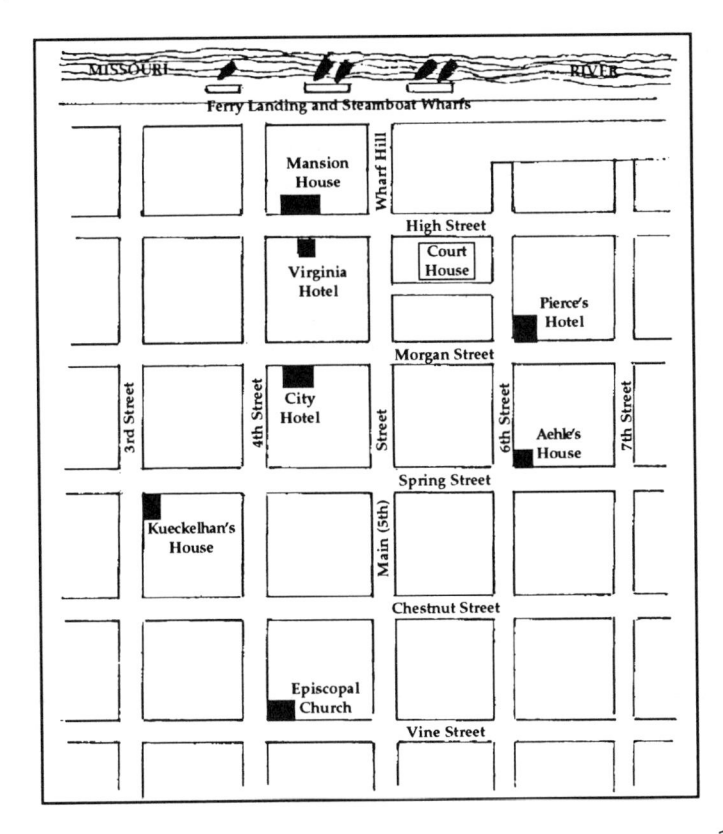

127

the hotel buildings he was actually staying in, though it seems reasonably certain that it was the hotel on the northeast corner of 6th and Morgan streets, just a block north of C.F. Aehle's log house on the northeast corner of 6th and Spring streets, and about four blocks northeast of Dr. Kueckelhan's house on the southeast corner of 3rd and Spring streets.

There is, however, a further problem with determining where, exactly, Paul stayed in Boonville, because Edward McPherson's City Hotel register contains what appears to be Paul's scrawled signature under the date December 10, 1851. It is possible that he was actually staying in Peter Pierce's Mansion House hotel, but went to dinner (or lunch, or breakfast) at McPherson's City Hotel and was asked to sign the register since he was a "notable" guest, or that, for some reason, he actually changed hotels during his stay in Boonville. My own guess is that the former explanation is the most likely. Duke Paul was interested in both steamboat and stagecoach accommodations, and while Pierce's Mansion House was the stage stop, McPherson's City Hotel seems to have been the place that kept most closely in touch with the movements of steamboats on the Missouri River.

Duke Paul's praise of Pierce as a host (especially his food) echoes the reminiscences of a writer who signed his name as "Peregrine" in the **Boonville Weekly Advertiser**, January 25, 1889. "Peregrine", who wrote a series of romantically nostalgic articles on early Boonville says:

Upon first reaching Cooper county [in the 1830s] *it appeared to him* [Pierce] *as a new Virginia, filling in as it was with almost daily accessions of fresh families from the sacred soil* [Virginia], *each one accompanied by long processions of negroes; so without further delay he purchased a square in a central locality of the young city...and proceeded to build a hotel of what seemed at that day, palatial dimensions. The "City Hotel," as the new establishment was christened, was managed...as an old style village inn, rather than a modern hotel, but no guest ever complained of lack of cleanliness and the board groaned daily beneath the weight of food.... The fame of the new hotel went abroad, and the traveling public made a point of reaching "Peter Pierce, Prince of Providers," partaking of his tempting fare, resting in his cool, sweet rooms, or lounging in the shaded grounds.... Here too, youths and maidens met to enjoy social evenings or to dance cotilions or the recently introduced Virginia reel and stately contradance.*

The most durable of the newspapers between 1840 and 1860 was the **Boonville Observer,** an outgrowth of Boonville's first journalistic venture, the **Boonville Herald,** that began in 1833 under James H. Middleton as a politically independent newspaper, and evolved into the **Western Emigrant,** an outspoken Whig paper under the editorship fo Robert T. Brent before being purchased and renamed the **Boonville Observer** in 1840 by C.W. Todd. It continued as a Whig organ until the demise of that party in the 1850s. A partial collection of the **Western Emigrant** and the **Boonville Observer** newspapers exists on microfilm at the State Historical Society of Missouri, but unfortunately there are no issues of the **Observer** for the period from June 1851 to March 1854, which, of course, includes the time of Paul's visit to Boonville. The Democratic voice in Boonville in 1850 was the **Boonville Democrat,** owned and operated by John Price. No issues of this paper for the time of Paul's visit exist either. Copies of newspapers from the nearby towns of Glasgow, Columbia and Jefferson City do exist for the time of Paul's visit to the area, but none of these papers mentions him.

The bastions of Southern religious tradition in

Boonville in 1850 were the Baptist, Methodist, Episcopal (which Paul calls "Anglican") and Presbyterian chuches, which held a virtual monopoly on religious worship, though the German emigrants had organized their own Lutheran, Evangelical, Catholic and Methodist congregations by this time and would soon begin erecting churches of their own before the decade was over.

The town's Southern heritage was also evident in the educational system, consisting of a number of private schools for young men and women. A number of the earlier private schools did not survive into the 1850s, but at least three schools established in the 1840s were still in operation and, indeed, flourishing, in the 1850s. Professor Joshua Tracy's "school for the instruction of young Ladies", the "Boonville Institute" opened in the spring of 1841 and by 1850 (the peak year) had an enrollment of over 200 young women and occupied several buildings along the south side of Vine near Fourth (across from the Episcopal Church) and the west side of Fourth near the corner of Fourth and Vine. In 1851 this school incorporated under the name "Boonville Female Institute" and in 1855 the name was changed again to "Adelphai College."

The main competition for Tracy's school was the "Boonville Female Seminary" founded about 1845 by the Rev. William G. Bell, Boonville's Presbyterian minister from 1840 until 1854. The success of this school can be partly gauged by the large and impressive building Bell erected about 1850 on the east side of Sixth Street near Locust. The school's name was later changed to "Pleasant Retreat Female Seminary" and then to "Missouri Female College" before it finally burned and went out of business in 1876.

The main boys boarding school in Boonville from

the mid-1840s until the mid-1850s was Frederick T. Kemper's "Boonville Male Academy" established in 1844 with five students, but rapidly increasing to about 50 students and then to about 100 in the early 1850s by which time the name had been changed to the "Male Collegiate Institute." Only a year after the school first opened in rented rooms in downtown Boonville, Kemper erected "an ample seminary of brick" on the west side of Third Street near Center. Although the school closed for a few years in the late 1850s when Kemper went to teach at Westminster College in Fulton, he reopened it again in 1861 and it has operated continuously from that time down to the present (1996), first under the name of "Kemper's Family School" and then as "Kemper Military School and College." Kemper, whose ancestors were part of the first great wave of German immigrants to America in the early 18th century, came to Boonville from Virginia, and his school has proved to be the most enduring symbol of Boonville's Southern educational traditions.

Another potent symbol of the town's Southern cultural traditions was Thespian Hall, an impressive, Greek Revival theatre building erected by the Boonville Thespian Society in 1856-57 on the corner of Main and Vine Streets and still used today as a center of cultural activities in the town. The Boonville Thespian Society was originally organized in the late 1830s by a group of some sixty young men representing the more prominent families at that time. Tradition has it that their first theater building was an "old hewn log structure (30 x 60 feet) that stood on the brow of the river hill, almost directly opposite the city Hotel." Later, the group moved to the old log store building formerly occupied by the town's first successful merchant, Jacob Wyan, on the

Joshua Tracy's "Boonville Female Institute," established 1841, as it appeared ca. 1850 at the corner of 4th and Vine Streets, across the street from the Episcopal Church where Duke Paul attended church services in December 1851 (Courtesy Friends of Historic Boonville)

Rev. William G. Bell's "Boonville Female Seminary," established ca. 1845, as it appeared in 1850 when this building was erected at the corner of 6th and Locust Streets (photograph taken ca. 1870s, courtesy Friends of Historic Boonville)

Boonville Wine Company and Central Brewery, William Haas, prop. (Dyer Collection)

corner of Main and High Streets (about a block away from the first theatre building), and then to rooms over Nathaniel Mack's store on the southeast corner of Main and Spring Streets.

The principal German organizations, other than the churches, for maintaining cultural and social traditions in Boonville were the singing and gymnastic societies known respectively as the "Gesang (singing) Vereins (clubs)" and the "Turn (gymnastic) Vereins (clubs)" established not long after the arrival of the first significant number of Germans in the late 1840s and early 1850s. These groups, which came to be known among the non-Germans in the community simply as the "Turners," traced their origin to the work of Father Friedrich Ludwig Jahn who established the first Turn Verein in Berlin in 1809 at the time Germany was being suppressed by Napoleon. Father Jahn supposedly formed the group to drill his followers in gymnastics and military tactics with the object of making them better soldiers. In later years, however, music, theatricals and oratory were added to the activities of the Turn Vereins and the organizations came to serve a more general social function in the German communities.

The first such organization formed in Boonville was the "Gesang Verein," a men's choral group established in the early 1850s. By the late 1850s the younger Germans in the community organized a "Turn Verein" and the two groups continued to meet regularly (except for some disruption during the period of the Civil War) into the first decades of the 20th century. Their first meeting place was apparently a brick building not far from the old log building where the Thespians got their start on High Street, but they soon moved to "Squire" Mack's saloon on the southeast corner of Main and

Spring (where the Thespians had also met for a period of time). In the years following the Civil War when the old Southern aristocracy of the town had lost much of their dominance over cultural activities, the Turners used Thespian Hall for a period of time as their main meeting place, and finally bought the old Baptist Church (built in 1847) on Vine Street in 1895 and converted it into "Turner Hall." This building, across Vine Street to the south of Thespian Hall, has survived down to the present and is now being restored to serve once more as a cultural gathering place.

Another symbol of German cultural traditions which has its roots in the period of the 1850s is Boonville's sobriquet "The Vine Clad City." Perhaps as early as the late 1840s German immigrants were planting vineyards in and around Boonville and were brewing beer as well as making wine. The most prominent of the Boonville vintners and brewers was William D. Haas who came here from Chicago in the late 1840s and established his "Central Brewery and Boonville Wine Company" on the banks of the Missouri River at the west edge of town. Beginning with only a few acres of Catawba grape vines his holdings expanded by the late 1850s to over a hundred acres on which were several large buildings with underground brick cellars and a steamboat landing. In 1854 his "Premium Catawba" received a complimentary notice in the report on the Missouri State Fair held at Boonville in October of that year, and not long after this his wine took a first premium in the native dry wine class at a national fair held in Philadelphia. Haas was born about 1800 in Darmstadt, Germany, and came to the United States about 1825 where he married Mary Schwind from Wuerttemberg, Germany. In 1839 he established a brewery in Chicago and then moved to Boonville in 1844.

He died here in 1862, and though others continued to operate his brewery and winery for another ten or fifteen years, its business declined after his death. The ruins of the Haas winery and brewery, including at least one large intact cellar, can still be seen in the thick foliage of a small valley on the west edge of Boonville.

This, then, was the setting for the arrival of Boonville's surprise royal visitor, Duke Paul of Wuerttemberg, in December of 1851.

* * *

8 December — *Toward morning it again became clearer and cooler. A German physician, Dr. Kueckelhan, was pointed out to me and I sought his acquaintance and that of a merchant, C.F. Aehle. These gentlemen showed me a great deal of cordial attention, and I spent a very pleasant evening in the former's charming family circle.*

The weather became wretched again. It rained throughout the entire night. My frost bitten feet burned me so that for a long time I could not sleep. The overland roads had become so abominable that travel by land was no longer conceivable. The passengers from the south and east, especially from Jefferson, complained a great deal about the mail stage and for the most part had covered the distance through the deep mud on foot without being able to board the stage.

9 December — *In the morning it rained and stormed, but it was warm. The river was bound to rise, and a steamer waited in anticipation. The board at the inn was excellent, and because of my suffering in the prairie, it was very essential for me to rest so that I would not fall victim to the type of sickly condition that is usually the result of winter hardships of the type from which I had escaped only with great difficulty.*

The overland route with which I was already acquainted leads northward via Columbia, seat of the University of Missouri, and Fulton to St. Charles. The Missouri must be crossed at Rocheport, about ten miles from Boonville. The road does not cross any important rivers except the Missouri; it leads mostly over prairie and is not so bad as the other road, which turns to the east on the south side of the stream via Jefferson City, the state capital. On the latter road—hilly and often totally bottomless—one must ferry across the Osage, Gasconade, Petite Femme Osage and other streams. In rainy weather these rivers are very swollen, and one must contend with high and steep banks as well as with deep mud. The mail stage for Jefferson leaves Boonville at 2 a.m., the one for St. Charles at 8:30 a.m. From the telegraph station I sent for information from St. Louis as to whether a steamer would be coming upriver this late in the season, and initially received very unfavorable news. From the stage office I was advised not to go via St. Charles but rather via Jefferson, for although the latter road was worse, it would be preferable to the extent that few if any passengers weighed down the wagon. This climbing out of the wagons in order to cross bottomless places could become very dangerous for me with my swollen and frost-bitten feet.

In the evenings I was invited out by my friendly countrymen. I was most splendidly entertained, and in the pleasant family circles of these gentlemen the evenings passed quickly. Life here in Boonville is very comfortable and nothing is wanting. Boonville is generally a lively, pleasant little city with significant commerce with the South. It has wide streets, sandy soil, several fine-looking brick houses and stately churches of all Protestant denominations: Anglican, Presbyterian, Methodist, Baptist, and so-called Christian (whose followers, commonly called Campbellites, only acknowledge the teaching of the New Testament and reject the Old Testament). It rained and blew violently without interruption during the entire *night.*

[Note: On this day, Duke Paul wrote two letters addressed to his friend, the Consul General of the Kingdom of Prussia in St. Louis, Ernest C. Angelroth, informing him of his survival and requesting that Angelroth inform the Royal Court in Stuttgart immediately, and to enclose the other letter. (The second letter has been preserved in the Wuerttemberg Hauptstaatsarchiv, file #55:49:40.) The reason for this immediacy was less one of concern for anyone at home, but one of pecuniary interest. The King and the courts had previously decided that Paul would receive a quarterly payment, the new apanage, upon which he could draw to live and pay off his old debts, but only as long as he would prove, in his own handwriting, that he was alive at the end of each quarter. Given the Duke's adventuresome lifestyle, the court wished not to incur any expenses if they could be avoided! These notes, in short, would be summarized as containing one very simple, and common, message: "Am Alive! Send money!"

Also on this day, Pierre Chouteau, Jr., in St. Louis, wrote to Andrew Drips at Fort John in his own orthography:

This morning we received your two favors of the 18th Octobr and the 1st Novr both at the same time — the former with the enclosed draft on Mess (ieurs) Angleroth & Barth from Prince Paul of Wertembergh for one Hundred and fifty eight 25/100 Dollars which amount was paid on Presentation, the amount Stands to the Credit of U.M.O. (Upper Missouri Outfit) Fort John, due this day, the Prince has not yet arrived in our City sead to be on his way down by Land from Independence on his return her, we shall Endeavor to make him pay the Small Acct of 3 50/100 which you ought to have sent us in due form. (Courtesy: Bancroft Library)]

10 December — *In the morning it froze and cleared up. The climatic conditions in this country are so changeable. In winter months it touches upon all extremes and it is not unusual to experience a 65° change in the thermometer within 24 hours.*

My hope of finding a steamer faded more and more. It was remarkable to me that there was not more competition among steamship operators in the Missouri Valley, considering the multitudes eager to utilize this relatively comfortable mode of transportation and considering the high passenger rates ($20 from St. Joseph to St. Louis this autumn). Although danger existed, uninterrupted running was assured since navigable water was still practical for small boats, as they require little more than 2 feet of water. With the south wind which has set in and the heavy masses of snow in the prairie tributaries, a rise in the Missouri must take place without the danger of drifting ice and even less of becoming ice-bound. For a considerable number of years the Mississippi downstream from St. Louis has remained navigable even in the colder years. The process of clearing the large forest masses in areas adjacent to the river, draining creeks and cultivating the land must considerably moderate those hard winters of the past which will recur only as an exception.

Boonville and its immediate environs are very healthful. By contrast Jefferson is the complete opposite. This is a striking manifestation, since both places are situated along the river on commanding heights. It is assumed that the difference is due to the former city's being built on a fairly level, hilly ridge, while the latter is spread out on very broken terrain containing damp ravines which discharge the miasma.

11 December — *The day was calm, the thermometer*

139

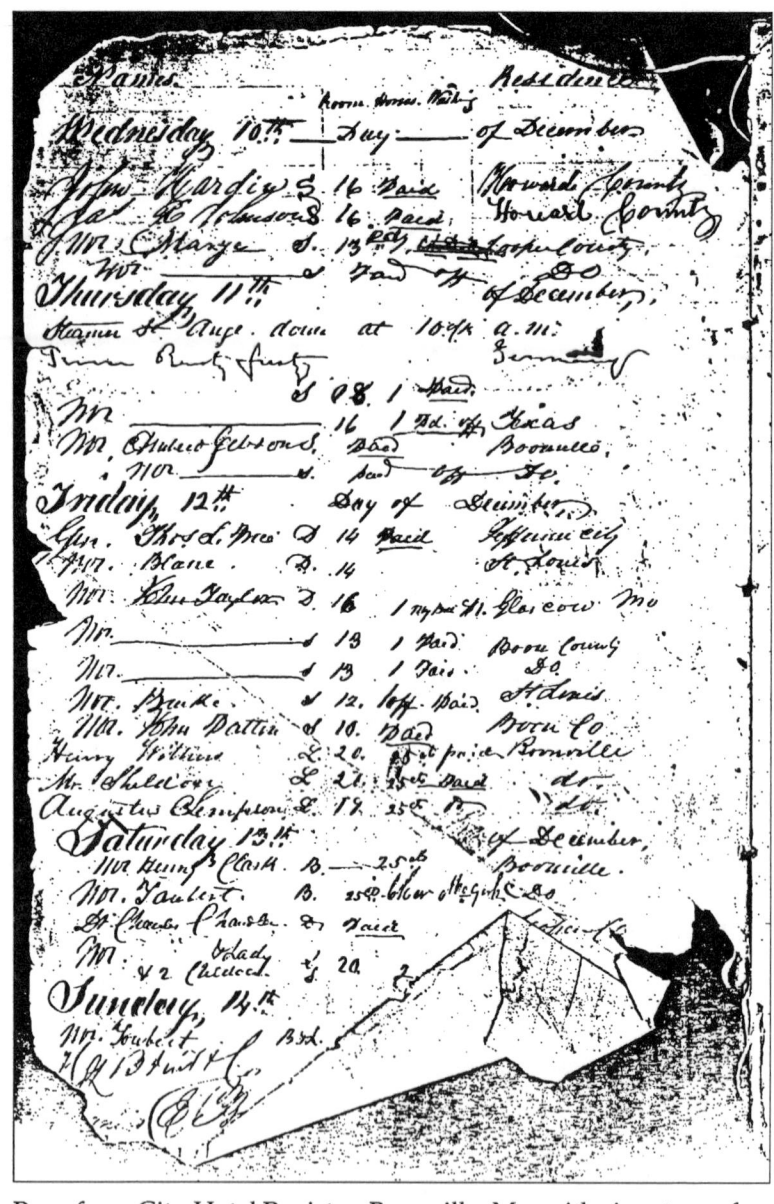

Page from City Hotel Register, Boonville, Mo. with signature of "Prince Paul Wurt. Germany," under entry for Thursday, 11th of December 1851. (Courtesy of Wilma Brengarth Bledsoe)

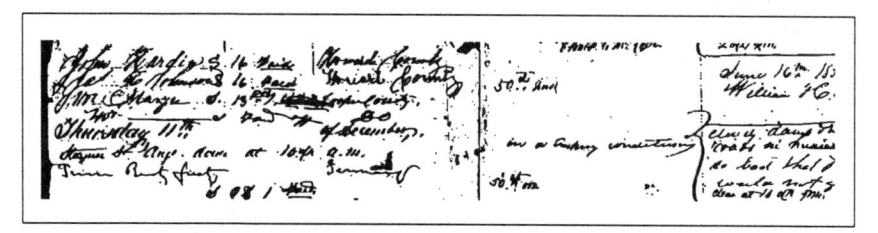

Detail from City Hotel Register for December 11, 1851, with scrawled signature of "Prince Paul Wurt Germany" and arrival of St. Ange "in a sinking condition."

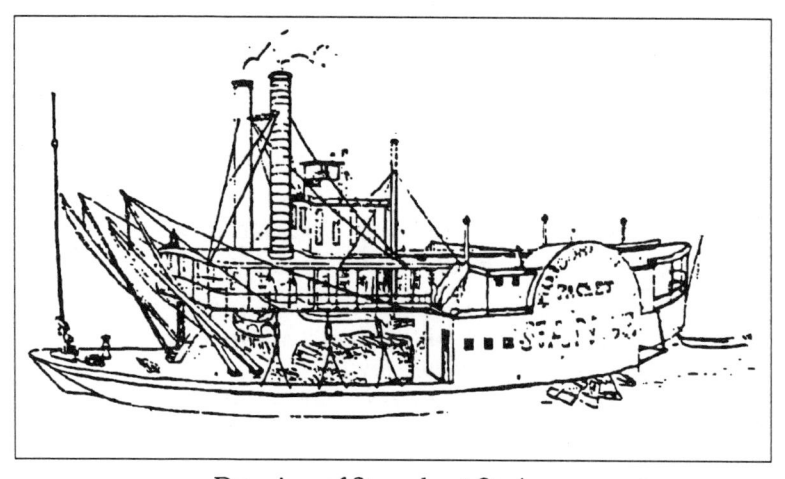

Drawing of Steamboat St. Ange
(Smithsonian Institution, National Anthropological Archives)

LATEST NEWS.

☞ We learn that the steamer St. Ange is sunk above Glasgow, on her downward trip. She had a large number of passengers on board, none of whom were injured.

Notice of St. Ange sinking, **Brunswicker**, December 6, 1851

141

stood at 32°F., the water had risen noticeably and the roads began to dry out again. The steamer **St. Ange**—notorious because of her last Yellowstone journey in the summer, when cholera had raged on board—came down stream after a snag had terribly damaged her. However she was so poorly equipped that I preferred to wait a little longer, since I might easily have been stranded on the river in this very leaky, waterlogged ship. The evening was cool and the thermometer stood at the freezing point. [Note: Duke Paul started writing his Letter from Boonville on this day.]

12 December — *Cold dreary morning. The Mansion Hotel in which I stayed was among the best in the provincial towns of the West, and since the running of its table could serve as a standard for all others, I wish to expend a few words describing it. The dining room, a very long proportionately narrow room, could accomodate 100 people, who congregated around a long 3 1/2 foot-wide table. Breakfast was served at 8 o'clock, dinner at 1 o'clock, and at 7 o'clock supper was eaten. Meals cost 25 cents each, daily board (heated room, bed and meals) $1 [per day], $4 per week and $12 monthly, a cheap way to live, since very ample meals were served and everything was forthcoming which the season offered.*

First of all the ladies — irrespective of their outward appearance — seat themselves around the hostess at the end of the table near the fireplace; then at a given signal the gentlemen pour in, take their places as quickly as possible and reach out where and however they can. They sit at the table for as short a time as possible, since eating for the Anglo-American is a <u>necessity,</u> not a <u>pleasure,</u> although in more recent times there is a great deal of consideration for good food. The Americans almost never drink wine with their meals, preferring coffee and tea, and now have an eye for good milk and butter. The better boarding houses boast good German soup for lunch. Service is good in the western and southern slave states, for they have mostly hired slaves who are clean and prompt. Here in Boonville the service personnel consisted of a half dozen clean women and nearly a dozen fellows and young boys. The head waiter was a free Negro, whom I liked very much, for he was obliging and intelligent. These domestic servants were treated very well. Hiring colored people cost $50 to $100 per year from the 1st of January to the 31st of December.

The day was clear but a cold wind whistled through the streets and dried the roads. However the deep mud froze and the wheels of the mail stage were frozen into disks. Incidentally it had already arrived at 5:30 o'clock, thus 2 1/2 hours earlier than our arrival. I had telegraphed to St. Louis but received no answer. This I could only attribute to a disturbance in the telegraph lines.

Since it was of some interest to me to learn somewhat more precisely about the price of farms in this country, I asked Mr. Aehle for particulars. From 60-1,200 acres with sufficient grass, including the dwelling and the necessary buildings, costs from $8-$12 per acre. I was offered a 200 acre farm situated near to the Missouri with excellent land for $5 per acre and a good frame house for $500 with an assorted inventory, for the lowest bid on credit terms. Many farms are for rent for from $50—$300 per year.

13 December — It had frozen very hard last night, and this morning it was cold and clear. I suffered intense pains from my frost injuries. At 11 o'clock I received a telegraphic dispatch dated Dec. 12 from my friend in St. Louis, stating that the steamer **Kansas** was scheduled to leave St. Louis early on the 13th. But it had become very cold since then, and it was likely that the steamer would be held back for fear of its becoming icebound.

[Note: Paul's friends in St. Louis were von Angelroth and Barth. The telegram has not yet been found.]

14 December — *Sunday. Complete thaw, almost cloudless sky and south wind. I visited the Anglican church with Mr. Aehle. The educated German Lutherans of religious inclination attend church for want of a Lutheran pastor because of its dignified services and the most excellent hymns, which are well-suited to conduce true devotion. In any event the high church holds a favorable position among the Protestant churches, not only through the status of its clergy but also because of it strict Christian bearing. Within its confines one can be truly devout and religious without serving pietistic hypocrisy.*
For the past several days many wild turkeys, geese and fish have been brought to market. The La Mine offers an unusually good yield of gray catfish and buffalo fish (Paul's note: *a carp of excellent flavor, often over 30# in weight and closely related to the Egyptian Dacmah).*
It became cold again toward noon. It rained and snowed at the same time and in the evening it froze hard again at 25°F. Simultaneously a strong N.W. wind blew which threatened to intensify the cold even more. The deep mud was transformed into a hard frozen crust, and thick ice covered the ponds. This alternation of warm mild air and raw western storms is a peculiarity of this winter climate and carries with it the germ of disease to the same degree as the humid summer heat and the miasma which is produced by the warm weather. Inflamation and respiratory diseases, severe rheumatism, diarrhea and nervous ailments prevail, especially among strangers who come from the South.

15 December — *The cold, accompanied by a strong wind, intensified by morning to 16°F. But without the wind*

Christ Episcopal Church, Boonville (1846). Duke Paul attended services in this church with C.F. Aehle on December 14, 1851. He calls it the "Anglican Church" in his diary. Photo taken ca. 1910. (Missouri Historical Society, St. Louis, Mo.)

Interior of Christ Episcopal Church, Boonville. Photo taken ca. 1910 (Missouri Historical Society, St. Louis, Mo.)

it would not have been so sharp at -13°F. Now the sky cleared up. Several mail stages failed to appear, since the roads were totally impassable. Despite the bright sunshine the cold intensified throughout the day, so that around the noon hour it was 10°F. Everything froze hard and the benumbed people who were little accustomed to severe cold ran over the streets at a trot.

  Most of the houses were so poorly constructed that the fireplaces and cast iron stoves served their purpose very deficiently. The Americans, especially in Pittsburgh, have advanced very far in the manufacture of iron stoves for cooking and heating and produce good, inexpensive but elegant merchandise. Their cook stoves—cast in all dimensions and costing from $14—$60 including all utensils and accessories—burn wood much more efficiently. One can cook conveniently in his room with one of the smaller models. There is space in them for many dishes, and frying and baking in them turns out very well.

  The cold continued and intensified to 5°F. The night was bright and calm, and since there was also no wind blowing in the morning, the cold abated somewhat.

  16 December — The sun came up brightly but wintery. Ice was everywhere. The windows were coated with it. The mail stages arrived behind schedule and in disarray. The cold intensified even more toward noon, and in the city of Boonville it began to create serious concern because of shortages of foodstuffs and firewood (in the midst of a virgin forest), since the farmers were not coming to town with their victuals because of bad roads. A small wagon of wood, about 1/4 cord, rose in price to $1.50, and apprehension even greater....

[Note: The surviving journal of Duke Paul ends here, in mid-sentence. Unfortunately, the remaining pages of the diary have not yet been rediscovered. During the years 1928-31, however, parts of the journals were transcribed, in old-German handwriting, by a Stuttgart archivist, Friedrich Bauser. As was mentioned earlier, this transcription has a number of serious problems, but since we have no other record of the remaining parts of this journey, we are including here a portion of Bauser's transcript as translated by Hans von Sachsen-Altenburg.]

[Bauser's entry for 16 December continues the above entry as follows:] ...*The news from St. Louis was not any better as one expected not only a freezing over of the Missouri, but also of the Mississippi. All commerce had broken down, neither by water nor by land was there any connection possible. A jar of water froze into a solid ice cube while standing close to my redhot oven. The mail from St. Charles had been late for three days.*

On the 19th (of December) brought beautiful sunshine, and since thanks to the frost the roads had become usable again, the market place was beginning to fill again. Here a few food prices: beef 2 1/2 cents (hereafter adjusted for American readers) per pound, pork 3 c, a dozen chicken $1.50, quails $0.50 a dozen, doves the same, rabbit 5 c, tame and wild cornish hen 30-35 c, a fat goose 25 c, wild duck 5-10 c, catfish of 15-40 pds—20-25 c, river bass 10-15 c, etc.

With the snowfall it got colder and colder. The involuntary spare time caused by the weather allowed me to review the possibilities of settling here. Single farmers own large tracts comprising up to several thousands of acres and they try to sell them subject to advantageous terms. The farms are well located. Since wood is still valuable one could invest in it. However, I believe a farm of 120-160 acres may be more profitable since one can manage it without much hired help, and it would supply enough fodder to sustain a nice stand of

147

cattle as well as a productive piggery (pig breeding operation). A large farm necessitates an all-encompassing knowledge of the American economic and commercial apparatus and a substantial population of negroes.

The rational establishment of a steamdriven saw- and flour-mill would also be a good investment. Furthermore, someone accomplished in working a saline, with sufficient capital, could produce salt, the quality and richness of it cannot be doubted when one considers the salty springs. Furthermore, this county contains coal and iron ore.

For a welcome change a coach arrived carrying a group of gentlemen who had left Santa Fe in October and thus had taken 55 days to reach Independence; they had suffered much from the cold. For one party they consisted of high officials with whom I had an in-depth conversation until late into the night; amongst them was the governor of New Mexico, G. Howton [Actually, the governor was James S. Calhoun; Joab Houghton was chief justice of the New Mexico Superior Court], *a most charming man who had mastered the Spanish language completely. On that night we also received the news of the coup d'etat of the princely president, Louis Napoleon, in Paris.*

[Note: Assuming that Bauser's rendition of Duke Paul's journal is correct, it is amazing but not impossible that the news of Louis Napoleon's coup d'etat traveled from Paris to Boonville in only three weeks. As so often in history or life, the significance of news is not immediately apparent. Almost certainly, Duke Paul would have made a great conversationalist on this subject—especially with an interesting circle of people such as the one that convened that night in Boonville.

With the reported military takeover of the government in France, Charles Louis Napoleon Bonaparte was to begin a cycle of events which—both in the beginning and the end—would lead to two major waves of German immigration to the United States. Paul had heard of this distant relative throughout all of his life; a trouble maker, a power hungry man with one single-minded vision—himself at the top—to restore the fading glory of the Napoleons.

Little Louis was the third son of Emperor Napoleon's brother, Louis, King of Holland, and his wife, Hortense de Beauharnais. Because Hortense was believed to have masterminded the Emperor's return from Elba, she was exiled from France and lost her oldest son after an embarrassing custody battle. Hiding with little Louis under the name of the Duchess of Saint Leu, she wandered through Southern Europe and eventually settled in a castle in Switzerland.

During the post-Napoleonic years the Bourbons had restored their powers thus creating a simplistic dichotomy of thinking not unknown throughout history: if you were supportive of the old system, no matter what its merits, and of the Bourbon family, you were considered to be conservative—and good. If you were supportive of the new systems which had arisen from the reforms of the dictator-turned-Emperor Napoleon, you were branded as a liberal and considered to be bad. So the teenager Louis was branded, by name and by thought, liberal, as would have been, by association, virtually all of American's population at the time.

Since members of the Napoleonic dynasty were legally banished from France, the young remained abroad and soon became involved with other liberals. The freedom-seeking revolution of 1830, which quickly spread to other countries, was an attempt by young and educated people to retain some of the civil liberties gained

149

since the Emperor's times. They were bright students like Aehle, Kueckelhan, and ten thousand others. They failed in their attempt for reforms, and these refugee-liberals—adopting and upholding American individual freedom—greatly increased the American population, even in remote places like Boonville. After the collapse of this intellectual revolution, young Louis was exiled by the Bourbons, and unceremoniously shipped off to the country of the "liberals," to be set free in New York.

Not to be deterred by a little setback, Louis returned to Europe immediately and hid in Switzerland and England until an opportunity of if-you-can't-lick-them-then-join-them allowed him to associate with the goverment which first demanded his departure, then elected him to a leadership position. With the classic bravado of a politician ("If the people impose duties upon me, I shall know how to fulfill them!"—Louis Napoleon) he endeared himself to the middle class, capitalizing more on the hatred against the conservative Bourbons than based on his own merits. Legally still banished, he had the law revoked, and soon the man who overtly styled himself after the first Napoleon, the dictator and self-proclaimed emperor, took the oath as the president of the Republic of France.

The explosion was preprogrammed. When the still conservative National Assembly limited suffrage and shackled the younger generation sufficiently to generate effervescent resentment, liberal Louis gained massive support just as he neared the end of his term. Constitutionally barred from re-election, he sought to have the constitution changed; the Assembly refused. After endless speeches, and maybe after reviewing the memoirs of the first Napoleon, Louis loaded his power bases, used his presidential powers to dismiss the Assembly, and had his military forces take over on December 2, 1851. Most had seen it coming, and quickly resistance waned. Such were the matters that might have been discussed in Boonville during that cold winter night after the news of Louis Napoleon's coup d'etat arrived. The new revolution spread like wildfire, igniting the aging young and the next generation of students. As always in periods of uncertainty and weak leadership, it was a time of proposals and visions of renewal and improvement. Karl Marx's vision was only one among dozens.

The wake of this flood of new ideas destroyed Duke Paul's own homebase. In most European countries liberal ideas were quickly and brutally thwarted, and again young men left their parents and spouses to escape the secret police of the conservatives. Back then they still had a place to go, and soon they nourished their souls on the American dream of liberal freedom, rarely to return to the old fatherland.

Exactly one year later, Louis became Emperor Napoleon III. With amazing speed he adopted the methods of the conservatives and maintained a republic tied to the monarchy for the next twenty years. His activities led to the execution of the ill-fated Maximilian, Emperor of Mexico, and numerous other international failures.

At the end of the third Napoleon's cycle, the immigration officers of America again worked overtime when, in 1870, he initiated a war against Prussia, necessitating a rigorous German draft which many young men sought to dodge by emigrating to America. Soon, Lady Liberty became the magnetic symbol of hope for all who refused to bow to the forces of conservatism and senseless militarism. The vision had been renewed again.]

After 17 days I was able to leave Boonville on the 24th of December. Now the expedition to Laramie had actually come to an end.

[Bauser then adds a description of the adventures of Balduin Moellhausen which the archivist had probably found in the local library. Since this description is presented as if it were part of the diary, the reader might incorrectly conclude that Duke Paul had written it, which is, of course, not true. After this interlude, Bauser continues to provide his version of the diary.]

The journey by mailstage first crossed standing timbers with high-stemmed oaks and foliage trees which would provide ideal food for pigs and sheep, and reached Jefferson, where at the occasion of Christmas Eve there was a happy and enjoyable gathering with fireworks and dancing. The Germans residing there gave a serenade in my honor. I found a lot of honest and honorable people among them, another proof that our people in the Western states are better than the ones in the East, where Germany has literally dumped the veritable scum of its population.

When we passed the Osage River by ferry we first had to wade—while sinking up to our knees—through deep mud and very loose and watery ice (slush). Only with great difficulties were the belongings put aboard while it continued to rain buckets. We spent an hour stopping at the settlement of a rich German widow who had lost her husband and four workers in one single day during the cholera epidemic last year. The weather had turned terrible, it was raining and storming during the pitchdark night.

The passengers had to ascend on foot a high, rocky and steep mountain, and on a ghastly road, through wooded hills and deep mud, we finally reached a house where I spent the night wrapped in my buffalo hide.

During the passage of the Gasconade River a part of the

baggage and some people broke through the ice and were exposed to great danger. The mail driver had simply thrown our baggage and the mail on the river's shores where they remained unguarded for several hours. If you ask an American whether this seems right, he will answer the security of the country proves it right, but he could not deny that the mail has often been robbed.

Meanwhile it had got dark and the wagon for our continuation of the trip had not arrived yet. The passengers had to spend the entire night in the small village without any place to overnight. [Note: As so often in Bauser's transcription, all personal and geographical names are omitted as he usually had difficulties deciphering them.]

*Beginning in the settlement of Adams the road became horrible beyond description, a terrible thunderstorm with monstrous amounts of rain cast upon us which lasted until deep into the night. When the stage reached its goal [**name omitted by Bauser**] at 11 o'clock at night, it had to wait until daybreak. I stayed in the wagon and slept as well as possible. Between Habitation Rodgers and Manchester the wagon got stuck, so we had to (change and) take a common economy coach (to continue our journey).*

On the 31st of December (1851) at 5 o'clock in the morning we reached St. Louis, after a trip of seven days.

* * *

In addition to Paul's diary description of the visit to Boonville, we are fortunate to have another account of the visit written by one of his hosts, Carl Franz Aehle. This account comes from a reminiscence written in 1898. The original is in the possession of Dr. Mike Aehle of St. Louis, a great great grandson of Carl Franz Aehle, and the following excerpt from pages 53-56 of that manuscript is used here with his permission.

Life in a small town must of necessity be more or less uneventful, yet in ours a meteor would occasionally brighten the sky, among which I might recount the often unheralded, totally unexpected arrival of lately imported musical celebrities, who seemed to have lost their bearings like erratic comets and landed or stranded here scarcely knowing themselves how or why, among whom I may include the incomparable Italian trombonist Rogacy, for years afterwards a shining member of the Thomas orchestra, the superb Polish tenor Sabatizky, left in this country by a dissolved Italian opera troupe and besides many others, the divine, absolutely unapproachable cellist Joe Deam, whose soulful playing still lingers in our memory.

But another notable star of an entirely different magnitude made suddenly and unannounced his appearance during the extremely cold winter of 1850 [actually 1851], *when the Keeper of our best hotel brought a gentleman to my store, whose courtly manners and magnificent physique betrayed him at once as a distinguished personage and who, to my surprise introduced himself as Prince Paul, brother of the reigning King of Wurtemberg. Not speaking English, though master of seven languages, he seemed much pleased to find me and explained that he was on his return trip from the Rocky mountains, whither he had gone at the urgent request of Baron von Humboldt and the Berlin scientific society with an escort of twenty five men to examine and, if possible, to determine the formation of Pikes Peak, a knowledge of which was considered of the utmost importance to solve a hitherto insoluble geological problem.*

All the country lying west of Independence—Kansas City not yet known—being then an almost unexplored wilderness in sole possession of the Indians, he lost twenty four of his men by one of their attacks, saving his and one of his men's life

Carl Franz Aehle and his wife, Elizabeth Jane Mack (daughter of Nathaniel W. Mack). Photos by Boonville photographer, O.D. Edwards (Courtesy of Dr. Mike Aehle, St. Louis, Mo.)

Upper right: Aehle Coat of Arms (Courtesy of Dr. Mike Aehle, St. Louis, Mo.)

Page 54 of Carl Franz Aehle Memoirs (1898) containing a portion of the account of Duke Paul's visit in 1851. Courtesy of Mike Aehle.

by an almost miraculous escape and having luckily reached civilization, he proposed to remain here until the opening of navigation. Abhorring hotel fare and refusing to know any one besides myself and Dr. Kueckelhan, he became an almost daily guest at our home and table, being especially pleasant with our cuisine and the quality of our wine, without which he considered a dinner simply unedible, delighting us in return by his highly cultured conversational powers and having traveled extensively among the exceedingly interesting ruins of upper Egypt, besides commanding an exploring expedition to the then unkown sources of the Nile, it is easily believed that we often listened spellbound till a late hour of the night to these "tales of a traveler" nor were we less captivated by his recitals of visits to the different European courts, to nearly all of whom he was in some manner related—calling the Queen of England cousin Victoria—frequently uncovering skeletons in the closets of Royal families, which the outside world would neither learn nor suspect.

It is useless to add that we almost dreaded the coming of the first steamboat, usually hailed with pleasure, knowing that it would carry away a guest, who had contributed so much to shorten an inclement winter.

* * *

Aehle's memory of what Duke Paul told him and Dr. Kueckelhan during his visit to Boonville contains a number of inconsistencies with the actual facts of Paul's life and his journey to and from Fort Laramie in the fall and winter of 1851. These inconsistencies are probably, for the most part, due to the fact that Aehle is remembering something that happened 47 years previously and is not always accurately remembering what was said. But the kinds of errors are interesting and they lead one to a general speculation about other matters the men might have discussed on those cold winter days and nights when Paul was wined and dined by his cultivated, German speaking hosts in their Boonville homes.

First of all, of course, Aehle is off by a year in his memory of when Paul came to Boonville. He says it was the winter of 1850 when, in fact, it was the winter of 1851. He also identifies Paul as the brother of the reigning king of Wuerttemberg, when, in fact, King Wilhelm and Paul were cousins.

Aehle says Paul did not speak English, even though he was a master of several other languages, including French, in addition to his native German. In fact he did speak some broken English, but he often preferred to converse in French or German. It is somewhat surprising that he did not speak better English given his obvious fascination with America and his several trips here, but it would not have been unusual at that time. French was still spoken fairly widely on the western frontier and there were a considerable number of Germans living in St. Louis and the lower Missouri River valley at this time, so he would have had very little difficulty communicating in these more familiar languages on his various journeys. In addition, he almost always travelled with someone who did speak English, as well as French and German. One might imagine, nevertheless, that Paul would have felt particularly comfortable when in the company of people like Aehle and Kueckelhan who spoke his native language, especially when those people were, like himself, well-educated and cultivated men.

The comment about Paul "abhorring hotel fare" may have been an accurate memory of what Paul told Aehle, but it is interesting to note in this respect that Paul makes a particular point in his diary of describing the Mansion House hotel where he stayed as "among the best in the provincial towns of the West." Paul also notes that he had a "good supper" on the night of his arrival in Boonville, and he gives a lengthy and complimentary description of the food and service at the hotel, though he does add the fact that "Americans almost never drink wine with their meals" and that "eating for the Anglo-American is a necessity, not a pleasure."

A further observation might be made in regards to Aehle's comment about Paul taking special pleasure in the "quality of our wine." Paul was, indeed, a connoisseur of fine wine, but he noted in his diary entries while at Hermann on the trip up the river in late August that he was far from enamored with the wine the Germans at Hermann were making from Catawba grapes. He referred to the Catawba as a "wild grape" without much stability or durability, and noted that the wine he tasted made from the Catawba grapes had a "peculiar aftertaste like black currants." Finally, he said that given the cheap price at which good white French and red wines were available at Hermann and other towns along the river, he could not understand why people were willing to pay more for the "home-grown" Catawba wines. One of the so-called "premium" Catawba wines Paul paid a higher than normal price for he found to be "entirely unpalatable, similar to a completely sour apple cider." Boonville, it might be noted, was at this time noted for its "premium" Catawba wines, produced by William Haas at his brewery and winery on the west edge of town, and many of the Germans in Boonville made their own beers and wines. What exactly Duke Paul was drinking with Aehle and Kueckelhan is not clearly stated, but one would assume they had access to the best wines and brandies that could be had in Boonville at that time, in addition to the "home grown" Catawbas. So Paul, undoubtedly, had his choice.

Aehle says that Paul explained that he was on a return trip from the Rocky mountains, "whither he had gone at the urgent request of Baron von Humboldt and the Berlin scientific society with an escort of twenty five men to examine and, if possible, to determine the formation of Pikes Peak, a knowledge of which was considered of the utmost importance to solve a hitherto insoluble geological problem." There are a number of inaccuracies in this statement, though it is not too hard to see how the inaccuracies may have occurred. Paul had not been sent to the Rocky Mountains by Baron von Humboldt and the Berlin scientific society, though he was well-acquainted with von Humboldt and his works as well as with the Berlin scientific society, of which he, himself, was a member. Baron von Humboldt was certainly one of the leading and best known German scientists of his day, and there was, indeed, much speculation at this time among European scientists about the flora, fauna, geology, archaeology and anthropology of the American lands west of the Mississippi. Paul did, in fact, gather much valuable information of this kind on his various journeys to America, but the specific nature of the 1851 expedition was to attend the major government conference with the Plains Indians being held at Fort Laramie. Paul did not, unfortunately, arrive in time to attend the conference, and he did do some exploring of the area before returning to St. Louis, but neither his diaries nor his **Letter from Boonville** reveal any very specific references to a "hitherto insoluble geological problem" connected with the formation of Pike's Peak. It is not hard to imagine, however, that Paul would have shared some of his scientific knowledge and observations of the far western lands with two cultivated and educated men such as Aehle and Kueckelhan, and that some mention of Pike's Peak might have occurred during the conversations.

The other curious error in this particular memory of Aehle's is the statement about the escort of twenty five men who supposedly accompanied Paul on the journey, along with the later statement he makes about twenty four of the men being lost to an Indian attack and the miraculous escape made by Paul and the remaining man. It is clear from Paul's diary that his only companions on the journey were a man named Zichlinsky, "a young immigrant from Saxony" whom Paul hired in New Orleans, but who was separated from Paul early in the journey and was not heard from again; and 26 year old Balduin Moellhausen, a writer and artist who later became a famous and much published author of Western travel literature in Germany.

It is, of course, true that Paul and Moellhausen were harrassed and attacked by Indians on their way back from Fort Laramie, and both men did manage to miraculously escape from a series of potentially fatal encounters, not only with Indians, but also with weather, sickness, accidents, and starvation. But where Aehle got the idea that Paul was accompanied by a twenty-five-man escort is not clear. Paul may have "embellished" the true nature of the journey in the warm glow of a winter's evening by the fire with good friends and some of Dr. Kueckelhan's fine brandy, or Aehle, himself may have "embellished" the story, or it may simply be a matter of Aehle's not remembering the story clearly after the passage of so many years.

Aehle's memories of Paul's other "tales of a traveler"—about visits to the ruins of upper Egypt and exploring the "unknown sources of the Nile"—are essentially accurate, and Paul was related to the European and English courts, so he could have easily recounted, as Aehle notes, numerous stories about "skeletons in the closets of Royal families" both in Germany and in England.

Perhaps equally fascinating as the things Aehle says they talked about during Paul's stay in Boonville, are the things Aehle does not mention. One can assume that since Paul was in Boonville for nearly three weeks he and his hosts talked about a wide range of topics, for there were many things of interest going on, not only in Missouri and America, but also in Cuba, England, Germany, and Europe at this time. Local newspapers, as well as the St. Louis newspapers, to which one can assume Paul, Aehle and Kueckelhan would all have had ready access (though, of course, Paul's reading of newspapers would have been largely confined to the German language papers from St. Louis), carried numerous articles about local, regional, national and international issues and events. Paul was obviously interested in many of these issues and events for he mentions them specifically in his **Letter from Boonville**.

One issue that he comments on several times is the "communistic revolutionary zeal" of certain of his countrymen in America, such as those in St. Louis, who, for the most part, migrated to America after the failure of the attempt at revolution in Germany, Hungary and other parts of Central Europe in 1848. Paul is especially critical of the activities and speeches of Lajos (Louis) Kossuth, a Hungarian patriot and revolutionary who was given a hero's welcome to America in December of 1851 just two years after his failed attempt to overthrow the Hapsburgs of Austria. He came to America in an attempt to raise financial and official political support for his cause, but was largely unsuccessful in this. News of Kossuth is prominent in all the newspapers in the months leading up to his arrival in America, and one can be certain that he would have been a topic of conversation between Paul and his Boonville hosts. In Paul's eyes these latter day revolutionaries stood in stark contrast to the older generation of more conservative, practical, stable, and industrious Germans like Aehle and Kueckelhan (though one should remember that Kueckelhan apparently dabbled with revolutionaries while a young student in Germany) who had migrated to America a decade earlier and who had made every effort to adapt themselves to the American social and political system. This earlier generation of Germans were, for the most part, Lutheran or Catholic in religious preference as opposed to the largely anti-religious intellectual revolutionaries and the narrowly and fanatically religious German Methodists who come in for particularly harsh criticism from Paul.

Paul is also harshly critical of the German press in St. Louis because of its bias for revolutionary propaganda, and he decries the fact that the "monarchical conservative party" in Germany does not have more of a voice in the American press. The newspaper he is referring to is the **Anzeiger des Westens**, founded in 1835 in St. Louis and largely guided, up to 1850, by the relatively conservative Wilhelm Weber. But in 1850 editorship of the paper was taken over by the openly radical Heinrich Boernstein who made it the voice for the "Forty-Eighter" platform of anti-slavery, anti-Prohibition and anti-Catholic revolutionaries who had managed to gain leadership of the German emigrant community in St. Louis.

One can imagine Duke Paul, Aehle and Kueckelhan condemning the, to them, empty, irreligious, and potentially destructive fanaticism of these young St. Louis revolutionaries and being thankful that towns like Boonville harbored representatives of the more enduring German traits of religious conservatism, social responsibility, industriousness, frugality, and a disciplined intellect.

Another somewhat related topic receiving considerable press in the period between August and October of 1851 when Paul was making his way to Fort Laramie, and a topic that might well have worked its way into his discussions with Aehle and Kueckelhan about the dangers of revolutionary fanaticism, was the volatile Cuban situation. After more than 300 years of Spanish domination a revolutionary movement gained increasing force in Cuba throughout the first half of the 19th century to make Cuba a separate nation state or, perhaps, even form an annexation agreement with the United States. The movement climaxed in the period between 1849 and 1851 when two abortive armed attempts were made by Cuban revolutionaries under the leadership of the Venezuelan expatriate Narcisco Lopez to overthrow Spanish rule in Cuba. Lopez launched his failed attempts from New Orleans and was joined by a number of American supporters (mostly Southerners) who favored the idea of annexing Cuba to the United States. The American government was, however, opposed to the actions of Lopez and did not support the idea of annexation. As it turned out, both expeditions were soundly defeated by the Spaniards and Lopez, along with a number of his supporters, were executed.

Paul mentions his own lack of support for the actions of Lopez and seems to view the whole revolutionary movement in Cuba as just another example of the dangerous, destabilizing activities of revolutionaries in general. It would be interesting to know what some of the transplanted Southerners living in Boonville at this time thought about the Cuban situation. Some might well have supported the idea of the overthrow of Spanish domination and the possible annexation of Cuba to the United States, but one can be sure that people like Aehle and Kueckelhan would have shared Paul's view of the situation.

Another volatile and potentially interesting topic of conversation between Paul and his Boonville hosts might well have been the whole matter of the increasing agitation in the United States over the spread of slavery to newly acquired territories west of the Mississippi River. This issue, which would eventually lead the nation into a bloody Civil War, had become a matter of considerable political importance throughout the nation, but especially in the lands west of the Mississippi River, in the late 1840s.

One of the opening salvos in the debate was the so-called Wilmot Proviso, named for an obscure Democratic congressman from Pennsylvania named David Wilmot, who proposed an amendment to the $2 million appropriation bill Congress was attempting to pass to bribe Santa Ana into ceding California to the United States. The Wilmot Proviso stated that in any territory so acquired "neither slavery nor involuntary servitude shall ever exist." Every Northern state legislature but one passed resolutions approving the Wilmot Proviso, but Southerners viewed it as an insult to them and the Proviso did not pass when it came to a vote in 1846.

The next major stage in the debate came in the fall of 1850 when five different bills were adopted by Congress related to proposals made by Senator Henry Clay in an attempt to reach a compromise between the opposing sides in the debate. Under the terms of this so-called Compromise of 1850: California would be admitted to the Union as a free state; New Mexico and Utah territories were organized with no restriction as to slavery; Texas boundaries were set and no restrictions were made as to slavery; the slave trade (but not slavery itself) would be abolished in Washington D.C., after January 1, 1851; and the Fugitive Slave Act would be strengthened.

Of America's two main political parties at the time, the Whigs were the party most friendly to this Compromise, while the Democrats, especially those in the South were, for the most part, strongly opposed. Indeed, passage of the compromise measures led to various meetings in the South where there was considerable talk about the South's right to secede from the Union. Agitation related to the Compromise (and its relationship to the earlier Wilmot Proviso) continued well into 1851 and was a frequent topic of discussion in the newspapers of the time.

Missouri was, of course, a slave state which had been largely settled by Southerners and it is interesting to note that though many of the German immigrants were opposed to the idea of slavery, the older generation of immigrants often seemed to quietly accept the behavior of their Southern neighbors in this regard and even to occasionally own, as did Aehle and his wife, a domestic slave or two themselves. Paul remarks on the fact of slavery in Missouri in his 1851 diary as he passes through, but he makes no overtly critical statements about it, and one would guess that if the topic arose during Paul's conversations with Aehle and Kueckelhan the prevailing attitude would most likely have been in favor of Clay's Compromise.

The spirit of compromise on this issue of slavery

would, however, be severely tested several more times before the decade reached its end, especially by the Kansas-Nebraska Act of 1854 and the subsequent bloody border dispute between Missouri and Kansas in the final years of the decade over the matter of whether or not Kansas would enter the Union as a slave or free state. And when Civil War finally erupted and Missourians began choosing which side they were on, conservative old line Germans like Aehle and Kueckelhan found themselves joining their more radical cohorts, like Boernstein in St. Louis, on the side of preserving the Union, abolishing slavery, and putting down the rebellion of the Southern "separatists." The firm stand of the Boonville and Cooper County Germans for the Union would, of course, set them irrevocably against the more dominant Southern culture of the area, and with the end of the war and the defeat of the South, Germans like Aehle and Kueckelhan would find themselves in positions of power and leadership largely unknown to them in the years before the war.

A less weighty, but no less interesting, topic of conversation between Paul and his hosts would, no doubt, have been the California Gold Rush and the general emigration of Americans to the far western territories, especially the Mormon emigration to Utah and the massive emigration into Oregon Territory. Paul had, himself, visited California prior to his journey to Fort Laramie and had been more or less disenchanted with the situation he had found at the gold fields. Missourians, including a considerable number of Boonville's citizens, Southerners and Germans alike, had joined the "Rush" to the gold fields in 1849 and 1850, but by 1851 a number of the "49ers" had returned empty handed and disillusioned by the hard work, violence, poor living conditions, inflated living costs, and generally poor odds for getting rich quick that they found when they arrived in California. Among Boonville's German immigrants, the only ones who seem to have clearly "struck it rich" in California were the Sombart brothers who returned to Boonville in 1851 with a considerable amount of money and used it to establish a large scale milling operation on the river that proved to be the first in a series of highly successful business ventures for them in the years to come. One wonders if the Sombarts were introduced to Paul and, if so, what views they may have shared with him about their experiences in California.

Another likely topic of conversation would have been the railroad question. One wishes Paul had made some specific comment about this issue in his diary or in his **Letter from Boonville,** but he didn't so we are left to surmise what his feelings might have been on the issue. One might infer from his many uncomfortable and sometimes dangerous experiences with travel by foot, horseback, wagon, keelboat, steamboat and stagecoach that he would have welcomed the advent of fast, efficient, relatively comfortable, and cheap rail transportation into the western lands. But in 1851 railroading in Missouri and beyond was more a dream than a reality, and one would guess that Paul's interest in studying the regions he passed through in as much detail as possible would not have made train travel as attractive as it might at first seem.

Aehle and Kueckelhan would likely have had mixed feelings about the railroads also. For anyone living in Boonville at that time, the economic focal point of the town was the river. Steamboat traffic was increasing year by year, as it had been since the late 1830s, and it would be another seven or eight years before it would reach its peak on the Missouri River. Railroads, on the other hand, were in their infancy in Missouri and many towns and counties were supicious of the "eastern capitalists" who seemed to be behind many of the railroad building schemes, and were unwilling to expend the rather large amounts of money being asked for by the railroads as incentives to route the rail lines through a particular community or region.

Some of Boonville's town fathers, like the banker Joseph L. Stephens, wanted to see the proposed cross state railroad on the south side of the river routed through Boonville. Others felt that the river would always be more important to the town than a railroad. Some believed that the railroad would be naturally routed through or close to the town whether or not the town and county provided financial incentives. These latter attitudes would come to predominate as negotiations for the route of the railroad continued over the next ten years, and the final result would be that when the cross state railroad south of the river finally became a reality in the years just prior to and following the Civil War, Boonville would be by-passed by the main line, and this, coupled with the decline of steamboating would result in a period of economic stagnation for the town.

In addition to these weightier issues Paul was also rather obviously preoccupied with more mundane local matters, such as stagecoach and steamboat schedules, the weather, the apparent inadequacies of local home construction methods and heating arrangements to deal with the extremely low temperatures being experienced at that time, the on-again-off-again service of the newly established telegraph connection with Jefferson City and St. Louis, church services, and local land values. All of these matters are mentioned at one time or another in the

169

diaries, and some of these matters also work their way into the **Letter from Boonville.**

It is unfortunate that no issues of the **Boonville Weekly Observer** newspaper have survived from the period of Paul's visit to Boonville for it may well have been that his presence and activities in the town, and perhaps even some account of his adventures on the plains, were reported in the local newspaper. On the other hand, it is indeed fortunate that we have as much information as we do about Duke Paul's visit. The **Letter from Boonville,** Paul's diaries, and the memoirs of Carl Franz Aehle present a rare look at a significant, but little known, aspect of life in a small midwestern town of the 19th century and the part it played in the life of an important European scientist and traveller.

CHAPTER 5
The Letter from Boonville

Duke Paul probably had never dreamed of writing a lengthy letter from a small town in western Missouri. But he had also never expected to have so narrowly escaped a series of life-threatening situations. When he arrived in Boonville, he was made to feel at home immediately. His own memories of his earliest visit in 1823, to which he explicitly referred in his letter, were thereby elevated to become an integral part of it.

For Paul, as for most travellers, the river was not a separating boundary between counties or between northern and southern Missouri. Instead, it was a unifying element, a stream-line which united St. Louis and Independence, and all settlements along the watery superhighway of the eighteen hundreds.

For Paul, the villages of Franklin and Boonville were turning points. On his first visit, Paul exchanged the swaying boat deck for the cart, the waves of water for the waves of the prairie. It was the beginning of Western trails, and of Duke Paul's more serious adventuresome travels.

On his last visit, Duke Paul was at the end of his trail and the end of his trials. Here, in Boonville, he had finally left the threatening wilderness behind and re-entered civilization. It was time to pause.

On this trip Paul had learned to recognize his limits; for the first time in his life he felt the burden of his age. This was more than he had wanted to endure, and he was grateful to "the great master builder of the universe" for delivering him, one more time. We cannot tell from his diary, but Paul would escape death a few more times to come. During the following year he would,

171

impatiently, leave a steamboat that would not sail on time, and survive its explosion that killed dozens of passengers. A few months later, he would drift aboard a storm-damaged boat from Africa to Brazil.

Very astutely, Paul forecast the shift of importance from Franklin/Boonville to Kansas City, in his first diary. In 1851, realizing himself to be in a maturing city, Paul provides us with a summary of everyday observations we cannot easily find anywhere else.

"Letters from" were as en vogue then as they still are today. Paul had repeatedly sent lengthy essays to friends, who would edit and publish them. There are letters from Nubia in Africa, Mazatlan in Mexico, and others. Travellers found it their duty to correspond with their home base, to tell of their discoveries and progress.

The **Letter from Boonville** contains the elements one would expect in a travelogue. In addition, however, it contained the message of sustainable life in Missouri, and of the untamed wilderness, social and climatic, beyond. Not even half a century had passed since the passing of Lewis and Clark, and much progress had been made in inching the white man's civilization westward, but one still could succumb to many dangers along the way. In comparison, Paul's four-month trip contained more danger on a daily basis than Lewis and Clark encountered in thirty months of their absence from St. Louis.

Paul fully intended the **Letter from Boonville** to contain several distinct messages. For his scientific colleagues there was the scientific part. For his king-cousin there was the suggestion to reconcile with German refugees. For the religiously effervescent there is a call to return to the simple teachings of Martin Luther, as Paul believed in them. To all there was the shout: I am alive,

Letter from Professor Wilhelm Plieninger to Baron von Maucler February 7, 1852, suggesting that Duke Paul's **Letter from Boonville** be printed without the personal and political references. Courtesy of Wuerttemberg State Archive.

and I am grateful. But was he trying to send yet another message to someone very dear to his heart?

The **Letter from Boonville** was addressed to Professor Wilhelm Plieninger, a friend of Duke Paul's. This fact was only discovered in 1995 when another letter from Professor Plieninger to Baron von Maucler mentioning the **Letter from Boonville** was found in the Wuerttemberg State Archives. Paul's **Letter from Boonville** was prefaced with a cover letter, and since the greetings were abbreviated and virtually illegible, historians had no idea to whom the **Letter from Boonville** was addressed. (Note: The cover letter to Professor Plieninger is reprinted courtesy of the Wuerttemberg Hauptstaatsarchiv, file E14:128:6:nn)

My most honorable Master and Professor,
Having luckily escaped from great dangers, with the help of the great master-builder of the wide world, I have the sweet duty to inform you, honorable professor and dear friend, and to include a simple report of my distant travels and adventures in the New World. This is a sequence to my earlier reports of this year from Buffalo, New York State, and St. Louis, Missouri State, which have described my travels through the North of the Union, the Eastern states, the Great Lakes (Superior, Michigan, Huron and Erie) as well as my excursion to Mennisota [sic] the upper Missisipi [sic], the Falls at St. Anthony and Lakes St. Croix and Pepin, a huge distance across the country which I traveled during summer, starting from the South.
I nearly came to a tragic end on an expedition to the western Rocky Mountain via Fort Laramie when I, under greatest threats to my life, barely escaped from a group of hostile Indians after an hour long, tough ordeal and mistreatment. At last I had to suffer from stiff and icy snowstorms, and had lost

my animals which had frozen to death. Close to death by hunger and cold, I was saved more by coincidence, from a fate that seemed nearly inescapable. The truly magnanimous support granted to me by American citizens in this lamentable situation compensated sufficiently for the suffering. My health improved significantly since I have reached the borders of civilization again.

The demands put upon the traveler are not foreign to you, a man of science, as one strides through the immeasurable territories of the West, which has its own poetry consisting of naked and wild Indians and of the buffalo. But since every trip into these almost mythical mountains is filled with adventure and might be of interest, I will add a report covering the timespan from August 20th through the beginning of December, comprising my last scientific trip of this year.

My dear colleagues and you, most honorable professor, surely want to share in my difficult goal I have pursued. Maybe you are following me on my path, and as my heart keeps imagining your support, which is so important to me, and as I send my prayers to thank the great creator of this world for his sustenance and support... [last sentence illegible]

Paul Wilhelm v. Wuerttemberg

We know the date when Paul started to write the **Letter from Boonville**—11 December 1851—but we don't know how it was transported and by what routing and exactly when it reached its addressee.

On 7 February 1852, Professor Plieninger wrote a letter to Baron von Maucler (whose father had been the administrator of the Wuerttembergian military invasion of Mergentheim half a century before). Politically correct, the younger Maucler would review Plieninger's and Paul's request for publication with His Majesty the King. Approval was not automatic but well considered, especially when the letter contained sensitive issues that exceeded the normal travelogues. Both the mail system and the royal permission came forth in record times, and both would warrant comparison to today's equivalent systems.

To the Director of the Royal Inner Cabinet
Baron von Maucler

Your Excellency!

A few days ago I received the enclosed news from Duke Paul Wilhelm, Highness. Before I fulfil the wish indicated at the end of the letter, I deem it my highest duty to submit the news first of all to the highest pleasure of His Majesty the King, especially in view of the recent rumors of the tragic fate which was said to have afflicted His Highness, and I beg your intermediation to that effect.

In case His Majesty would be pleased to grant permission for such publication, I would assume it to be self-evident that those parts referring to the personal circumstances of the high traveller, but also his political views regarding the European and North American situations—especially since the latter might embarrass himself in North America—might be subject to omission, leaving just the scientific and the travel parts to be printed. First of all, as they contain interesting and in part new facts, secondly, as they actually contain a correction to those rumors which have led to much concern in wide circles.

If it pleases His Majesty, I would suggest the Augsburg General Newspaper for this publication.

With most excellent devotion,
Stuttgart 7 Febr. 1852

Prof. Plieninger

[According to a note on top of page 1 of this letter, this request was approved on 9. Febr. 52, signed F.v.M.]

Professor Plieninger had barely received the desired permission when the text was already typeset and printed. Meanwhile, the professor had struck out a series of sentences that were, as he had indicated, too personal or too political to be printed. Plieninger probably exercised his own discretion and was not subject to guidance in this exercise. We are lucky to have both the handwritten and the printed version of the **Letter from Boonville**, allowing us to compare the extent of change and omission.

I have disregarded minor changes, which would be better labeled corrections, in Duke Paul's often negligent orthography or in his occasionally awkward choice of words. These changes are, I believe, improvements bearing insignificant changes in meaning. The omissions are skillfully cut out, not allowing the reader of the printed version to notice a break in logic or style. These alterations of the letter must not be seen as censorship intended to suppress Paul, but rather as a protective step in his own interest vis a vis those that would have misused his statements for their own purposes in Germany. Plieninger, however, cleverly transfered these German concerns to America by saying that he had left out "those parts...[that] might embarrass himself in North America."

The published version of Duke Paul's **Letter from Boonville** was translated by Dr. Raymond J. Spahn, and is printed here courtesy of the Research Collections, University Archives, Lovejoy Library, Southern Illinois University at Edwardsville. Omitted sections from the original letter are inserted in italics and were translated by Hans von Sachsen-Altenburg.

Letter from Boonville, December 11, 1851, Part I Supplement to No. 51 of the *Allgemeine Zeitung*, Friday, February 20, 1852.

Letter of Duke Paul Wilhelm of Wuerttemberg, from Boonville, Missouri, approx. Lat. 38° 52' N. Long. Greenw. 92° 46' W. Dec. 11, 1851.

(This letter, sent to a colleague in the Fatherland, is published here to refute a recently circulated rumor that the noble traveler had met a tragic fate and to make available his copious scientific and ethnographic observations.)

I left the State of Illinois in the middle of August, shortly after my return from the Upper Mississippi. I reported to you in July about the latter trip, which was quite pleasant and favored by good weather, high water, etc. My plan for the remainder of the year, after having ordered my considerable collections and notes, was to visit the Rocky Mountains in the West or the spurs attached to the tertiary formations at the Upper La Platte River. This is a distance of almost 1500 English miles from St. Louis, the way leading mostly through the vast prairies of the West.

Only lesser rivers, tributaries of the Kanzas and the La Platte flow through it, forming a narrow, wooded, and watered strip in the often entirely waterless prairie, providing shelter and nourishment for man and animal during the tremendously scorching heat in the summer or the deadly winter cold of a snow storm.

These monotonous plains, so well-known through the reports of [Stephen H.] Long, [Benjamin L. E. de] Bonneville, and [John C.] Fremont, as well as romantically amplified and enlivened by two masters of writing (Washington Irving and [James Fenimore] Cooper) — these plains open up a tremendous scientific field to the traveller despite their monotony. Resembling the waves

Excerpt from original German edition of the **Letter from Boonville** published in the **Augsburger Allgemeine Zeitung**, February 20, 1852.

of the ocean, they are enclosed by the large natural wall that nature has drawn from North to South, from the Polar Sea to the Southern Ocean, through the long continent for a distance of nearly 120 degrees of latitude.

As is known, this natural partition is so high that its higher ridges extend into the icy snow line through all the climates of our universe, and its peaks are enthroned in the splendor of eternal snow. Only at two places do they slope to form lower hills or plateaus. One of them is between 40° and 38° N.L. where the South Pass, now well-known because of the California pilgrims, forms only a moderate mountain ridge, the highest water shed of which is hardly 4000' above the Pacific Ocean. Here is the source of the Gila River. The other low place in the chain is where the mountains of the Isthmus [of Panama] join together both new worlds.

In the various zones and climates I have seen vast, long stretches of these gigantic **cordilleras** with their white conical peaks and rocky jags. To study them is always a renewed attraction for me, to cross them a favorite task, either in the formidable **presacas** and **cañadas** which lead to the main passes in tropical America, or in the Rockies of the temperate zone, where they tend to be more undulating and assume phantastic, tower-like shapes.

These lime masses of Neptunian formation along the main range in the east form a belt running from the Missouri to the South Fork of the La Platte. They are so rich in grotesque shapes that they offer the eye a variety of scenery possibly unequaled by any other mountains on this planet. The master hand of [Karl] Bodmer, who accompanied Prince [Maximilian] of Neuwied on his North American trip, presents us with good sketches of the northern branching-out, which I visited in 1830. Then in 1851 I saw the southern spurs of these clay and lime mountains, the peculiar groups of which are even richer in characteristic formations. A natural rock column well-known since Fremont's travels, the Chimney Rock (La cheminee) has acquired a world-wide reputation which it richly deserves. More about it later.

When one approaches the Rocky Mountains from the northern arm of the flat [Platte] River, one is amazed to see in front of these white mountain groups the black rock masses of the Black Hills and the Wind River Mountains, the heavily-wooded Laramie Peak, approximately the height of Mt. Aetna, and the lofty James and Snow[mass] Peaks, covered with eternal snow and resembling huge sugar cones. Bordering the vast plains, they seem like natural boundaries between an Eastern and Western new world.

Then there is the peculiarity of the climactic differences between East and West within the same latitudes, as well as the peculiar distribution of animals and plants. The latter take on an almost tropical character as one approaches the Rocky Mountains, despite the high altitude and the cold that prevails six months of the year. The types of the cacti (**Mamillaria** and **Opuntia**), of the **Loasa** (**Bartonis**), of the tree-like **Liliaceae** (yucca), and of the **Papaveraceae** (a plant unknown to me, which is like an **Argemone**) attest to this, as do the conifers to be found here in the mountains and along the streams in the place of the deciduous trees that predominate in the East.

The animal kingdom also changes its forms the closer one approaches 100° W.L., Greenwich. The bison, elk, or the giant red deer [**Cervus elaphus**], the antelope with forked antlers, the mountain sheep, the mountain goat, the black, long-eared stag (**Dama [Cervus] macrotis**), the black prairie wolf (resembling the **Canis lycaon** of eastern Asia), the spermophiles, the grizzly bear, the American badger (**Meles labradorius**), the Rocky Mountain wolverine **Gulo occidentalis**, nob. [?]), more than twice as large as the one of Lapland, and many more four-footed animals belong to this eastern border zone of the mountains, and are part of a unique organic change that

181

is evidently due to specific causes.

The western world between 52° and 40° N. L. takes on its own character which has many similarities with the warmer Europe of the same latitudes. It is rich in forests and water, unfolding into meadows, none of them vast, continuous prairies; conifers often are predominant with their huge shapes.

Then there is California, which is a part of the United States, from 40° to 32° N. L. and from the Utah (Salt) Lake (the seat of the Mormons) to the Gila River and westward to the great ocean. This comprises countless wooded areas, meadows, stony deserts, mountains, and rows of hills where various deciduous trees (oaks, plane trees, bayberry bushes, and clethras) again predominate, but where coniferous trees are worthily represented by individual giants of the conifers (**Taxodium giganteum** and **Pinus lambertiana**).

In this western region, which incidentally provides ample nourishment, the mammalia are less frequently represented. The buck becomes rarer, as does the argali (**Ovis montana**), while the mountain goat (**Capra americana**), on the other hand, appears more frequently, the antelope (**Dicranoceros furcifera**) appears in groups; the American elk (**Cervus major**, Say) is to be seen in herds from time to time, the gray bear (**Ursus ferox**) often in annoying numbers, but the wolf less often.

The spermophiles of the eastern plains are replaced by other species with a similar manner of life, including a gray ground squirrel with a white collar, quite commonly found as far west as the coast, from 30° to 45° N. L. Curiously, in this part of the country it appears mostly where entire areas, including the mountains, are literally covered with some sort of oats, forming natural fields of unbelievable extent. Since it grows even in the woods, it affords the animals an excellent source of nourishment. The habitat of other vertebrate-animals in the West also is different from that in the bordering eastern areas.

Concerning birds, there appears a new kind, headed by the large California carrion-vulture (**Cathartes californianus**). As for gallinaceous birds, the West Coast is poorer than the East, which is rich in kinds and species. **Centrocerus urophasianus** and the pretty **Ortyxeris tata** are the only representatives of the milder West. Of the corvine birds the small western crow, not much larger than a blackbird (but no daw, of which there are two kinds in Mexico), and the bare-cheeked magpie (**Pica gymnogenys**, nob. [?]) are the most important. Among the woodpeckers the large imperial woodpecker (**Picus imperialis**, Gould) heads the list. Besides it, the most peculiar kind is a bird belonging to the **Prionitis**, from the family of **Meropedae**, which represents this South American form in the Northern Hemisphere and is found as far as southern California.

On the waves of the ocean often appears an albatross with black beak and feet (**Diomedea melanorrhyncha**) and from the eastern oceans of northern Asia there are the peculiar kinds of **Uria, Alta [Alca**?], and **Mormon**, which enliven the inland seas of Fuca[?] and San Francisco. A lack of **Sauria** and **Ophidia** is evident compared to the rich eastern part of the continent. The **Agama** are represented by the **Phrynosoma orbicularis**, the pleurodont lizards by a beautiful blue-throated **Anolius [Anolis]**, and **Polychrus** by a small kind completely unknown to me. Among the **Batrachia** there is the large green **Hyla**, marked with two silver-colored lateral stripes, and a gray/green, dark-speckled **Cystignatus**. The **Chelonia** include a **Testudo** and two

Emys, rather wide-spread, which also appear farther east. Of the **Ophidia** there is to be mentioned Say's **Crotalus tergeminus**, a gray black-speckled **Calamaria**, **Coluber flaviventris**, **guttatus**, Say, Tropidonatus (**Psammophis** [**Thammophis**] **saurita** or **syrtalis** and a **Dipsas** or **Dendrophis**, not known to me.

Among the invertebrates there is to be found an unknown treasure, but one that requires time and careful pursuit if one wishes to acquire a rich collection. The fish, to be found in large numbers in rivers and lakes, are confined to sturgeon, salmon, and whitefish, the species of which already are known to science, and the numerous coastal fish, which live in this great ocean from the north to the south. They have been observed often and specimens given to our museums. Since I lack all scientific references here, I have to rely on my memory, and I add this free-hand sketch with apologies for not being more detailed or systematic; but since it is my purpose to give only a synopsis, I trust you will forgive me.

Now that I have made a comparison of both regions, basing it on the wealth of my own research in the East and the West, I shall go into the historical part of my last trip and give an account of my best adventures and events. A more strictly scientific presentation will follow later, since I cannot even use my diary here. I am handicapped also in establishing degrees of latitude and longitude, because these have been taken from the notes of Fremont and other travellers. My own written observations are in the small part of my baggage I was fortunate enough to have saved.

A page from Duke Paul's original handwritten **Letter from Boonville** with hand drawn landscapes of the Scott's Bluff region made by Duke Paul.

Letter from Boonville, Dec. 11, 1851, Part II
Supplement to No. 52, *Allgemeine Zeitung*, February 21, 1852

During the middle of August [1851] I left St. Louis in a steamboat, accompanied by the amiable and excellent Prussian Consul C. E. Angrodt [Ernst Karl Angelroth] with whom I had a close friendship, as well as many young countrymen, who wanted to bid me farewell on the Mississippi, wishing me God's protection for a dangerous undertaking.

[*Due to my financial circumstances, thanks to the gallant procedure of the Second Chamber of 1849, which decided to cut off my legal property, I cannot equip my excursions in a princely manner and not even in the manner of an ordinary citizen. But since one only knows me here as an energetic, entrepreneurial man, not as a noble lord, I accomodate myself and am not ashamed when my equipment appears rather poor.*] A rather common one-horse carriage with an indispensable supply of provisions and tools, weapons, and ammunition was going to have to be sufficient for me, since I was going to play the role of a backwoodsman again.

I had with me a riding horse for my companion, a volunteer, for I had insufficient means to employ an engagé, Mr. H[einrich] B[alduin] Möllhausen, a Prussian of good family and education who had been lending me a helping hand since the previous spring. He was cooperative and faithful as well as good at sketching.

A certain Mr. Zichlinsky, originally from Dresden, whom I myself paid, joined him. He was a young man from New Orleans, who endeared himself to me very much and who wanted to remain with me. Unfortunately when his wagon broke down later, we missed one another, but I am glad that he did not have to share our severe trials, and I only hope that he survived.

I proceeded up the Missouri and had a comparatively pleasant trip as far as the mouth of the Kansas River, the provisional destination of my river trip, 380 miles from the mouth of the Missouri. You are probably well acquainted with the banks of the great river through some of my earlier printed travel accounts. Though mountains and rivers have not changed since 1823 and 1830, the areas of the country under cultivation, the settlements, and the population have changed indeed. Where formerly vast wooded areas and wilderness bordered the valley of the Missouri, there now are many successful farms with some elegant wooden and brick houses, and they are stocked with thriving horses, cattle, sheep, and swine, surrounded by the most magnificent fields which supply a rich harvest of corn, wheat, oats, barley, cabbage, and legumes, as well as delicious fruit consisting of excellent apples and peaches.

Because the State of Missouri is slave country, the more successful farms are cultivated entirely by blacks. The owners therefore do not have to be dependent upon hired hands, which in the United States are perhaps even worse than in our country. The hired hands, who serve for approximately 8 to 10 dollars per month, including meals, are mostly German, Irish, or Swiss. The latter are usually good people; the former, if from the old stock, useful and industrious, but if refugees, mostly lazy, arrogant, shiftless people. They are even less eager to conform to the institutions of the Union than to those of their fatherland. They use the communistic revolutionary zeal only for their own purpose, namely to live off others, and are truly a nuisance. If I accuse the Hungarians of carrying on an unjustified and badly-led revolution, I must admit that subjective though they may be concerning conditions in their [old] country, they generally strive to be just and diligent. Most of them speak respectfully of the imperial house and still revere the monarchical principles more than they do communism.

The Irish are [—*because of their bad priests*—] almost all degraded, fanatic, quarrelsome, thievish rabble. They make up a group of people from which rowdies and loafers are organized—truly a plague in the land. The American looks with respect upon the older German population, mostly pious, well-to-do, thrifty, and diligent landowners or craftsmen. They own farms, are model managers, industrious craftsmen and merchants, and are helping the country to flourish.

In the West the American is still of the good old stock, sturdy, stout-hearted, diligent, honest, and God-fearing, comprising the foundation of a population that is growing with tremendous strength, spreading from one ocean to another, from North to South, through woods and across rivers and mountains. The people are intelligent, ingenious, not afraid to face danger when necessary, and even if crafty and speculative in business, yet honest and honorable. The exceptions, which include Yankee tricksters and humbugs, are more or less found in the East and the South; the West is not yet so demoralized; the hypocrisy and sanctimony of smart sabbath-breakers cannot prevail in the face of the fundamentally sound citizenry, so they tend to graze with the herd of our German bigots who were led astray in the Abraham's bosom of [John] Wesley's teachings or who found a new heaven with the Methodists and those addicted to meetings, and who spend their time feuding with all of the other Christian congregations.

Though I do not like to speak about our politically confused countrymen, [*since I cannot but remember the sad, revolutionary situation of our German fatherland with all the consequences which are so destructive to me, and which have left me without the comfort and a quiet estate for old age. Now that my estate in Mergentheim has been defiled and I have no chair left to rest my old body after having fulfilled the last, difficult tasks, I will have to light my warming chimney in a distant land. That is the reason I feel enmity against these adventurers, but*] I do feel the need to explain that many of them have approached me quite honestly, and that not all belong to the aforementioned group. In the United States I have not been insulted by these people. I believe that in due time a limited amnesty would do some good, and many a lost soul could be won back for the fatherland [*and it would cure them from their current principles, punish the leaders and bring together the lost ones, I propose; the gruesome persecution will only have the opposite result than the intended cleansing of the state, just like the laughable*] ovations presented to the [*most insignificant*] Hungarian agitatior [*Kossuth*] led to different results [*in England and in the USA*] than the adulatory party expected [*i.e., the Magyars (Hungarians), a proud, strong people do not see a hero in this high rising Pesther Jurate, since Kossuth never fought like a victorious warrior for the cause itself, but instigated intrigues in his own interest and thus the penniless man created a fortune for himself. Hate and envy are secretly catching up with him, and soon his adversaries will publicly confront and ruin him. Therefore our*] hardened German revolutionary heroes, namely those of Baden, are fighting one another furiously and calling each other scoundrels and cheats, [*which shows that they often are both insincere people*].

The best Germans I discovered in the United

States are settlers in Wisconsin and in western Missouri. If I ever had to choose a home in the Union it would be there. The charming location of Cedar Lake, for instance, which is north of Milwaukee, and where many countrymen live under the protection and influence of an excellent gentleman, Mr. Schleisinger-Weil, really caught my attention. I spent a few most pleasant days with the charming family of this upright man from Strassburg.

Inviting as the State of Illinois is, its climate and soil fertile, its necessities of life inexpensive, I would not want to live there. I cannot advise any strict follower of our Lutheran Church to settle [*his family*] there among the Germans. Either they belong to the so-called independent people who disregard all religious order, and who, through the influence of these principles infect the education of the youth and try to lure them away from Christianity, or they are pietistic Methodists, who interfere with family life through their ridiculous and foolish exaggerations. They pursue with inquisitorial criticism anyone who thinks differently, and evoke dissension and mistrust among the German settlers. This sect, which combines much hypocrisy with strict asceticism, is much more intolerant than the Roman Catholic Church.

They try to make converts, using an iron hand and any other disgusting and intolerable means. They hate the Lutheran and reformed Protestants; their preachers, often coming from the lowest and least educated layer of the people, use the most nonsensical sermons against the well-established congregations. [*Unfortunately they try to proselytize in our fatherland and it would be an incredible mistake to give them even a small chance. They would be even more dangerous than all other groups of these frenzied sects, even more so as their naive (make believe) virtuousness has an infectuous effect on others, thwarts true and passionate reli-*

gion and despises the genuine and decent teachings of Martin Luther.

I know very well that some South German pastors are secretly corresponding with delegates of German Wesleyans, and that they show a tendency toward this false teaching. The upper levels of the church should be more attentive to such regressions.

The American Methodists are much more reasonable than the German ones and] some of the American Methodists live quietly indeed, that is they hold only their lamp and night meetings. In some of the larger cities they have good speakers and honorable preachers, which the fanatic German **Michel** does not tolerate among his self-created clergy.

The Roman Catholic Church is making great strides in the Union, and its **ecclesia militans** consists mainly of the Irish. Even though there are honorable men among their priests, there are also schemers and greedy clergymen. In general, they are much better than they appear, and the malicious attacks of the German press against the Catholic clergy are more the result of envy than of conviction. Unfortunately the German newspaper is entirely under the influence of a fleeting democracy of which it is the instrument. The revolutionary propaganda, as I well know, wants to call forth a new insurrectional movement, but finds itself controlled by a conservative clergy, and in turn tries to cast a slur on it. [*By the way, the German governments have good reasons to be careful, because the revolutionary party in the USA includes very active and ambitious members, and no opposition is likely to reach out for the most extreme means than the one of the German refugees. There is no limit to the barbaric persecution and murderous destruction that could be caused by a renewed insurrection in Germany. If a revolution was to take place* within the German federated states, it would lead them all back to the fatherland, provided there was even a glimpse of a victory for these exiles. The leaders of the Puritan revolution in England and of the Jacobite one in France would be surpassed with their indomitable feeling of revenge. I often had to listen to how the leaders of the German revolution were publicly accused as traitors, and they were accused of squeamishness because they had not supported the general slaughter of princes and the higher aristocracy. Even though I feel too unimportant to give any advice to the German sovereigns, I still dare to state with concern for their interest that the smartest step would be to possibly try to win the most courageous heads of the insurrection, like, for example, Hecker, who in his private life is a straight man who even has some aristocratic manners (even though I don't know him) and who is a determined adversary to communist tendencies, at least at the moment. Boernstein, the editor of the* Anzeiger des Westens, *a dangerous opponent to the catholic clergy, is a man of great talent too, and even though he is a determined democrat, he is an enemy of the Jacobite communists. There is still a possibility to convince him of moderation, even if he cannot be won over.*] It is unfortunate that the monarchial conservative party in Germany does not have a solid and good paper in America, in order to squelch any vicious slander and abuse.

[*Maybe you will criticize me for my extreme treatment of the political and religious matters of our beloved German fatherland and for testing your patience. But my affection for the monarchy and for the crowned heads is but too natural and too definite to remain silent. I am in a country that has become kind of a second fatherland for Germans and that is of most decisive influence on the old fatherland. I am not writing this for the sake of my side, which you and the one for whom I write this do support, but because the public must be informed of the danger which confronts them.*]

The Anglo-American, whether Whig or Democrat, is a friend of ostentatious demonstrations, yet is a conservative and an enemy of communist activity. Therefore it is easily understood that our freedom fighters find only negative aid. For the American, money is not to be made through communism, as it is through a demonstration in Texas or Cuba. Even the smart Yankee who is not easily embarrassed as to how he makes his money, will not give aid to [Gottfried] Kinkel so that he can get a loan for the cause of the German revolution. This German humbug is indeed too obvious and unskilled to arouse the interest of a sharp American speculator, the government in Washington too honest and conservative not to oppose this speculation [*,which borders on deceit,*] when confronted by the danger as with the manipulations against Spain and Cuba.

[*But where is the public organ which should alert President Fillmore, definitely a man of honor, to Kinkel's manipulation, led by a miserable, would-be celebrity. This manipulation, closely examined, is the very same criminal act, on a small scale to be sure, as Lopez's sensational raid on Cuba. The very nature of the invective hurled at the government in Washington should show the Whigs that such calumny is foreign to the great majority of Germans. I believe that I can flatter myself that my convictions are known in the Union and that it is known here that although I'm closely bound to the monarchy, I would be happy to endorse the policy of the federal government in Washington in so far as the interests of my fatherland permit.*]

Letter from Boonville, Dec. 11, 1851, Part III.
Supplement to No. 53, *Allgemeine Zeitung*, Feb. 22, 1852

Before I pursue the historical events of my travels, I would like to add a few remarks about the State of Missouri's economic life, because this is of utmost importance to those who want to settle here, and because Missouri and Arkansas are the two western neighboring states best suited for German settlements. [*I believe I owe my observations to my countrymen wishing to emigrate.*]

The State of Missouri, which covers a vast, well-irrigated area of woods and prairies between 36° and 39° [north] latitude, is well-known as far as its geographical and geological conditions are concerned. We have good maps and topographical descriptions made by diligent Americans who have been appointed by the government as men who know their craft. They have engaged busily in their task and performed it excellently. The area has been surveyed, its resources evaluated, and all of the land suitable for cultivation (almost the entire state, excluding a few rocky sections) has either been settled (is held by specific owners) or (the lesser part) still may be bought from the state at 1 1/3 Doll. per acre in parcels of 160 acres each.

The vast wooded areas contain some of the most magnificent building materials; they comprise not only "bottom" (tall forests in the bottom lands along rivers, especially the Missouri, the Osage, the Gasconade, the Grand Riviere, the Fish River, and the Kanzas, where there are the giant-like representatives of the aspen, sycamore, ash, and storax trees with their brilliant undergrowth, girded and overgrown with climbers and wild grapes), but they also consist of "timbers" (woods of deciduous trees on higher ground, on hills, and on greater elevations). These are mainly oaks, nut trees, ash, now and then cedars, **Juniperus oxycedrus**, [Juniperus] **virginianus**, and tulip trees, locust trees, **Gleditschia tria[ca]nthos, Robinia pseudo-acacia,** Preedwood [redwood], **Cercis canadensis;** [Kentucky coffee tree,] **Gymnocladus canadensis;** Porcelia [Asmina] **triloba**, papaw; **Dyospyros virginianus**, persimmon; as well as shrubs, climbing plants, and many trees, bushes, and plants utilized in medicine and technology.

The vegetation can be compared with that in Illinois, [i.e.,] with the same types. The southern part of the state sees a transition from a colder climate to one in which the winters are mild with little bitter weather or snow. The counties in the south contain large cypress woods (**Taxodium distichum**). These trees, whose trunks are known for their huge dimensions, are found from 36° 30' [N.L.] to the tropics and even on the Mexican plateau; in Chapultepec in Mexico, for example, they get very old and can be seen in the deep swamps. The central areas of the state, between St. Louis and Herculan[e]um have vast areas of **Lyriodendron tulipifera**, and the sassafras (**S.** [**Laurus**] **officinale sassafras,** Linn[aeus]) grows on the fertile land of the lowlands and the rocky bluffs, as does the dogwood (**Cornus florida**).

From all of this you can see that there is a variety of trees and shrubs, as well as herbs and plants in the forests and on the prairies. The most magnificent riot of blooms covers the fields eight months of the year, with endless varieties and changing colors, offering a vast field to the expert. The fertility of these Western states as concerns natural nourishment for man and animal is immense; nature's productivity is incredible, and the humus in part inexhaustible.

The grain, without exception European varieties,

is extremely abundant; but also garden root vegetables, potatoes, tobacco, castor beans (**Ricinus communis et viridis**), cotton (the small variety of **Gossypium herbaceum**), beans peas, chickpeas, lentils, peanuts, and sweet potatoes (**Convolvulus batatas**), cucumbers, many varieties of pumpkin, watermelon, and sweet melon grow beautifully. Therefore the land is extremely suitable for economical cultivation, even on a large scale, because there is the additional advantage of many mills and a profusion of waterways which during the warmer months of the year very greatly facilitate and expedite the transportation of produce.

I admired [original: *was astounded by*] the many head of livestock, the extremely well-fed herds of cattle, horses, and flocks of sheep, as well as the droves of swine. The tremendous size and plumpness of the latter amazed me; it is no rarity to see pigs weighing between 600 and 800 pounds. The animals live mainly on the plants of the woods and need only some supplementary corn in order to be fattened and later sent to the pork slaughter houses. There they are butchered daily by the hundreds, prepared, cured, and smoked. This explains the low price of smoked pork at 5 to 7 cents per pound, and the increasing improvement of the meat, which can be compared favorably with Westphalian and Bayonne meats, but at half the price. In the West, life's necessities become less expensive day by day; competition among factories and steamboats facilitates trade and traffic, and lowers the price of goods, so that almost all of them are much below the European market.

Hand-made goods are still expensive, as well as the better products of tailors and shoemakers. Due to the fact that the pay is still high (approximately $10 to $15 per month), everyone willing to work can lead a decent life with good food; there should be no vagabonds. Unfortunately there are many foreigners who do not like to work, and to this category belong most of our fugitive freedom fighters!

In the slave states it is easy to hire colored people. For approximately $150 to $50 one can work with them easily according to their capacity, without having to spend the large amount of $400 to $1200 to buy one. Land for sale is $3 to $15 per acre, including living quarters and farm buildings. Entire inventories of agricultural implements and livestock often are sold either at public auction or by private owners, mostly on credit, with securities or pledges to pay within one year.

In recent years some attention has been given to wine-growing in Illinois and Missouri. But as long as even our German wine-growers in Hermann on the Missouri River plant the wild Catawba [albeit] in perfected form, I, as a friend of oeneological progress, cannot approve, because any praise of such fruit is based on ignorance or on the desire to speculate. On the other hand, the improving of fruit trees and the correct preparation of apple cider has provided good results. In the United States the price of grapes is so low and freight by sea so reasonable that it hardly pays to grow grapes, except for eating; these can be sold on the market at a high price. I loathe these Catawba grapes, which by no means measure up to our magnificent perfected European grapes.

My journey up the Missouri River on one of the better steamboats took place without incident. I had the opportunity again, after several years, to see the parts of the lower valley of the river about which I had written earlier. I also noticed the development of new places as well as the disappearance of old ones such as Franklin.

Some of the most important new towns on the banks of the river are: Hermann, Jefferson, Boonville, and Glasgow. Favored by their location, they increase in size continually. In Hermann, the Germans are excellent wine growers. Further upstream [there are] Kanzas, at the mouth of the river with the same name; Weston; and St. Joseph, almost entirely belonging to the Robidoux family and named after Joseph Robidoux, of importance near Black Snake Creek (serpent noir), where I had a meeting with the chief [Black Hawk] of the Sakis [Sacs or Sauks] and Fox (Otogami) Indians.

I landed in Kanzas [sic] which is a main center like Westport and Independence. From there, trains and expeditions leave for the West (S[an]ta Fe, [Fort] Laramie, Salt Lake, California, and Oregon) to start their long and dangerous trek. It had been extremely hot during the last days of August when I was completing preparations for my departure. There were severe thunderstorms and heavy rains, but they hardly affected the heat (26° to 28° R[eaumur]), although they increased the world of tormenting, winged insects. I had acquired two light wagons and loaded them mainly with provisions and the necessary weapons and ammunition.

As soon as one reaches the border of the State of Missouri, the prairie begins; however, it is not the short grassy prairie of the West but the kind with tall grass and beautiful flowers, intermingled with low shrubs, oak, and sumach. For quite a distance this land still belongs to Indians who have come from the East, and with whom the United States has signed treaties. From Westport to the River Wakarussi and westward, the land belongs to the Sha[w]nees, who are mainly Christians. They have Presbyterian, Baptist, and Methodist missions which serve as places of worship and conversion, because the pious zeal of the Anglo-Americans is concerned not only with spreading Christianity among the redskins but unfortunately also with the spreading of sects. In this way the country is surrounded by friendly, half-civilized Indians.

Because I followed Captain Freemont's [Paul actually spelled the name correctly—Fremont—in his original letter] travel route, which now is considered the real California road, I arrived after 90 English miles and after having waded through many little creeks and small wood-bordered rivers, at an important settlement of the Puttowatomi [sic], called Union Town. There I crossed the Kanzas River, which at this point is wider than the [river] Neckar at Heilbronn. After ten more English miles there is the last settlement, a Catholic mission, where a titular bishop [the Rt. Rev. John B. Miege] resides, and where boys and girls, children of the Indians, are instructed in religious and secular subjects. This institution is making good progress. It is approximately 240 English miles to the La Platte River. The land is undulating, with many deep creeks and little streams, all tree-lined and flowing into the Kanzas River, cutting furrows through an endless ocean of lovely grass, which for long stretches has little life, with but few kinds of birds and burrowing animals, but many wolves.

Among the fowl, prairie chickens (**Tetrao cupido**) are frequent, the horned lark (**Otocoris bilosa**), the cowbird (**Molothrus pecoris**) the yellow-headed oriole (**Leistes icterocephalus** [?]), and the American harrier (**Strigiceps uliginosus**) similar to our gray hite (**Str.** [**Circus**] **pygargus L[innaeus]** or **cyaneus**). Among the four-footed animals we see, in addition to the three kinds of wolves in the West, the polecat (**Mephitis chinche** [chincha?], the badger (**Meles labradorius**), the mygale, the **Spermophilus hoodi**[?], and various kinds of mice. The tree-lined waterways maintain sources of nourishment for deer, turkeys, and some hares (**Lepus nanus**) [and] rare antelope, which are more abundant at the Platte River.

Letter from Boonville, Dec. 11, 1851, Part IV.
Supplement to No. 55, *Allgemeine Zeitung*, February 24, 1852

The streams, which are either small rivers or large creeks are: the Big Vermillion, the Little Rock River, the Big Blue, the Little Vermillion, the Big Rock River, and the Little Blue, which is 80 miles long and where the bison sometimes wander astray. It is only 20 to 25 miles from the Little Blue River to the valley of the flat [Platte] River; from the steppe-plain of the La Platte River it is only 12 English miles to the military establishment of the government, Fort Kearny, where a captain and 200 soldiers are stationed, where there is a store and a post office, and where the trains and the emigrants have their first rest stop. I covered the distance from Kanzas to this point in 19 days, but I had the misfortune to have a broken wagon, which could have been repaired easily; however, my young companions felt too sick. Here I realized my blunder in having permitted these volunteers to persuade me to take them along, instead of taking qualified hired men, who have to do what they are ordered to do, and who are capable of withstanding the torture of climate and mosquitos.

From Fort Kearney we managed to cover a good 25 to 35 English miles a day on a way that led along the North and South Forks of the La Platte River, a plain without trees and often without water. One meets large herds of bison up to the ford, where the broad but quicksand-like Southern Fork (the Padouca River), coming from the **cordillera** of the mountains of New Spain, winds through a broad, grassy plain that is surrounded by low limestone elevations. I waded through the shallow river and after 20 miles reached the North Fork, also known as the north arm of the La Platte River, which after flowing almost 700 English miles from the Rocky Mountains, connects with the other fork.

Strange tertiary limestone formations with phantastic, shapes begin here and extend to the Missouri River. A deep ravine, bordered by high elevations and covered with cedars and ash trees (the Ashhalla, pronounced Aescholer), **Creux des freres [le creux aux frenaie]** of the Creoles), runs through a sandy valley to the river. [Note: Paul had spelled the name "Ash hollow" correctly] Accumulations of sand spread out along the slopes of all the spurs of North America's mountains and along the banks of rivers, filled with the debris of quartz, limestone, pebbles, and breccia, often piling up in such a way as to impede travel. The soil in these prairies where the grass is short is a mixture of clay and sand particles; during the dry season it forms a cement as hard as a barn floor.

In these areas, populated by countless buffaloes, are innumerable paths, resembling foot paths, made by these giant animals. Having traveled frequently through the areas in question and being well-acquainted with these wild bison and their life style because of my long presence among them, I must reject categorically the opinion of European zoologists who identify the American bison with the European **aurochs**. Their opinion is based on total ignorance of both animals. Exact measurements of the dimensions and zootomical autopsy have shown that both species of the subgenus **Urus** comprise but a small group of the bovine genus. As little as the **Urus antiquorum[?] (Bos urus)** is the ancestor of the tame ox, so little is the **Urus americanus** one and the same kind as the wild forest ox which lived in our German areas in ancient times and which today is confined to the swampy primeval forests of Poland and Siberia. One need only examine the spine, the fore-part of the skull, the **Hornstock**[?], and the teeth of both animals, as well as their dimensions and tracks.

From the aforementioned pass of Ashhalla [Note: this time Paul spelled the name "Ashhallo" in his original letter], which forms a deep dell and is covered with much timber and shrubs—not at all in character with the surrounding region—the way leads away from the North Fork of the La Platte River. The southern bank is bordered by steep rock walls and strangely shaped tertiary formations. However, along the southern bank are undulating hills. The dry beds of mountain torrents and two small rivers with water in them, the Horse Creeks, empty into the La Platte River at this point. Approximately 60 miles from the ravine, groups of the most picturesquely-shaped elevations have their beginning, largely covered by a heavy layer of clay. In outer appearance they are not to be equalled anywhere else on this planet. To this group belongs the famous Chimney Rock (**la cheminée**) and the Scotbluffs. [*Since a sketch of formations with such contours is more effective than any description, I have copied some of these groups from my diary on to the next page, including two views of the group to which Chimney Rock belongs. From them you will see that*] Fremont and Dr. [Charles] Preuss did not exaggerate, and if one considers that at one time Chimney Rock must have been at least 100 feet higher, judging by the debris, it is evident that it belongs to one of the wonders of the world and alone is worth a trip to these western areas.

The Scotbluffs also make up a large, peculiar circle-shaped group which slopes away in the north toward the La Platte River, encircles an oval plain 10 miles wide, and is surrounded in the south, west, and

Chimney Rock, sketch by Duke Paul

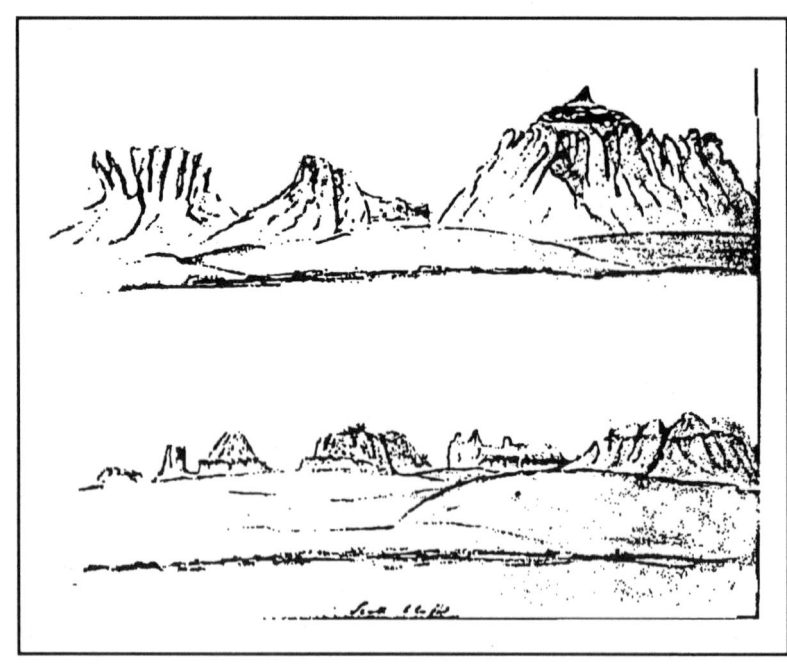

Scotts Bluff, sketches by Duke Paul

northwest by other mountains, partly covered with conifers, which are steep-walled, full of ravines, rugged, coffin-like, and shaped like cones and towers. From the north-northwest side of the Scotbluffs, which at their highest point are approximately 4200 feet above sea level, one can see ranges of the Rocky Mountains running from southwest to northwest, among them the Black Hills and Laramie Peak, which rises approximately 9000 feet above sea level. These are dark, wooded mountains which seem to be covered with snow on the western side all year round. Large coniferous woods cover their ravines, beautiful meadows their valleys. Gray bear and elk populate [*add life*] to these hunting grounds.

Behind Laramie Peak rise the Wind River Mountains, as well as the cone of Snow[mass] Peak [*Pic*], always covered with snow and ice. The latter is perhaps the highest mountain of the American alpine region, and bordering on it are the heads of the three Knops [Tetons?]. From this point the Rocky Mountains slope down; a slanting plain connects the western spurs running toward the south with the watershed of the Columbia River, the Lewis River, the [Multamahau] River, the Rio Gila, Multnaurdha (Green River), which runs into the Sea of Cortez (mar vermeja [bermeja]) from the South Pass, over which the gradually rising way leads across Utah to California. [Note: Paul provided the "translation" of Rio Gila in his letter as "Green River".]

South of this pass or trans-Californian plateau dividing East and West, rise the Andes of New Mexico, vying with the snow-covered tops of James and Long[s] Peaks. Where the Laramie River empties into the La Platte River is the fortification of the same name [Fort Laramie]. It flows through the mountains and plains of the eastern slope. The Padouca River, which is the South

Fork of the La Platte, follows the same water shed, but somewhat more to the south. The military establishment of the United States at the Laramie is therefore the key to communication between the Eastern states and California as well as Oregon.

The important area of land at the Salt Lakes (Utah), lying like a fertile oasis amidst very rugged country, halfway between the La Platte River and California, is ruled by [Brigham] Young, the restless King of the Mormons and his apostles. This large, aggressive sect, typical of the aimless direction of our century's religious-political life, is beginning to incommode seriously the government in Washington. Public opinion in the states against these "rebels" differs widely from the sentimental ovations offered Mr. [Lajos] Kossuth, who, viewed in the light of day, is only an adventurer as far as big words are concerned, while the Mormons, though I can by no means excuse either their attitudes or their political direction, are men of deeds [*who carry through what they propose, and if they set themselves apart, at least they don't aim to overthrow the existing order, and they don't brutally ruin anyone and circulate bogus paper money like the Magyar agitator*].

I explored portions of the area around [Fort] Laramie, where I met the English traveller, Lord Fitz-William [Charles W. W. Fitzwilliam] and had the opportunity to see more tribes of Indians that I had missed on earlier journeys. I therefore make note of the tribes who traverse these areas; while some of them are hostile, others are friendly toward the white people. At the La Platte River, namely at the North Fork of the Laramie River, there are two Dacotah tribes, the Ogelala [Oglala] and the people of the burnt posteriors (**cul brule**), now friendly, formerly of a hostile reputation.

Then, in a southerly direction toward the South Fork, the Chayennes [Cheyennes], a poor, in part often scattered and thievish band of people; farther south toward the James Peak are the Arapahos, a stately and good nation; south of them, the Icarellis, named after a cloth Ica-ra, a tribe of Apaches, mostly hostile toward whites if they meet the latter singly; the Kiowas, a treacherous mob, equally cowardly and blood-thirsty; the Crows, tall and stately warriors, now friendly; the Snake Indians Shoshonee, harmless; and the Utahs, a treacherous and cowardly tribe that has murdered many white people and is therefore greatly feared.

These Indians traverse the areas I visited in the fall, and I saw members of all of the tribes in varying numbers. One can meet redskins from most of these tribes without danger, in their wigwams as well as when trading with them, but it is still dangerous to meet their war parties. Especially as concerns tribes that are hostile or whose friendliness is dubious, the individual traveler is almost always facing death if he meets such roving bands of the barbarians. Even if he saves his life, he runs the risk of being totally robbed and badly mistreated.

Early in October I had finished my western excursions and started the journey back; however I was obliged to stop longer than I wished at the settlements of the fur traders at Fort Johns as well as at the factorship of old friends, the Brothers Robidoux. The purchase of new horses, the trade of my light wagon for a more reliable one, a covered wagon, as well as the continued illness of my companion, delayed for two weeks the date I had planned to leave the area of Scot-Bluffs. The trip back to the South Fork was without incident, but as soon as we arrived there, I was confronted with a number of trials and unhappy events from which only God's help saved me and kept me alive.

 My companion, riding ahead, missed the ford of the La Platte River in the darkness, and my wagon hit quicksand, making it impossible to get it beyond the middle of the river. With great difficulty we got the horses out, but I had to spend the night there in the wagon during a storm that left a heavy snowfall. Chayenne Indians who came, made every effort to get the wagon out by hitching their animals to it, but in vain. Fortunately, after some time a convoy from Fort Laramie came by and rescued me. A few days later I met war parties of Ogelalas and Arapahos from which I managed to escape

 Early in the morning of October 26, however, not far from where the South Fork of the La Platte empties into the north one, I fell into the hands of Indians. At first they approached me with apparent friendliness, but they soon showed themselves to be a hostile tribe. They treated me and my companion in such a barbarous manner that it was sheer luck that I was not shot with my own rifle and that I was able to get away from these rowdies through presence of mind and some unexpected circumstances. It seems that these Indians had murdered a group of United States soldiers shortly before, because they were carrying the weapons of the latter and bragging about the deed.

 In spite of the beautiful sunshine, it got colder day after day; each night the water froze because of north-northeasterly, north-northwesterly winds. These winds acquired the force of storm, the fires on the prairie got out of hand and moved with incredible force and speed, so that the entire northeastern horizon was red at night, and by day the atmosphere seemed to be wrapped in heavy clouds of smoke. The banks of the South Fork of the La

Platte River are almost treeless, while the North Fork has many wooded, often large, islands, and even the banks are not always devoid of trees.

In and around Fort Kearney I found many Pahnis. A group of approximately 800 to 1,000 was encamped ten miles downstream, and my path led close to their camp. These savages were very obtrusive, and they begged and otherwise bothered me the entire day with their extremely troublesome presence, holding me back, stealing most of my provisions, and causing me much damage.

From the La Platte River to the Little Blue River the weather was bearable, although a strong easterly storm, changing into a southerly one, caused a prairie fire to follow me. This fire would have devoured everything if I had not been able to flee to a small island which had been formed by a brook. It took three days to cover the distance I traveled along the Little Blue River. The prairie had been burned everywhere. I had hardly left the river, when the weather changed entirely; between November 10 and 12 winter set in, with heavy snowfall and cold temperatures of 8° to 10° R [50° to 55° F.], accompanied by strong east and west winds. The normally hard roads became bad, and the animals suffered terribly.

On November 14 a violent snowstorm began, and it became bitterly cold. I camped for the night not far from a small, almost dry brook. It was hardly possible to light a fire, and I had scarcely any means to protect myself from freezing to death. Soon three horses froze to death, and the rest of the animals suffered cruelly. I succeeded in dragging myself another 15 English miles, but at a point still 180 miles from the Kanzas, I had to stop at a torrent, Big Sandy Creek. The grueling winter killed all but one of the horses, and left alone without nourishment in a burned prairie, exposed to extreme cold and the fiercest storms with almost no protection, I faced death hour after hour. My limbs were so damaged by the cold and my body so exhausted from hunger that I could hardly move.

In this condition God sent help. Those individuals who even in the winter take care of western mail from Fort Laramie, along with some of their companions, found me and took me to Independence, the westernmost town in the State of Missouri. But I had to camp out for ten more nights in grim, cold weather or in snow that was wet from having been thawed by the wind. I suffered badly from frostbite and extreme exhaustion. I must praise the people of Independence who helped me in every way. Many offered to support me if I needed financial help. I left the hospitable place with the mail stage, one of those miserable farm wagons called mud wagon, used where there are no hard roads.

In this manner I proceeded through Lexington, Marshall, and Arrow Rock to Boonville, a distance of 104 miles; however, I was so exhausted that I decided to rest in the excellent inn at Boonville (opposite Franklin) in order to regain strength and to wait for more favorable weather conditions. Two Germans, Dr. Knekelhan [Kueckelhan] from Hannover and the merchant Stehle [Aehle] from Gera, offered me extremely friendly hospitality. I plan to leave in a few days, to travel directly to New Orleans, but to get to St. Louis, I still have to cover 180 miles of bad roads with bad wagons, quite a difficult test for an exhausted traveler.

[*This coming spring probably will find me in the West again, where I still hope to find a good many things to see and collect. Particularly of interest to me are the fish of the little lakes.*

The fall of 1852 probably will find me in the South

again, and in January and February (1853) I intend to explore the Straits of Magellan and the southwest coast of Chile, and return by way of the Dutch Indies and spend a short time in the fatherland to check whether my large natural history collection escaped the storm which the Revolution of 1848 and the 1849 representatives of the country so sympathetic to royal princes, had brought upon my poor head. However, the treatment accorded my residence in Mergentheim has made such a painful impression on me that I will never again step into my chambers in Mergentheim and I will restrict my activities to doing what I can to add to my collection, for I am not at odds with natural science, but only with callous persons.

Although I possess no property in the United States I love the land, and it will be difficult for me to leave it and my friends here behind. I would give up everything for a quiet little house and a small farm. After the experiences of 1848 and 1849, my hearth, my title, etc. no longer have much worth to me. I have through no fault of my own been condemned to such adverse fate that I have lost heart, and I no longer consider my title, etc. worth while. My diligence in the interest of natural science has not been favorably regarded! Haven't I served as the butt of the most profane wit?

With your usual discretion utilize whatever you wish for publication or for passing on to my friends in the fatherland, which I still regard as warmly as ever.]

God protect you and our Wuerttemberg, always dear to me.

Paul Wilhelm, Duke of Wuerttemberg

Postscript: The cold is increasing hourly to a degree unknown even to the oldest inhabitants. The thermometer already has fallen to -15° R. [-2° F.]. Because of bad roads and the interrupted ship traffic, it is difficult for the inhabitants of towns to get a supply of provisions and firewood, even though there are woods all around. The prevailing wind is north-northwest with clear skies and no snow. Because of poorly-built houses, one suffers a great deal in the cold weather. Fireplaces and stoves give heat close by, but there is ice on the doors, walls, and windows.

EPILOGUE

THE LATER YEARS

Hans von Sachsen-Altenburg

Once Paul had left Boonville, he passed through Jefferson City where the German population somehow recognized him and, according to Paul's diary, the local Gesangsverein, the choir, gave him a melodious homage, but there does not appear to be any local record of this unusual occurence on Christmas Day of 1851.

Back in St. Louis, Paul recuperated at the mansion of his rich friend Angelroth, the Prussian Consul General, after whom a St. Louis street is named.

Never tired of travelling and forever restless, Paul visited the Midwest and New York later in 1852. Returning to St. Louis again, he had to rush to New Orleans to meet Pauline who had followed him to the United States. Undaunted, Paul placed her in the charge of Pastor Spiess in Mascoutah, Illinois, and set off on a voyage to Australia.

Again disaster and luck were not far apart. Paul's ship reached Africa but it was blown off course in a vicious storm. Virtually unnavigable and subjected to prevailing winds and currents, the ship reached northern Brazil. Again, an artist in survival, Paul spent nearly a year touring Montevideo, the Uruguay River, Tierra del Fuego, Chile, and returned via Panama to New Orleans and Illinois.

His diaries and letters betray some homesickness, but the time to return home had not yet come. So Paul visited the southeastern U.S., the north to see Niagara Falls, the midwest to see his friends, and he visited Texas again. A dizzying circle and repetition of visits and excursions, until in 1856 he returned to Mergentheim amidst unexpected shouts of welcome. His published **Letter from Boonville** and several smaller trip reports, but especially his friend's smooth handling of the financial settlements, had again endeared the famous man. Paul was made honorary citizen of Mergentheim, a stark contrast to the way he left seven years before.

But if one would expect Paul to now lead a quieter, more contemplative life, one would be mistaken. After his return to Germany Paul seems to have embarked on a round of visits of ever increasing speed between Silesia, Mergentheim, Bremen, Berlin, and other places. He was cataloging, writing, revising, planning and thinking. The halls of his medieval castle were stuffed with thousands of objects ranging from bugs to roots, from skeletons to stuffed snakes. "The largest collection of its kind in the world," Paul once boasted to a friend, and the savants would later come to the same conclusion. At the same time, the restless man added a wing to the castle in Carlsruhe, called the Paulsburg, and worked day and night, writing, reading, traveling.

One more trip to America, hasty and purposeful, to New York and the St. Louis region, and back to New York. A speedy ship took him, nonstop, around Tierra del Fiego to Australia. Once again, as on past trips, he attempted to travel incognito, as Count von Heidenheim, yet he was apparently recognized by all who listened to whispers. Now over sixty years old, Duke Paul seemed to speed up. He visited Melbourne, Tasmania, and the huge, unknown continent, as well as Ceylon, India, Aden, Italy, and Vienna, before returning to Mergentheim.

But his restlessness continued. In the port town of Bremen he rented two rooms and filled them with very special items collected throughout the years. Again,

Carlsruhe in Silesia, the Paulsburg was finished—and the bills kept coming in.

Amidst the haste, as suddenly and spontaneously as nearly everything else he had ever done in his life, Duke Paul died. The cause of his death is not certain, and there is reason for speculation. The creditors were haunting him; it was a good time to leave.

A frightening efficiency of bureaucracy and implementation took over; like clockwork, as if planned and prepared for ahead of time, arrangements for Paul's funeral were executed. Within a few days he was buried in the family vaults of a Stuttgart church. By the end of 1860 it was all over, and then the estate liquidators took on their duties.

For years the castle of Mergentheim remained untouched, and the valuable scientific collection, books, manuscripts and notes remained enshrined, almost untouchable. Until Paul's son, Duke Maximilian, in need of money, sold it all. Unlabled, unrecorded, unconnected, the greatest scientific collection of its time was dispersed to the winds, never to be found again. In the last ten years, evidence and records have connected a few pieces, maybe five dozen, to Duke Paul's love for collecting things from worlds not yet quite discovered. They can be found in the vaults and showcases of the British Museum, the Ethnological Museum of Berlin, the Linden [Ethnological] Museum of Stuttgart, and maybe in dozens of others, of unknown provenance.

It seems that Duke Paul's legacy was lost. Yet he had been a ferocious writer of diaries and letters; and he filled thousands of pages with notes, drawings, meteorological observations, lists of animals and plants—a treasure trove of knowledge collected by a man who wanted to know it all. Paul emulated and corresponded with the greatest men of his times, but very few of his letters seem to have survived. His manuscripts were misplaced. The last remains were said to have been destroyed in a bombing raid in 1945, unpublished. The Paulsburg was dynamited by vengeful Russian and Polish soldiers after the end of World War II.

A lost legacy is depriving us all of experience once gained. In Germany, there is no proud, visible record of Paul's life.

But if the legacy appears lost, it may merely not meet the eye. Since nothing is ever lost unless its entire physical and spiritual destruction is complete, archaeologists and historians can find hope in tracing dust and footprints. Based on diligent research and many coincidences, his legacy is experiencing a renaissance.

Parts of this book are based on records not thought to have existed or survived. The first visit to America in 1823 was recorded and published by Duke Paul himself. His notes on the second trip were undoubtedly recorded somewhere, but have not yet been recovered. An unwritten diary, however, is preserved in hundreds of secondary notes by others, and in his own later memories, as partially quoted in this book.

Paul's unknown legacy lives on in many ways. His beloved Pauline, who never returned to Germany, became the proud ancestor of a clan of Americans, some of whom still reside in Missouri.

To many Americans, Paul is the enigmatic European prince who took the son of Sacagawea to Germany. As such, Duke Paul has already become part of the American saga of westward expansion. His last notes and diaries are now being published for the first time.

Amongst the greatest elements of his legacy may have been the love he expressed about the land, the nature, and the people of Missouri. For Paul, Boonville was more than just a small frontier town. For him it was freedom, hope, and the future.

THE FLORA AND FAUNA OF DUKE PAUL'S MISSOURI: A NATURAL LANDSCAPE IN TRANSITION

Jason Fridley

As a devoted natural scientist and explorer of the American West, Duke Friedrich Paul Wilhelm found a natural treasure in the Lower Missouri River of Missouri. Contained in his journal entries for this area are beautifully detailed accounts of the trees, herbs, and wildflowers that he encountered and collected, such as the common moisture-loving sycamore and the resplendent columbine. Also illustrated are past and present members of Missouri's fauna, including the widespread groundhog and the now extinct Carolina parakeet. Indeed, although many plants and animals described by Duke Paul can be found in similar numbers along the Missouri River today, others are found more frequently, less frequently, or are absent altogether. For these reasons, his journals are an invaluable resource for reconstructing the natural history of Missouri. The following assessment, taken from journal entries made in central Missouri during the late spring and early summer of 1823 (**Travels in North America 1822-1824**, translated by W.R. Nitske and edited by S. Lottinville, University of Oklahoma Press, Norman, Oklahoma, 1973) and journals kept during the late summer of 1851 ("From St. Louis to Kansas City," translated by Dr. David Miller), is a testimony to the journals as a resource and the determination and fruition of Duke Paul as explorer and naturalist.

Flora: trees

As one navigated the Missouri River in the nineteenth-century, giant trees appeared to fortify the banks, growing in veritable walls sometimes more than a hundred feet tall. Thus, many long-lived plants have adapted to life on the wet, sandy riverbank despite sporadic inundation and changes in the river's course. It could be argued that some even have the capacity to change the habitats in which they live. The black willow *(Salix nigra)*, for instance, stabilizes soil along riverbanks with its long, interlacing roots. In this manner a group of willows may anchor an entire bank and keep soil from washing downriver. Thousands of black willows support the walls of trees that line the Missouri. Growing next to them are the towering cottonwoods *(Populus deltoides)*, which, like the willows, are moisture-loving and well-suited to frequently disturbed habitat. Cottonwoods are fast-growing, short-lived opportunists that are quick to invade new shore space.

Over 150 years ago Duke Paul saw much the same picture. On 6 June 1823, upriver from Jefferson City, he observed, "cottonwoods and willows soon prosper on the ground where giant tree trunks decay and are covered with layers of clay by flooding, the fertile soil hastening their growth."(**Travels**, p. 242) He also noted the predominance of willows on small islands around Boonville. The frequency with which he mentions these two species leaves little doubt that they were as common along the Missouri then as they are today.

Closely related to the cottonwood, the quaking aspen *(Populus tremuloides)* is also a species of poplar. At slightly higher altitudes and latitudes than the Missouri River of the Midwest, quaking aspens dominate the early succession of old fields and logged forests. They can do this by cloning, meaning that they do not have to reproduce sexually, and thus many stands of aspen are actually a single plant. Aspen also sprout after fire. In Missouri, fire is suppressed much more today than it was 150 years ago, and aspen are rare. Duke Paul mentions aspen twice in the Boonville area in 1851, located on "level shores...often covered only with low willows and aspen, often with sandy meadows,"(Spahn, p. 11) and on a row of hills downriver from Lexington, which is a more typical habitat for aspen. In addition to aspen and cottonwood, Duke Paul mentions other poplars, some of which "bear the stamp of unhindered growth, [having the] most slender shapes."(**Travels**, p. 260)

Another Missouri tree common in river habitats is the familiar sycamore *(Platanus occidentalis)*, which attains the greatest diameter of any hardwood. The sycamore is tolerant of wet soil conditions, often found with cottonwoods and willows as well as elms and maples, and it too is a pioneer of disturbed habitat. Sycamores are found along the Missouri and all major rivers in the state. Duke Paul attests to their splendor along the river numerous times. After landing in Franklin to embark on land to Arrow Rock, he records "magnificent and luxuriant"(**Travels**, p. 258) sycamores. Two days before, he and his crew narrowly avoided a giant sycamore trunk floating as driftwood.

On his short trip to Arrow Rock by trail, Duke Paul mentions many trees that are common in Missouri today. Among these is the honey locust *(Gleditsia triacanthos)*, thought of most commonly as an ornamental, though native to Missouri. It cannot withstand floods but favors rich, moist soils in bottomlands. It also is a pioneer of disturbed habitat and is remarkable in its ability to resist disease and insect attack. Another tree favoring rich, moist bottomlands is the Kentucky coffee tree *(Gymnocladus dioicus)*, which grew with the honey locust that Duke Paul observed. Although it does not grow coffee beans, its own beans used to be roasted and brewed as a coffee substitute (though it doesn't taste much like coffee). Growing with the honey locust and Kentucky coffee tree was the slightly more palatable sassafras *(Sassafras albidum)*. Today sassafras is known for its good root tea and beer and its capacity for quickly invading old fields.

A tree that Duke Paul mentions almost as much as cottonwoods, willows, and sycamores is the linden tree or basswood *(Tilia americana)*. Although typically not as big as the sycamore, basswood is one of the giants of the forest, and is found over most of Missouri. As an ornamental it is valued as a shade tree and for the beautiful lattice design of its bark. Underneath the sycamores, Kentucky coffee trees, honey locusts, and sassafras trees were the pawpaws *(Asimina triloba)*, which rarely grow over 20 feet tall. The pawpaw, found throughout Missouri, is a northern member of a tropical family with unmistakable large leaves. The fruit, which resemble small bananas in appearance and taste, are popular in dessert dishes. Unfortunately, the fruit is difficult to obtain (at least ripe) due to rodent predators.

In addition to the pawpaw, Duke Paul mentions other smaller trees on his way to Arrow Rock. Hop hornbeam or ironwood *(Ostrya virginiana)*, usually no wider than 12 inches, is so-called because of its extremely hard, heavy wood. It is common on rocky cliffs and hillsides under hardwoods such as basswood; this is, in fact, where it was observed by Duke Paul. West of Arrow Rock, he observed three species that are most commonly found as low bushes in Missouri: smooth sumac *(Rhus glabra)*, shining sumac *(Rhus copallina)*, and elderberry *(Sambucus canadensis)*. For Duke Paul, sumac proved to be a nuisance, as it overgrew the trail in many places. Many today know smooth sumac in similar fashion due to its tendency to vigorously invade unburned prairies and abandoned fields. Shining sumac has the same propensity but is smaller and shrubbier than its cousin. Elderberry, more adapted to moist soils, is more commonly found lining rivers and streams and in moist forests. All three can be found throughout Missouri.

In many of the natural accounts given by Duke Paul, it is difficult to determine the specific plant or animal to which he is referring. In some cases, Paul himself is not specific, but more often the use of outdated terminology obscures the reference. Frequently, Paul refers to an organism by its scientific name (or gives it one himself). Unfortunately, scientific names have changed markedly in the past 150 years, and in Duke Paul's time they were far from universal. Thus for many accounts, and particularly those of plants, the object of observation must be deduced from Paul's description and what is known about Missouri flora and fauna today.

What Paul calls "nut trees" are mentioned occasionally, and from our current perspective one would speculate that he is describing the lofty hickories (of which Missouri has more than any other state). It is impossible to differentiate among the shellbarks, shagbarks, mockernuts, bitternuts, pignuts, pecans, and black hickories from his descriptions, but he does identify pignut hickories *(Carya glabra)* outside of Arrow Rock. Along with black hickories, pignut hickories prefer dry, upland soils, not the moist bottomland soils preferred by other hickories. Accordingly, Duke Paul's nut trees grew on a "high, steep hill where the timber becomes thinner."(**Travels**, p. 259) Also adapted to the drier, limestone glade areas is the eastern red cedar *(Juniperus virginiana)*, the most widespread Missouri conifer. Upriver from the mouth of the Little Saline River, around Wooldridge, Duke Paul wrote that the "thick growth of deciduous trees and the dark green of the cedars against a limestone background enhanced the landscape's beauty."(Spahn, p. 9) Like most of the trees growing in the dynamic Missouri river valley, the red cedar grows quickly and is a frequent invader of old fields and fence rows.

Duke Paul was also nonspecific when describing ashes. Three ash species are found in Missouri today: white ash *(Fraxinus americana)*, green ash (F. *pennsylvanica)*, and blue ash *(quadrangulata)*. Along the river, Duke Paul probably saw green ash, as it is commonly found among cottonwoods, bur oak and pin oak. Also found close to the river is white ash, though it is more common in upland areas with black oak, red oak, basswood, and sugar maple. Green and white ash are very common throughout Missouri. Blue ash is not so common, and it prefers dry limestone hillsides with others such as ironwood, shagbark hickory, and post oak.

The trees most difficult to identify precisely from Duke Paul are the oaks *(Quercus)*. In the eastern and midwestern United States there are about 34 species of oak, most of which are found in Missouri (which also has more oak species than any other state). Sometimes it is possible to discern an observation from Paul as referring to a white or red oak species, but anything further proves impossible. Traveling the same route today, one would most likely encounter bur oak, swamp white oak, pin oak, and shumard oak along the river, while further upland in drier areas and along ridges one would find white oak, post oak, chinkapin oak, northern red oak, black oak, blackjack oak, and shingle oak.

Because trees are generally highly visible and long-lived, it is worthwhile to include a discussion of the trees that exist in the area today but were not mentioned by Duke Paul. Most significant in this category are the maples. Today, four maple species are found in Missouri: red maple *(Acer rubrum)*, black maple (A. *nigrum)*, silver maple (A. *saccharinum)*, and sugar maple (A. *saccharum)*. Closely related is the ashleaf maple or box-elder (A. *negundo)*, also widespread in Missouri. In central Missouri silver, red, and ashleaf maple are very common along the river and sugar maple is common away from the shore. It is surprising that Duke Paul did not record any observations concerning this group of trees, especially considering their unmistakable appearance. Were they as common as they are today, and Duke Paul felt that their mention would be unnecessary? This is unlikely (he was, after all, a naturalist), but it seems even more unlikely that these native Missouri trees were out of Duke Paul's view. Thus, for some reason, it appears that around Boonville Paul found no reason to document the presence of maples.

Missouri's widespread elms, the American elm *(Ulmus americana)* and the slippery elm *(U. rubra)*, also are not mentioned in central Missouri by Duke Paul. Both are common bottomland species and can be found in every county. Though today their numbers are declining due to elm phloem necrosis (the death of food-transport tissues due to disease) and "Dutch" elm disease (a debilitating fungus spread by a beetle introduced to North America from Eurasia), it is expected that they were prevalent along the river over 150 years ago. Moreover,

Missouri's river birches *(Betula nigra)*, fairly similar to the elms, are also absent from his journals. Other common bottomland trees that escaped comment by Duke Paul are the red mulberry *(Morus rubra)* and the hackberry *(Celtis occidentalis)*. It would be inappropriate to make general conclusions about the nature of Missouri's landscape 150 years ago based on one source, yet Paul's meticulous description of the landscape makes this source particularly good. Given the fact that many current elms and maples predate Duke Paul's time, one must conclude that either they were not as visible along the Missouri as the species cited in his journals, or Paul found their mention unnecessary.

Flora: wildflowers, herbs

The frequency with which Duke Paul mentions non-woody plants is slightly less than that of Missouri's trees, and this may be due to the fact that trees are simply more visible than many herbs and wildflowers. Additionally, the immediate identification of these plants often requires that the plants be in bloom, which for most wildflowers is a specific, brief interval between early spring and late fall. Note that 150 years ago, before a system of locks and dams was created on the upper Missouri to regulate water flow, the Missouri was swollen with melting snow from the Rockies each spring. Floating the river at this time proved a dangerous ordeal, and as a result Duke Paul, like most river travelers, began his trips in late spring or summer. Thus he would typically miss spring's bloomings on the upper Missouri.

In the Boonville area, the most detailed descriptions of wildflowers and herbs from Duke Paul come from his trip to Arrow Rock from Franklin in 1823.

Among these were: riverbank grape *(Vitis riparia)*, with small green flowers; cupseed *(Calycocarpum lyoni)*, a vine with black berries that, like riverbank grape, is common along rivers and streams; and moonseed *(Menispermum canadense)*, also a vine but with white flowers and found in woods and thickets. Found with the vines was coral berry or Indian currant *(Symphoricarpos orbiculatus)*, a small shrub with coral-pink berries found along riverbanks throughout Missouri.

An interesting and perhaps even frightening observation made by Duke Paul in 1823 is the presence of yarrow or milfoil *(Achillea Millefolium)* along the Missouri. Milfoil is common along shores and roadsides today, but it was introduced by European settlers. From Duke Paul's journal, it appears that this foreign weed achieved dominance in the New World quickly, reaching far beyond the Mississippi more than 170 years ago. This is further evidence of the susceptibility of native plants and animals to attack from foreign invaders. Typical of river banks and rocky woods is the prickly ash or toothache tree *(Zanthoxylum americanum)*, so-called because its bark and fruit can be used to relieve toothache. Of the rue family, prickly ash is an aromatic shrub found throughout the state, blooming in late spring. Duke Paul observed it in June, and may have just caught it in bloom. Along the woody banks he found the starry campion *(Silene stellata)*, found also in open woods. Most likely he was too early to view the flowering of this herb, as its small white flowers are visible only in late summer.

    He also might have been too early to see the flowers of white avens *(Geum canadense)* of the rose family. White avens is a perennial herb that grows among bushes on river banks, and typically does not bloom until early fall. What were blooming in mid-June were the forget-me-nots. Duke Paul observed a white-flowering species *(Myosotis virginica)*, fairly common on dry banks and in rocky woods throughout most of the country.

The flooded lowlands Duke Paul traversed were apparently dominated by the herbs that commonly dominate them today. Clearweed *(Pilea pumila)* and other nettles, according to Paul, "covered all low situated land that was subject to flooding."(**Travels**, p. 258) Today clearweed is found in similar habitats throughout the eastern and central United States. Another common marsh inhabitant is the familiar cattail *(Typha latifolia)*, found throughout North America. Duke Paul observed them, "cover[ing] the stagnant water of a swamp next to the road."(**Travels**, p. 258) The end of the 'tail' is actually two distinct groups of flowers—male flowers (staminate) located on top, and female flowers (pistillate) on the bottom. Among the cattails were the pondweeds *(Potamogeton)*, of which there are about 30 species in the central United States alone. Most of these species have their leaves completely submerged in water. Duke Paul additionally includes an account of docks or sorrels *(Rumex)*, green-flowered herbs observed in swampy lowland alongside the road, but again it is impossible to pinpoint a specific plant because there are as many as 13 species of docks in the Midwest. Finally, Paul mentions the "beautiful, flowering" water-lilies *(Nymphaea)*. The delicate white flowers of the water-lily have petals in numerous rows, blooming in the summer and early fall.

The other plants that Duke Paul recorded on his short trip to Arrow Rock were presumably found farther upland in the open woods or fields. These include: the green-flowered forked chickweed *(Paronychia canadensis)* of the whitlow-wort family, found throughout the eastern and central United States; pale Indian plantain *(Cacalia atriplicafolia)* of the composite family, common in the Midwest; the beautiful, purple-flowered blazing star *(Liatris pycnostachya)*, also of the composite family and common in the Midwest though more of a true prairie species; and the large purple cone-flower *(Echinacea purpurea)*, another composite and partial to open woods in the central United States. Another identification made is *Amaranthus*, or the genus of the amaranths (pigweed, tumbleweed, etc.), herbs with inconspicuous flowers, of which there exist about ten different species in Missouri.

A few days past Arrow Rock and closer to Marshall, Duke Paul, still on land, wrote more wildflower entries in his journal. Today, what Missouri naturalist's journal would be complete without the entry of Missouri's striking columbine *(Aquilegia)*? In bloom, columbine's large, drooping flowers are unmistakable. The showiness of this buttercup family member, common in the northern Midwest and Missouri, was apparent to Paul as well. Another species of amaranth identified by Duke Paul is water-hemp *(Acnida cannabina)*. A resident of the Mid- and Southwest, water-hemp prefers swamps or alluvial soils. Paul contends that his specimens "attained a height of five to six feet forming an edge around the forest... [giving] way to short prairie grasses."(**Travels**, p. 260) Slightly less pleasant is jimson weed *(Datura stramonium)*, a narcotic, ranksmelling nightshade (potato family). It is a native of Asia, but today it can be found throughout the eastern United States in waste places. Also mentioned were the coneflowers *(Rudbeckia)*, similar in appearance to the sunflower. Though it is difficult to pinpoint a particular species from Duke Paul's description, it gives a good account of the area and his difficulty identifying wildflowers: "This prairie is also poor in herbaceous plants with very few blossoming, among those Rudbeckia, this species with large underdeveloped flowers...roots smell like rattlesnake during mating season."(**Travels,** p. 262)

Finally, Duke Paul reports that the growth of horsetails *(Equisetum),* one of Missouri's common fern allies, had overrun an island in the Missouri downriver from Boonville. Horsetails are common residents of bottomland areas today.

Discussion of the significance of herbs and wildflowers that were not recorded in Paul's journals would be unwarranted, as those that are not in bloom are difficult to identify, and even those that are in bloom are usually not immediately visible to those who are not specifically looking for them. It is clear, however, that many were in bloom and were easily identified by Duke Paul when he ventured upon them. Indeed, the amount of description given to plants in general provides further insight into Paul's interest and talent in botany.

Fauna: birds

On Duke Paul's trips up the Missouri much of his time was spent on the river itself. Hunting for food or preservable specimens also took up a large amount of time. It is easy to see, then, why a large proportion of the birds recorded by Duke Paul are water and game species. In fact, in the Boonville area, no songbirds are recorded at all.

The most frequently observed bird on Duke Paul's trips through the Midwest was the wild turkey *(Meleagris gallopavo).* Near Lexington in 1823, Paul remarked, "the country teems with. . . wild turkeys, extremely tame—

they sunned themselves and their broods close to the house and were not disturbed."(**Travels**, p. 266) In 1851 near Camden, he again depicts "countless" turkeys. Today, the wild turkey is fairly common in Missouri, though its range nationwide is much smaller than it was in Duke Paul's time due to intense hunting over the past century. Also common on the river and adjacent streams was the wood duck (Aix *sponsa)*, which flew over Paul in large flocks. Today the wood duck is found throughout the eastern United States, with Missouri being its western range limit.

Duke Paul recorded two members of the family Areidae (herons and bitterns) in the Boonville area: the great blue heron *(Ardea herodias)* and the least bittern *(Ixobrychus exilis)*. As Paul passed Miami in August of 1851, great blue herons "rose up awkwardly from the sandbanks," in their flock. (Miller, p. 13) They were probably hunting for fish, which constitute their main food. Today great blue herons are found throughout the United States with the exception of the Rockies. The least bittern is a much more reclusive bird, and though it does not typically lounge on open shores, Duke Paul's men caught one alive downriver from Boonville in 1823. Paul gives it a lengthy description, expressing that the bird was, "so extremely vicious that we could hardly come near it. This bird stayed alive a long time, took the food we offered him, and finally became quite tame."(**Travels**, p. 246)

But one of the most intriguing sightings that Duke Paul recorded in the Boonville area was near Lexington in 1823. On 15 June, Paul records in his journal, "Hardly ever have I seen so many parrots in one place. When I shot one of these from a tree, where hundreds of these birds were sitting, the others did not fly away but were merely satisfied to make a frightful outcry."(**Travels**, p. 277) Paul called these parrots *Psittacus carolinensis*, and he has accounts of these huge flocks in other parts of the country as well. Today the Carolina parakeet is extinct. It was North America's only native parrot species, and disappeared from eastern forests in the late 1800s as a result of intense hunting. Unlike other recently-extinct bird species (such as North America's passenger pigeon) that were hunted as game, the Carolina parakeet was routinely destroyed because it was considered an agricultural pest, consuming stockpiles of grain and the fruit of entire orchards. The last Carolina parakeet died in the Cincinatti Zoo in 1914.

Fauna: mammals

One animal that has benefitted from hundreds of years of European settlement in North America is the woodchuck or groundhog *(Marmota monax)*. The woodchuck population, because it was formerly a prairie species, has expanded due to the cuttlng of forests. In fact, chances are good that a short walk through a forest meadow will result in a glimpse of one. Downriver from Boonville in 1823, Duke Paul dug a woodchuck out of its den, an "extraordinarily large [15 Ibs.]... pregnant female whose young were not fully matured. The meat of this American marmot is fat and edible. It [was] desirable food for me."(**Travels**, p. 246)

Once hunted to the brink of extinction in the northeastern states and the Midwest was the white-tailed deer *(Odocoileus virginianus)*, today the most important game animal in the United States. Duke Paul called the native white-tailed deer "fallow deer" (the European equivalent) and encountered them frequently in the Boonville area (almost as much as he did Cottonwood trees). Today in many areas of the eastern United States these deer are considered overpopulated—but they are only overpopulated so much as they are a threat to the expanding human population. Only by destroying forestland and restricting their feeding to concentrated areas does overbrowsing become a problem, though their numbers continue to increase.

What was eradicated from the Midwest and all the prairie states was the American elk or wapiti *(Cervus canadensis)*, a prairie dweller in the early nineteenth-century whose range extended into Missouri. Near Arrow Rock in 1823, Duke Paul described a sighting of elk "which at a distance of one thousand paces fled shyly from us," and was "[America's] finest member of the entire deer family."(**Travels**, p. 262) By 1830, elk were scarce in Missouri, as large herds could only be found in the northwestern and southeastern parts of the state. By the onset of the twentieth century, elk were all but eradicated from the entire eastern United States. Today, despite reintroduction attempts east of the Mississippi, the American elk is primarily a mountain dweller, ranging from California to the northern Rocky Mountains and into western Canada.

Fauna: insects

The manner in which Duke Paul writes of mosquitoes convinces us that they may have been one of the worst hardships he experienced navigating the Missouri. No plant or animal is mentioned more often, and none with such a feeling of abjection and despair. Paul "could not rest because of mosquitoes."(**Travels**, p. 266) "In the night [Paul and his men] had to endure a slight rain with a sultriness which attracted an insufferable number of flies and mosquitoes. Despite the utmost weariness [they] could not sleep."(**Travels**, p. 252) His testimony to the pain and misery inflicted on his group by these "bloodthirsty" insects is manifest in a journal entry made upriver from Boonville in 1823: "From the nearness of the stagnant water, I could easily explain the excessive number of mosquitoes that during the night had stung me so horribly. My whole skin was inflamed as if from the sting of nettles."(**Travels**, p. 262) Moreover, various flies added to the agony. "Our poor, tired horse swam in his own blood from the countless bites of gadflies and horseflies."(**Travels**, p. 266)

There are over 100 species of mosquitoes in the United States today, and despite the torment they cause and the diseases they carry, mosquitoes are an important food source for birds and bats, and mosquito eggs feed freshwater vertebrates, including many species of fish. It is impossible to determine for certain whether they were more or less frequent 150 years ago, but certain environmental changes provide clues that allow speculation. For instance, mosquitoes lay their eggs on still water, and their abundance is typically determined by the amount of still water in an area (such as small ponds and ephemeral forest pools). The number of such wetlands has greatly decreased since Duke Paul's time, primarily due to agricultural clearing. Along the Missouri River, dikes and levees have further diminished the amount of Missouri's wetlands. It is likely, then, that mosquitoes are less abundant around the Missouri River today than they were 150 years ago.

Conclusion

From his descriptions of Missouri's extirpated elk to his observation of the newly-introduced milfoil from Europe, the journals of Duke Friedrich Paul Wilhelm are remarkably valuable in assessing the natural landscape of Missouri in the early- and mid-nineteenth century. Unfortunately, the journals have been rarely used in this respect, largely due to the fact that many of Paul's writings have never been published. Other writings have been published only recently, and newly discovered is an inventory list of Duke Paul's flora and fauna collection, containing a multitude of preserved specimens. The examination of this collection will further substantiate the observations presented in this chapter. It will also help to positively identify those journal descriptions that are unclear.

When comparing the information obtained from Duke Paul with the flora and fauna of Missouri today, it is easy to note the obvious differences: the Carolina parakeet is now extinct; elk no longer graze Missouri's forests and plains; turkeys have learned to fear people; aspen are now rare in Missouri. In many cases, it is also easy to reason why. Game animals have declined as a result of over-hunting. Other forest animals have seen their habitat disappear as more land is needed for agriculture. Numerous native plants and animals have been displaced by foreign invaders: Eurasian carp have conquered our rivers and streams; European milfoil dominates our roadsides; our American elm has been decimated by "Dutch" elm disease. In each of these examples, the vehicle of environmental change was man. European settlers introduced, passively in most cases, these new plants and animals that endanger so many native species. Hunters like Duke Paul himself depleted forests of game, ultimately threatening their own livelihood. Yet they were not trying to exhaust these natural resources; rather, they lived at a time when these resources appeared to be in infinite supply.

This theme of an unbounded nature lies at the forefront of Duke Paul's writings, shaping humble natural observations into a captivating account of nineteenth-century exploration. Most descriptions are larger than life: his horse swam in his own blood; hundreds of parakeets were observed on a single tree. Thus, the importance of these writings is not merely academic; a significant aesthetic aspect remains. Together, they transform a journal of Missouri River travel into a meaningful, majestic depiction of the natural landscape of Missouri's past.

Acknowledgments:
I would like to thank Dr. Kerry Woods and Mr. Roland Brusseau for their very helpful suggestions, most of which were incorporated into this chapter.

[Note: Jason Fridley, a descendant of Duke Paul von Wuerttemberg, is a Ph.D. candidate at the University of North Carolina at Chapel Hill, North Carolina.]

CHRONOLOGY

November 6, 1754
Birth of Friedrich, who would become King of Wuerttemberg in 1805.
August 15, 1759
Birth of Napoleon Bonaparte
September 27, 1781
Birth of Prince Heir Wilhelm
May 18, 1797
Marriage of Friedrich von Wuerttemberg and Charlotte, daughter of George III of Great Britain.
June 25, 1797
Birth of Friedrich Paul Wilhelm von Wuerttemberg, in Carlsruhe Silesia
March 4, 1800
Birth of Sophie (Marie S. Dorothea Caroline) von Thurn und Taxis
February 11, 1805
Birth of Jean Baptiste "Pomp" Charbonneau at Ft. Mandan on the Missouri River
November 7, 1805
Meriwether Lewis and William Clark reach the Pacific Ocean
December 26, 1805
Kingdom of Wuerttemberg established
January 1, 1806
Proclamation Kingdom of Bavaria, Kingdom of Wuerttemberg
January 14, 1806
Marriage of Auguste, Princess of Bavaria, and Eugene Beauharnaise
May 1806
Friedrich King of Wuerttemberg makes Paul Wilhelm Commander a la suite

August 22, 1807
Marriage of Katharine von Wuerttemberg, daughter of Friedrich I, and Hieronymus Bonaparte, King of Westphalia
April 20, 1809
Wuerttemberg Regiment takes possession of Mergentheim
October 16, 1813
Napoleon defeated at the Battle of Leipzig
November 2, 1813
King of Wuerttemberg joins the confederation against Napoleon
1814
Paul Wilhelm Hauptmann a la suite in the cavalry
October 30, 1816
Friedrich I, King of Wuerttemberg suceeded by his son, Wilhelm I
May 20, 1817
Paul Wilhelm resigns from Wuerttemberg military as Major General
January 25, 1820
Paul Wilhelm becomes a member of the House of Lords of Wuerttemberg
August 21, 1821
Treaty of Cordoba grants Mexico her independence
September 27, 1821
Mexico independent
May 19, 1822
Augustin I de Iturbide proclaimed Emperor of Mexico
July 19, 1822
Berthold, Pratte & Chouteau receive license to trade with the Indians
October 17, 1822
Paul Wilhelm leaves Hamburg for New Orleans

aboard the *Hyglander*
December 21, 1822
Paul Wilhelm arrives in New Orleans as Baron de Hohenberg
January 10, 1823
Paul Wilhelm off Cuba, entering Havana
March 4, 1823
Paul Wilhelm arrives in New Orleans again
March 19, 1823
Augustin I de Iturbide abdicates as Emperor of Mexico
April 1823
Paul Wilhelm ascends the Mississippi and Ohio Rivers
May 5, 1823
Paul Wilhelm visits William Clark in St. Louis to obtain passport to Missouri/Columbia River region
May 6, 1823
Paul Wilhelm at Chouteau estate in St. Louis
May 14, 1823
Paul Wilhelm at Chauvin's Ferry at St. Charles
June 11, 1823
Paul Wilhelm in Franklin, 5 p.m., notes Boonville
June 21, 1823
Paul Wilhelm meets John Baptiste Charbonneau at Curtis and Wood trading post
October 9, 1823
Paul Wilhelm picks up Pomp at Curtis and Wood trading post
October 19, 1823
Paul Wilhelm and Pomp pass Franklin and Boonville on their way to St. Louis
October 24, 1823
Paul Wilhelm and Pomp arrive in St. Louis
November 5, 1823
Paul Wilhelm and Pomp board the steamboat *Cincinnati* in St. Louis

November 6, 1823
Steamboat *Cincinnati* wrecks in Mississippi River near Ste. Genevieve
December 5, 1823
Steamboat *Mandan* leaves St. Louis
December 24, 1823
Paul Wilhelm and Pomp board the steamship *Smyrna* and leave New Orleans
January 10, 1824
Steamship *Smyrna* off the coast of Cuba
January 29, 1824
Steamship *Smyrna* off the coast of Newfoundland
February 11, 1824
Pomp's 19th birthday
February 14, 1824
Steamship *Smyrna* arrives at Casquet, Harfleur, France
March 4, 1824
Paul Wilhelm and Pomp arrive in Stuttgart
1826
Spring flood on the Missouri River inundates the town of Franklin
July 8, 1826
King Wilhelm von Wuerttemberg writes to Secretary of State granting Paul Wilhelm apanage
September 1, 1826
Caroline von Schiller becomes governess at Carlsruhe
January 18, 1827
King of Wuerttemberg appoints Castle Mergentheim for Paul Wilhelm
March 27, 1827
Beethoven dies
April 17, 1827
Paul Wilhelm marries Sophie von Thurn und Taxis

1828
Paul Wilhelm's first proofs of diary of first trip to America printed
October 6, 1828
Death of Charlotte, Queen of Wuerttemberg, daughter of George III of Great Britain
April 27, 1829
Separation of Paul Wilhelm and Sophie by contract
May 1829
Paul Wilhelm and Pomp to Paris, Bordeaux, Spain, and back to Bordeaux
August 5, 1829
Paul Wilhelm and Pomp in San Domingo
December 1, 1829
Paul Wilhelm and Pomp arrive in St. Louis
December 23, 1829
Paul Wilhelm leaves St. Louis to ascend the Missouri
January 5, 1830
Paul Wilhelm reaches the Kansas River
January 6, 1830
Paul Wilhelm arrives at garrison Leavenworth
May 19, 1830
Paul Wilhelm and Pomp at Ft. Union
September 1830
Paul Wilhelm floats downriver in pirogue with tame eagle and buys flour in Lexington
October 30, 1830
Paul Wilhelm arrives in St. Louis and leaves for New Orleans
November 1, 1830
Paul Wilhelm on the steamboat *New Jersey*, which is snagged near Ste. Genevieve
December 21, 1830
Paul Wilhelm departs New Orleans for Tampico

* * *

August 21, 1851
Paul Wilhelm leaves St. Louis on the steamboat **Pocahontas** for the Missouri River
August 24, 1851
Paul Wilhelm passes Boonville, Franklin, Glasgow, Brunswick and Miami on his trip up the Missouri River aboard the **Pocahontas**
November 4, 1851
Paul Wilhelm returning from Ft. Laramie; reaches Little Blue River; snowing
November 9, 1851
Reaches Blue River; snowstorm
November 11, 1851
Horse dies; snowstorm
November 12, 1851
Second horse dies during icestorm
November 26, 1851
Paul Wilhelm leaves Big Sandy Creek in mail stage; new snowstorm
December 2, 1851
Louis Napoleon coup d'etat in Paris
December 6, 1851
Paul Wilhelm leaves Independence on mail stage via Wellington and Lexington
December 7, 1851
Paul Wilhelm passes through Marshall and Arrow Rock, and arrives in Boonville
December 8, 1851
Paul Wilhelm visits Dr. Kueckelhan and Carl Franz Aehle
December 9, 1851
Paul Wilhelm visits Dr. Kueckelhan, writes, and checks out mail stage

December 11, 1851
Paul Wilhelm makes entry in City Hotel register, and decides not to take the steamboat **St. Ange** to St. Louis

December 12, 1851
Paul Wilhelm sends his **Letter from Boonville** (published February 1852)

December 13, 1851
E.C. Angelroth of St. Louis sends letter to von Neurath, Stuttgart, on survival of Paul Wilhelm

December 14, 1851
Paul Wilhelm at Aehle's; church visit

December 15, 1851
Paul Wilhelm suffering badly from cold

December 16, 1851
Paul Wilhelm makes observations about Boonville

December 17, 1851
Reynold, Houghton, etc. arrive in Boonville, or later [?]

December 20, 1851
Paul Wilhelm notes arrival of "Gov. Howton" in Boonville (55 days from Santa Fe)

February 20, 21, 22, and 24, 1852
Letter from Boonville published

August 28, 1856
Paul Wilhelm writes Moellhausen and attributes their survival to "divine providence"

November 21, 1860
Paul Wilhelm falls ill at Castle Mergentheim

November 25, 1860
Death of Paul Wilhelm, Duke von Wuerttemberg

SELECT BIBLIOGRAPHY

Aehle, Edwin H. *Complete Genealogy and True Original Crest of the Aehle Family*, privately printed, collection of the State Historical Society of Missouri, Columbia, Mo.

Anderson, Hattie M. "The Evolution of a Frontier Society in Missouri, 1815-1828," *Missouri Historical Review*, 32 (April 1938 and July 1938), and 33 (October 1938).

Barry, Louise. *The Beginning of the West*. Topeka, Kansas State Historical Society, 1972.

Bauser, Friedrich. "The Journeys of Duke Paul, the Records Concerning Them and Their Literary Value," *South Dakota Historical Collection*, 1938.

"The Boonslick Country." compilation of materials by Charles van Ravenswaay, et. al. *Bulletin of the Missouri Historical Society*, 6 (July 1950).

Boonville (Mo.) *Weekly Observer*. Selected issues 1840-1861. State Historical Society of Missouri Collection, Columbia, Mo.

Bray, Robert T. "Historical-Archaeological Investigations in Central Missouri: Boone's Lick Salt Works, 1805-33," *The Missouri Archaeologist*, 48 (December 1987)

Butscher, Louis C. "A Brief Biography of Prince Paul Wilhelm of Wuerttemberg, and An Account of Adventures in the Great American Desert by His Royal Highness, Duke Paul Wilhelm von Wuerttemberg," *New Mexico Historical Review*, 17 (July 1942)

Brunswicker (Brunswick, Mo.) Selected issues, 1847-1857. State Historical Society of Missouri Collection, Columbia, Mo.

Chappell, Phil E. "A History of the Missouri River." *Kansas State Historical Collections*, 9 (1906).

Clark, Charles Upson. "Excerpts from the Journals of Prince

Paul of Württemberg," *Southwestern Historical Quarterly*, 15 (1959).
Commercial Bulletin (Boonville, Mo.) Selected issues, 1846-1847. State Historical Society of Missouri Collection, Columbia, Mo.
Cooper County Papers. Joint Collection University of Missouri Western Historical Manuscripts Collection-Columbia, State Historical Society of Missouri Manuscripts.
Deed Books, Cooper County Recorder of Deeds, Boonville, Mo.
Deed Books, Howard County Recorder of Deeds, Fayette, Mo.
DeSmet, Father Pierre J. *Life, Letters and Travels*, ed. H.M. Chittenden. 4 vols., Cleveland, 1905.
Duden, Gottfried. *Report on a Journey to the Western States of North America....* Trans. by George H. Kellner, Elsa Nagel, Adolf E. Schroeder and W.M. Senner, Columbia, State Historical Society of Missouri and University of Missouri Press, 1980.
"Duke Paul Wilhelm Collection in The British Museum," *American Indian Art*, 7.
Dyer, Robert L. *Boonville: An Illustrated History*. Boonville, Pekitanoui Publications, 1986.
Esbach, Friedrich-Carl. *Das herzogliche Haus Württemberg zu Carlsruhe in Schlesien*. Stuttgart, Kohlhammer, 1906.
Flint, Timothy. *Recollections of the Last Ten Years in the Valley of the Mississippi*. Carbondale, Southern Illinois University Press, 1968.
Fremont, John C. *The Exploring Expedition to the Rocky Mountains*, Washington D.C., Smithsonian Institute, 1988.
Glasgow (Mo.) *Times*, selected issues, 1848-1861. State Historical Society of Missouri Collection, Columbia, Mo.
Graf, Andreas. *Der Tod der Wölfe*. Berlin, Dunker & Humbolt, 1991.

_____. *Abenteuer und Geheimnis, Die Romane Balduin Möllhausens*. Freiburg/Breisgau Gy, Rombach, 1993.
Gregg, Jane. "Historical Sketch: Christ Church, Boonville, 1835-1935," pamphlet, no publisher given.
Guest Register, City Hotel, Boonville, Mo., Wilma Brengarth Bledsoe Collection, Kansas City, Mo.
Hebard, Grace R. *Sacajawea, a Guide and Interpreter of the Lewis and Clark Expedition...* Glendale, Arthur H. Clark Company, 1933.
"Historic Survey of Boonville, Missouri," Report prepared by the Friends of Historic Boonville for the Missouri State Office of Historic Preservation, 1979-1980.
History of Howard and Cooper Counties, Missouri. St. Louis, National Historical Company, 1883.
Hoffhaus, Charles E. *Chez Les Canses: Three Centuries at Kawsmouth, The French Foundations of Metropolitan Kansas City.* Kansas City, The Lowell Press, 1984.
Houck, Louis. *History of Missouri.* 3 vols. Chicago, R.R. Donnelley and Sons Company, 1908.
Howard, Harold P. *Sacajawea.* Norman, University of Oklahoma Press, 1971.
Hussey, John, and Michael Harrison, eds. *Early Sacramento, Glimpses of John Augustus Sutter, The Hok Farm and Neighboring Indian Tribes by Prince Paul H.R.H. Duke Paul Wilhelm of Württemberg.* Sacramento, Ca., The Sacramento Book Collector's Club, 1973.
Illustrated Atlas Map of Cooper County, Missouri. St. Louis, Atlas Publishing Co., 1877
Immigration Records, Cooper County Recorder of Deeds, Boonville, Mo.
James, Edwin, comp. *Account of an Expedition from Pittsburgh to the Rocky Mountains, Performed in the Years 1819 and '20: Under Command of Major Stephen H. Long. From the Notes of Major Long, Mr. T. Say, and Other Gentle-

men of the Exploring Party. 2 vols. Philadelphia, H.C. Carey and I. Lea, 1822-23.

Johnson, Ella. *The Economic Development of the Boonslick Country (as reflected in the Missouri Intelligencer).* M.A. Thesis, University of Missouri, 1931.

Johnson, W.F. *History of Cooper County, Missouri.* Topeka, Historical Publishing Company, 1919.

"Journal of William L. Sublette," in *Mississippi Valley Historical Review*, 6, (June 1919).

Karl Bodmer's America. Introduction by William H. Goetzmann, annotations by David C. Hunt and Marsha V. Gallagher, and artist's biography by William J. Orr. Omaha, Neb., Joslyn Art Museum and University of Nebraska Press, 1984.

Kellner, George H. *The German Element on the Urban Frontier: St. Louis 1830-1860.* Ph.D. diss., University of Missouri, 1973.

Kennerly, William Clark, as told to Bessie K. Russell. "My Hunting Trip to the Rockies in 1843," *Colorado Magazine*, XXII (January 1945).

Levens, Henry C. and Nathaniel M. Drake. *A History of Cooper County, Missouri...* St. Louis, Perrin & Smith, 1876.

Lewis, Meriwether, and William Clark. *History of the Expedition under the Command of Lewis and Clark.* Ed. by Elliott Coues. 4 vols. New York, Francis P. Harper, 1893.

Lucas Papers. Missouri Historical Society, St. Louis.

McDermott, John Francis. *George Caleb Bingham, River Portraitist.* Norman, University of Oklahoma Press, 1959.

_____. editor. *Travelers on the Western Frontier.* Urbana, University of Illinois Press, 1970.

Mattes, Merrill J. *The Great Platte River Road.* Lincoln, University of Nebraska Press, 1969.

Memoirs of Carl Franz Aehle, 1898. Private collection of Mike Aehle, St. Louis, Mo.

Miller, David H. *Trip to Fort Laramy*, ms, translation of transcripts made from Camp photos, SIUE.

Missouri Census, 1810 through 1880, including "Products of Industry for Boonville," 1840-1880, and "Slave Census," 1850-1860. Columbia, State Historical Society of Missouri.

Missouri Intelligencer and Boon's Lick Advertiser, selected issues, 1819-1830. State Historical Society of Missouri Collection, Columbia, Mo.

Missouri Register (Boonville, Mo.) Selected issues, 1840-1845. State Historical Society of Missouri Collection, Columbia, Mo.

Missouri Republican (St. Louis, Mo.) Selected issues, 1836-1865. State Historical Society of Missouri Collection, Columbia, Mo.

Möllhausen, Heinrich Balduin. "Account of an Adventure in the Great American Desert," *New Mexico Historical Review*, 17 (July 1942)

_____. *Diary of a Journey from the Mississippi to the Coasts of the Pacific.* London, 1858.

Morgan, Dale L. *The West of William H. Ashley, 1822-1838.* Denver, Old West Publishing Company, 1964.

Oglesby, Richard E. *Manuel Lisa and the Opening of the Missouri Fur Trade.* Norman, University of Oklahoma Press, 1963.

Paillou, Emile R. *Home Town Sketches.* Boston, The Stratford Co., 1926.

Pike, Zebulon Montgomery. *Journals, with Letters and Related Documents.* Edited by Donald Jackson. 2 vols. Norman, University of Oklahoma Press, 1966.

Primm, James Neal. *Lion of the Valley: St. Louis, Missouri.* Boulder, Colo., Pruett Publishing Co., 1981.

Rafferty, Milton D. *Historical Atlas of Missouri.* Norman, University of Oklahoma Press, 1982.

Robins, Ruby Matson, ed. "Americans in the Valley." 14 part series in consecutive issues of *Missouri Historical Review*, 45 (October 1950) through 48 (January 1954).

Rowan, Steven. Selected and translated by. *Germans for a Free Missouri: Translations from the St. Louis Radical Press, 1857-1862.* Columbia, University of Missouri Press, 1983.

Sachsen-Altenburg, Hans, Prince von. "Duke Paul von Wuerttemberg in St. Louis, 1823-1858," unpublished ms., 1997

———. "History in the Making: A Fraudulent Manuscript of a German Duke's Visit in 1850 to California," unpublished ms., 1995

———. "The Ducal Houses of Sachsen-Altenburg," unpublished ms., 1996

St. Louis Enquirer. Selected issues, 1818-1824. State Historical Society of Missouri Collection, Columbia, Mo.

St. Louis Intelligencer. Selected issues, 1850-1857. State Historical Society of Missouri Collection, Columbia, Mo.

Scharf, John Thomas. *History of St. Louis City and County, from the Earliest Periods to the Present Day.* 2 vols. Philadelphia, L.H. Everts & Company, 1883.

Schroeder, Walter A. "Spread of Settlement in Howard County: 1810-1859," *Missouri Historical Review*, 63 (October 1968).

Spahn, Raymond Juergen. "German Accounts of Early Nineteenth Century." *Papers on Language & Literature*, 14 (1978)

Thorp, Judge Joseph. *Early Days in the West: Along the*

Missouri One Hundred Years Ago. Liberty, Mo., Irving Gilmer, publisher, 1924.

Trexler, Harrison A. *Slavery in Missouri:1804-1865*, Baltimore, Johns Hopkins Press, 1914.

Vestal, Stanley. *The Missouri.* New York, Farrar & Rinehart, 1945.

Van Ravenswaay, Charles H. *The Arts and Architecture of German Settlements in Missouri.* Columbia, University of Missouri Press, 1977.

_____. *Papers.* Joint Collection University of Missouri Western Historical Manuscripts Collection-Columbia and State Historical Society of Missouri.

_____. *Papers.* Missouri Historical Society, St. Louis.

Viles, Jonas. "Old Franklin: A Frontier Town of the Twenties," *Mississippi Valley Historical Review*, 9 (March 1923).

Voss, Stuart F. "Town Growth in Central Missouri: 1815-1880," *Missouri Historical Review*, 64 (October 1969, January 1970 and April 1970).

Wagner, Henry R., and Charles L. Camp. *The Plains and the Rockies: A Bibliography of Original Narratives of Travel and Adventure, 1800-1865.* San Francisco, Grabhorn Press, 1937.

Walker, Mack. *Germany and the Emigration.* Cambridge, Harvard University Press, 1964.

Western Emigrant (Boonville, Mo.). Selected issues, 1839-1840. State Historical Society of Missouri Collection, Columbia, Mo.

Weekly Democrat (Boonville, Mo.) Selected issues, 1848-1850. State Historical Society of Missouri Collection, Columbia, Mo.

Wetmore, Alphonso. *Gazetteer of the State of Missouri*, St. Louis, C. Keemle, 1837.

Wied-Neuwied, Maximilian Alexander Philipp, Prinz von.

Reise in das innere Nord-Amerika in den Jahren 1832 bis 1834. 2 B., mit Bild Atlas. Coblenz, J. Haelscher, 1839-41.

_____. *Travels in the Interior North America....* Tr. by Hannibal Evans Lloyd, ed. by Reuben Gold Thawaites. 4 vols. in Early Western Travel Series, Vols. XXI-XXIV. Cleveland, Arthur H. Clark Company, 1906.

Wittke, Carl. *Refugees of Revolution: The German Forty-Eighters in America.* Westport, Conn., Greenwood, 1952.

Worms, Elfred M. *A Condensed History of Mascoutah,* Illinois, typewritten ms., no date.

Württemberg, Paul Wilhelm, Duke of. *Erste Reise nach dem nordlichen Amerika in den Jahren 1822 bis 1824.* Stuttgart und Teubingen, Verlag der J.G. Cotta'schen Buchhandlung, 1835.

_____. *First Journey to North America in the Years 1822 to 1824.* Tr. by William G. Bek. *South Dakota Historical Collections,* 19 (1938).

_____. *Travels in North America 1822-1824.* Translated by W. Robert Nitske. Edited by Savoie Lottinville. Norman, University of Oklahoma Press, 1973.

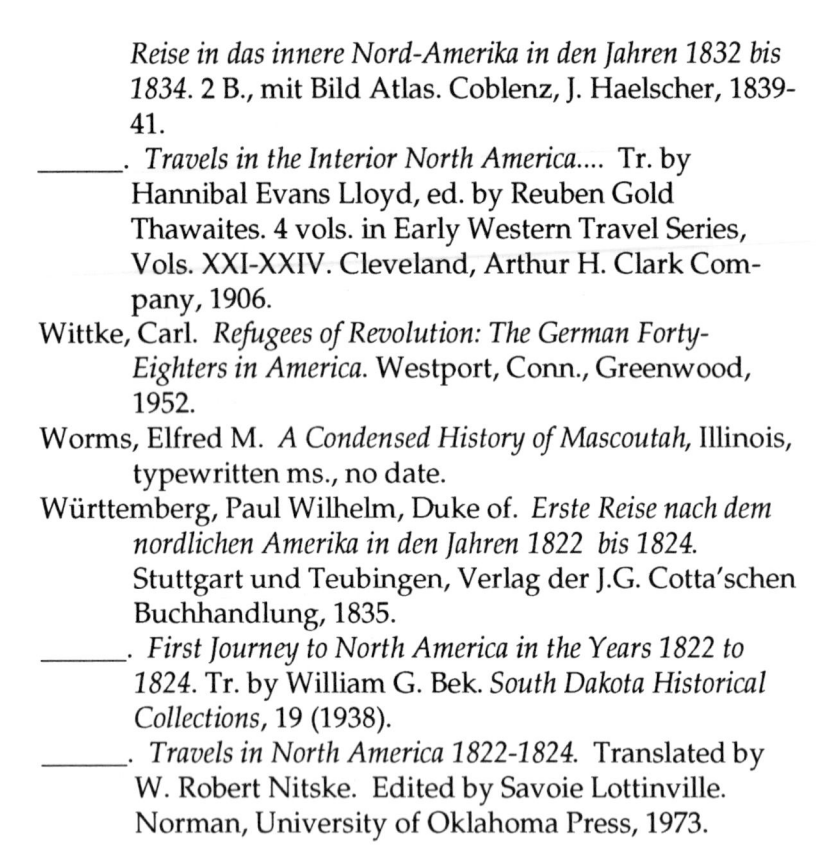

Index

[Note: No effort has been made to provide comprehensive index entries for **Boonville**, **Duke Paul**, or the **Missouri River** since such references are pervasive in the book. Most **botanical** and **zoological** terms are grouped under those general headings.]

Adams, settlement of 153
Adelphai College 130
Aden 214
Aehle, Carl Franz (Charles F.) 5, 14-15, 22, 117, 119-120, 123, 128, 136, 143-145, 150, 153, 155-158, 161-168, 170, 210, 242-243
Aehle Coat of Arms 155
Aehle, Dunnica & Co. 121
Aehle, E. F. 121
Aehle, Edwin H. 119
Aehle, Elizabeth 117
Aehle, Ernst August 119
Aehle, Mike
  7, 14, 22, 117, 153, 155, 156
Africa 25, 172, 213
Allgemeine Zeitung (Augsburg General Newspaper) 176, 178, 186, 194, 201
Altenburg 14, 81
Amalie, Auguste 35
Angelroth, Ernst Karl 138, 144, 186, 213, 243
Anglican 130, 144, 145, 137
Anzeiger des Westens 163, 192
Apaches 207
Arapaho Indians 207, 208
Arikara Indians 79, 90
Arkansas 194
Arrow Rock (Pierre de la Fleche) 55, 67-69, 74, 103, 112, 210, 221, 223, 226, 228-229, 233, 242
Ash Hollow 110, 111, 202
Ashley, Gen. William H. 53, 79, 90
Asia 25
Audubon 26
Australia 25, 29, 213, 214
Austria 123, 162

Babcock, Rufus 48
Baden 118, 119, 122, 189
Bailey's Mansion House 124-125
Balmer and Weber 120
Baltimore, Md. 115, 120
Bancroft Library 139
Baptist (church; religion) 15, 48, 121, 130, 135, 137, 198
Barth 144
Barton, David 53
Basque country 83
Battayano, Cuba 63
Battle of Leipzig 238
Bauser, Friedrich 98, 147-148, 152-153
Bavaria 34, 35, 95, 115, 119, 122
Bavaria, Princess of (Auguste Amalie) 35
Bayonne meats 196
Beauharnais, Eugene 35
Beauharnais, Hortense de 149
Becknell, William 50
Beethoven 82
Bell, Rev. William G. 130, 132
Bendele, Louis 118
Benouai, Mr. 11, 54, 64, 66
Benton, Thomas Hart 53, 55
Berlin 13, 26, 97, 214
Berlin Scientific Society 154, 160
Bernard, John 119
Berthold, Pratte & Chouteau 40, 238
Big Blue River 201
Big Canoe People (Missouri Indians) 5, 21
Big Manitou Creek 62, 103
Big Rock River 201
Big Sandy Creek 111, 209, 242
Big Vermillion River 201
Bingham, George Caleb 50
Bingham, Henry 50
Black Elk Speaks 20
Black Hawk 198
Black Hills 181, 205
Black Snake Creek 198
blizzard 15, 16, 17, 28, 30, 111
Blue Mill 108
Blue River 110, 242

Blufftown 76, 77
Bodmer, Karl 25, 89, 180
Boernstein, Heinrich 163, 167, 192
Boggs, Lilburn W. 53
Boller, John H. 119
Bonaparte, Hieronymus, King of Westphalia 35, 238
Bonaparte, Napoleon (see Napoleon)
Bonn 97
Bonne Femme River 48, 49, 63
Bonneville, Benjamin L. E. de] 178
Boone 123
Boone County, Mo. 49
Boone, Daniel 43
Boone, Daniel Morgan 43
Boone, Nathan 43
Boone's Lick (Boon's Lick, Boonslick) 15, 19, 22, 30, 43-44, 47-50, 54-55, 109, 113
Boonslick Historical Society 15, 23, 84
Boonville Democrat 129
Boonville Herald 129
Boonville schools 130-132
Boonville Thespian Society 131
Boonville Weekly Advertiser 128
Boonville Weekly Observer 116, 117, 127, 129, 170
Bordeaux, France 83, 241
border dispute between Missouri and Kansas 167
Bosnia 83
botanical garden 11, 55
botanical observations (Duke Paul) 67-69, 181, 195-198
bottom lands 194
Bourbons 30, 149, 150
Brackenridge 25
Bradbury, John 25, 47, 48, 49
Braunschweig 14
Brazil 172, 213
Bremen 92, 120, 214
Brent, Robert T. 129
brewing beer 135, 136
Brington 74
British Museum 13, 26, 92, 93, 94, 215
Brule (Sioux) Indians 206

Brunswick 104, 115, 242
Brunswicker 141
Brusseau, Roland 236
Buffalo, New York 174
Burnett, Peter 90
butterflies 6, 62, 63

Caillou 54, 61, 64, 66, 67, 75, 79
Calhoun, James S. 148
California 90, 95, 97, 165, 166, 168, 182, 198, 205, 206
California Gold Rush 96, 118, 167
California pilgrims 180
California road 199
Callaway County, Mo. 49
Camden, Mo. 107
Camp, Charles 97
Campbell, William M. 84
Campbellites 137
cañadas 180
Cap à l'Ail 102
Caribbean islands 83
Carlsruhe, Silesia 32, 33, 81, 88, 214, 215, 237, 240
Carolina parakeet 105, 219, 232, 235
Carson, Christopher "Kit" 11, 44, 52, 54
Carson, Lindsay 44
Cassel 120
cast iron stoves 146
Catawba grapes (see also wine) 98, 135, 159, 197
Catesby 26
Catherine the Great 33
Catholic 130, 163, 190, 191
Catholic mission 199
Cedar Creek 49, 54, 90
Cedar Lake 190
census 121-124
Central Brewery and Boonville Wine Company 135
Ceylon 214
Chapultepec 195
Charbonneau, Jean Baptiste "Pomp" 5, 13, 27, 33, 345-36, 38, 40, 79,

254

81-84, 88-90, 111, 237, 239-241
Charbonneau, Toussaint 79
Chariton River 48, 104
Chauvin's Ferry 239
Cheyenne Indians 207, 208
Chicago, Il. 135
Chile 211
Chimney Rock 110, 180, 203, 204
Chouteau, Pierre 27, 40, 138, 239
Chouteau Trading Post, 43
Christ Episcopal Church 145
Cincinatti Zoo 232
Cincinnati, Oh. 39, 87, 120
City Hotel 5, 124-126, 128-129, 131, 140, 243
Civil War 118, 134, 135, 165, 167, 169
Clark, William 27, 40, 237, 239
Clay, Senator Henry 165
Clay's Compromise 166
Cole, Hannah 44, 113
Cole, Stephen 44, 113
Cole, William Temple 44
Colorado 88
Colorado River 97
Columbia, Mo. 16, 129, 137
Columbia River 205
columbine 229
Columbus, Christopher 62
Comanche Indians 92
Commercial Hotel 126
communist activity 193
communistic revolutionary zeal 162
Compromise of 1850 166
Constantinople 88
Continental Divide 35
Cooper, Benjamin 44, 113
Cooper County 15, 19, 56, 57, 84, 114, 122, 123, 128, 167
Cooper County Circuit Court 122
Cooper, James Fenimore 179
cordilleras 180
Côte sans Dessein, Mo. 100
Council Bluffs 53, 79
Courthouse Rock 110
Creole 54, 75, 78, 108, 202
Crimea 33
Crow Indians 207

Cuba 39, 62, 63, 162, 164, 165, 193, 239, 240
Curtis and Wood trading post 239
Cycle of the West 20

Dacotah Indian tribes 206
Dade's [John] Hotel 124-125
Darmstadt 135
de Smet, Father 89, 110
Deam, Joe 154
Declaration of Independence 34
Democrats 166, 193
divorce procedings 87
Dresden 186
Drips, Andrew 138
DuBourg, Bishop 39
Duchess of Saint Leu 149
Duden, Gottfried 115
Duke of Parma, Italy 35
Duke Paul Wilhelm Collection (British Museum) 92-94
Dunnica, W. F. 121
Dutch elm disease 225, 235
Dutch Indies 211

eagle 6, 85, 94, 106, 241
Edwards, O. D. 155
Egypt 87, 157, 161
Elba 149
Elm Grove 90
Elster River 120
England 33, 150, 162, 192
environmental museum 81
Episcopal 15, 121, 130, 132
Eppstein, Viet and Joseph 118
Erfurt 120
Ethnological Museum of Berlin 215
Europe 25
European zoologists 202
Evangelical 130

Falkenstein, Baroness von 97
falls 87
Falls at St. Anthony 174

family farms 123
Femme Osage River 43
Ferrill family 68
ferry boat 112
Fillmore, President 193
fires on the prairie 208
Fish Creek 77, 107, 194
Fitzwilliam, Charles W. W. 110, 206
Flint, Timothy 44
floods 10, 19, 28, 56, 113, 24
flora and fauna analysis (Jason Fridley) 219-236
flora and fauna collection (Duke Paul's) 235
Florissant, Mo. 40
Force, Christian 118
Fort John 110, 138, 207
Fort Kearney 201, 209
Fort Laramie 28, 30, 91, 96-97, 109, 110, 152, 157, 160-161, 164, 167, 174, 198, 205-206, 208, 210, 242
Fort Laramie Treaty council 109
Fort Mandan 237
Fort Osage 107, 108
Fort Union 85, 241
Forty-Eighter 163
Franklin, Mo. 11-12, 18-22, 27-28, 42, 46, 49-51, 55-56, 63-68, 84, 103, 113, 171-172, 197, 210, 226, 239, 242
Franks, Augustus Woolaston 92
Fremont, John C. 90, 111 178, 180, 199, 203
French Hugenot 115
French Revolution 34
Friends of Historic Boonville 132
frost injuries 136, 143, 210
Fruitage Farm 55, 56
Fuchs, Anthony 118
Fugitive Slave Act 166
Fulton, Mo. 131, 137
Fur Traders Descending the Missouri 13

Gamble, Hamilton 53
Gasconade River 137, 152, 194

geographical and geological observations (Duke Paul) 178-181, 202-205
George III, King of Great Britain 34, 237, 241
Gera 119, 120, 210
German bigots 188
German cultural traditions 135
German immigrants 115, 122, 130, 131, 135, 166, 168
German Lutherans 144
German Methodists 163
German press 163, 191
German refugees 172
German revolution 192
German revolutionary heroes 189
German wine-growers 197
Gesangvereins (singing clubs) 15, 134, 213
Gila River 180, 182
Glasgow , Mo. 48, 103-104, 121, 129, 198, 242
Goettingen 115
Gotha 120
Grand Chariton 103
Grand River 48, 78, 104, 194
Grande Bonne Femme Creek 62, 63
Grande Passe 105
Great Lakes 174
Great Platte River Road 96
Green River 205
Gross, Phillip 119

Haas, William D. 119, 135, 136, 159
Hain, George 15, 118
Hamburg 92, 238
Hameln 120
Hammond, Allen 125
Hannover 33, 115, 118, 120, 210
Hapsburg family 162
Hardeman, John 11, 54-56
Hardeman's Garden 68
Harding, Chester 50
Harrison, Michael 98
Havana 96, 239
Heidenheim, Count of 33, 214

256

Heisrich, Reinhard 118
Herculaneum 195
Hermann, Mo. 98, 101, 103, 115, 159, 197-198
Hesse-Darmstadt 119, 122
Hesse-Wartegg, Ernst Baron von 26
Hicklin Lake 74
hired hands 187
Hirth, Abraham 118
Hohenberg, Baron von 33, 84
Holland, Louis, King of 149
Holzminden 115
Horse Creek 109, 203
horseflies (gadflies) 77, 234
Houck, Louis 68
Houghton, Joab 148, 243
Howard County, Mo. 15, 52, 123
Humboldt, Baron Alexander von 26, 97, 154, 160
Hungarians 187, 189
Hussey, John 98

Ile aux Cèdres 101
Illinois 96, 178, 190, 195, 197
immigration records 122
Independence, Mo.
    28, 50, 53, 112, 138, 148, 154, 171, 198, 210, 242
India 214
Indian mounds 11
Indian painting 62
Indian Treaty Council (Ft. Laramie) 96
Indiana 89
Iowa Indians 104
Irish 49, 52, 63, 187-188
Irving, Washington 179
Italy 214
Iturbide, Emperor of Mexico 238-239
Ives, Lt. Joseph C. 97

Jackson, Claiborne F. 53
Jacobite communists 192
Jahn, Friedrich Ludwig 134
James Peak 181, 205, 207
Jefferson City 55, 98, 101, 129, 136-137, 139, 152, 169, 198, 213, 220
Jesuits 110, 112
Joncar 102

Kansas City, Mo. 11, 16, 43, 57, 109, 154, 172
Kansas (Kaw) River 27, 40, 43, 54, 64-65, 67, 78-79, 81, 83, 187, 199, 239 (Curtis and Wood trading post on the), 241
Kansas-Nebraska Act of 1854 167
Kanzas 43, 178, 194, 198
keelboat 27, 54, 168
Keil, Christian 118
Kemper, Frederick T. (and his school) 21, 131, 133
Kennerly, William Clark 91
Kentucky 44, 52, 113
Kinkel, Gottfried 193
Kinney, Joseph 15
Kiowa Indians 92, 111, 207
Kline, Leonard 118
Knights of the Teutonic Order 35
Kossuth, Lajos (Louis) 162-163, 189, 206,
Kueckelhan, Dr. Augustus 5, 13-15, 115-116, 118-119, 121, 128, 136, 150, 157-159, 161-168, 210, 242
Kueckelhan, Henry 115

La Côte du Soldat de Duchaine 74
Lamine River 68, 112, 118, 144
Lakes St. Croix and Pepin 174
land values 123
Laramie Peak 205
Laramie River 73, 110, 205
Leavenworth, Ks. 241
Lewis and Clark 25, 35, 43, 172
Lewis, Meriwether 27, 237
Lewis River 205
Lexington, Mo.
    85, 106, 210, 221, 230, 231, 242
Liberty, Mo. 57, 77, 78, 109
Liberty Landing 108
limestone 101-102 (bluffs), 202 (strange

tertiary formations), 224 (glade areas)
Linden Ethnological Museum of Stuttgart 215
Lisa, Manuel 47
Little Blue River 201, 209, 242
Little Manitou Creek 102
Little Rock River 201
Little Vermillion 201
Long, Major Stephen 25, 50, 178
Long's Peak 205
Lopez, Narcisco 164, 193
Lorraine 119, 123
Lottinville, S. 219
Louis, King of Holland 149
Louisiana 34
Lovejoy Library, Southern Illinois University 177
Luther, Martin 172, 191
Lutheran 96, 130, 163, 190

Mack, Elizabeth Jane 121, 155
Mack, Nathaniel 121, 134, 155
Magellan, Straits of 211
Magyar agitator 206
mail stage 111, 136, 137, 143, 146, 152, 242
Male Collegiate Institute 131
Manchester 153
Manitou, Ile du Grand, and La Côte du Grand 60
Mansion House hotel 5, 13, 113, 124-128, 142, 158
Marais du Sorcier 74
Marshall, Mo. 112, 210, 229, 242
Marx, Karl 151
Maryland 89
Mascoutah, Il. 213
Massachusetts 52
Mato Tatanka (Bull Bear) 93
Maucler, Baron von 173, 174, 175, 176
Maximilian, Emperor of Mexico 151
Mazatlan 96, 172
McPherson, Edward 5, 126, 128
McPherson, Mary J. "Auntie" 125
Melbourne, Australia 214

Minnesota 174
Mergentheim 35-37, 82, 87-88, 95, 175, 189, 211, 214-215, 238, 240, 243
Methodists 130, 137, 190-191, 198
Mexico 87, 172, 183, 195, 238
Miami 105, 231, 242
Middleton, James H. 129
Miege, Rev. John B. 199
Miller, Alfred Jacob 89
Miller, Dr. David 85, 97
Miller, John 53
Mills, Dr. William 118
Milwaukee, Wi. 190
missions 198
Mississippi River 26, 34, 39, 105-106, 139, 147, 160, 165, 178, 186, 239
Mississippi Valley Historical Association 51
Missouri Female College 130
Missouri Historical Society 12, 145
Missouri Indians 21
Missouri Intelligencer 11, 49, 54, 55, 56, 83, 85
Missouri State Fair 135
Missouri's economic life 194
Moellhausen, Balduin 28, 96-98, 110-112, 152, 161, 186, 243
Monarch & Co. 120
monarchial conservative party 163, 192
Montevideo 213
Mormon emigration 167, 182
Moslems 83
mosquitoes 31, 60, 67, 72, 77, 201, 233
mountains of New Spain 201
Mozart 82
Mt. Aetna 181
Mueller, Amelia 119
Multamahau River 205
Murthly Castle, Scotland 88

Napoleon Bonaparte 29-30, 32-35, 38, 81, 119, 148-151, 237-238, 242
Nashville, Tn. 102
Nassau 119

National Assembly 150
naturalization 122
Neihardt, John G. 20
Neurath, von 243
New Franklin, Mo. 53, 84
New Mexico 148, 166
New Orleans, La. 39, 79-80, 83, 87, 89, 96, 107, 161, 164, 186, 210, 213, 238-241
New York 150, 213-214
Newfoundland 240
Niagara Falls 213
Nile 157, 161
Nitske, W. R. 219
Nolte, Vincente 80
Nuttall 26

O'Fallon, John 55
Oglala (Sioux) Indians 93, 206, 208
Ohio River 39, 239
Oktoberfest 82
Oregon 167, 198, 206
Oregon Trail 16, 90, 96, 111
Osage bow, arrows and quiver 94
Osage Indians 40, 78
Osage Orange wood 94
Osage River 48, 49, 64, 102, 137, 152, 194
Otten, John 118

Pacific Ocean 35, 180, 237
Padouca River 201, 205
Panama 96, 180, 213
Paris, France 83, 95, 148, 241
Patterson, Nicholas 49
Paul, Czar of Russia 33
Pauline 30, 95, 213, 216
Paulsburg 214-216
Pawnee Indians 111, 209
Peck, John Mason 48-49
Pekitanoui (Missouri River) 5, 21
Pennsylvania 165
Pennsylvania Dutch 52
Penultima 55
Perthshire 88

Petit Manitou 102
Petite Bonne Femme Creek 63, 102
Petite Femme Osage Creek 137
Petite Saline Creek (Little Saline or Little Salt) 57, 59, 102, 224
petroglyphs 6
Philadelphia, Pa. 135
Pierce, Peter (and his hotels) 5, 113, 125-129
Pikes Peak 154, 160-161
pipe organ 121
pirogue 13, 106, 241
Pittsburgh , Pa. 146
Plains Indians 20, 160
Platte River 28, 30, 96, 110, 178, 180-181, 199-203, 205-206, 208, 209
Pleasant Retreat Female Seminary 130
Plieninger, Professor Wilhelm 29, 173-177
Pointe à Ducharme 102
Poland 203
Polar Sea 179
Pomp (see Charbonneau)
pork slaughter houses 196
Portum 118
post wagons 113
Pottowatomi Indians 199
prairie 69, 72, 73, 136, 171, 195, 198, 202, 209, 223, 229
Prairie à la Mine 69
prairie fire 111, 209
Presbyterian 49, 130, 137, 198
Preuss, Dr. Charles 203
price of farms 123, 143
price of grapes 197
private schools 130
products of industry 124
Protestants, reformed 190
Prussia 33, 118-119, 122, 138, 151, 186
Prussian Consul General 213
Puritan revolution 192

Quarles, Margaret 118
quicksand 208

railroads 168-169
Red River 105
refugee-liberals 150
Regensburg 82
Reppley, George 119
Republic of France 150
Reuss, principality of 119
Revolution of 1848 211
revolutionary propaganda 191
Reynold 243
Rhine River 35
Richfield (Wayne City), Mo. 108
riding quirt 92
Rio Gila, 205
River of the Big Canoes 21
Rivercene 15
Rivière des Grands Os of the Creoles 100
Robideaux 110, 198, 207
Rocheport, Mo. 103, 137
Rocky Mountains
   39, 79, 85, 96, 106, 154, 160, 174, 178, 180-181, 202, 205
Roeschel, Ernest 119
Round Grove 90
Rousseau (Jean Jacques) 38
Russia 33, 38
Russian and Polish soldiers 216

Sabatizky, Polish tenor 154
sabbath-breakers 188
Sacagawea 5, 12, 27, 35, 40, 216
Sachsen-Altenburg, Dukes of, Duchy of 33, 119
Sachsen-Coburg (Saxe-Coburg) 118
Sachsen-Hildburghausen, Therese Duchess of 82
Sachsen-Weimar-Eisenach, Bernard, Duke of 26
Sacramento Book Collector's Club 98
Sacramento, Ca. 98
Sahm, George 119
Saline Creek 112
Salt Lake 182, 198, 206
salt spring 43
San Domingo 241

San Francisco, Ca. 96, 183
sandy meadows 221
Santa Ana (General) 165
Santa Fe 50, 52, 53, 148, 198
Sauk and Fox (Otogami) Indians 198
sawyers (river snags) 105
Saxony 96, 122
Schiller, Caroline von 33, 240
Schiller, Friedrich von 33
Schleisinger-Weil 190
Schumacher 95
Schwind, Mary 135
scientific collection 215
Scotland 88
Scotts Bluff 185, 203-205, 207
Sea of Cortez 205
Seultzer, Alexander 118
Shawnee Indians 198
Shaw, Henry 55
Shoshone Indian 27, 91, 207
Siberia 203
Sibley, Mo. 108
Sierras 96
Silesia 214, 215, 237
singing and gymnastic societies (Gesang-und Turnvereine) 134-135
Sioux Indians 111
slaves 52, 122-123, 165-166, 187
slave states 143, 166, 197
Smithsonian Institution 141
Snake Indians 207
snow storm 178, 209, 242
Snowmass Peak 181, 205
snowblindness 111
Soldier River 91
Sombart, Charles and Julius 168
South America 25, 29
South Pass 180, 205
South Platte River 89, 111
Southern aristocracy 135
Southern culture 167
Southern educational traditions 131
Southern religious tradition 129
South's right to secede 166
Spahn, Betty Alderton 97
Spahn, Dr. Raymond J. 97, 177

Spain 34, 35, 43, 83, 193, 241
Speed, William P. 125
Spiess, Pastor 213
Square and Compass (inn) 50
St. Charles, Mo. 19, 43, 47, 50, 84, 137, 147, 239
St. Joseph, Mo. 139, 198
St. Louis, Mo. 11, 13, 16, 22, 27-28, 30, 39-40, 43, 47, 55, 66, 79, 84-85, 87-90, 98, 113, 115, 118, 120-121, 137-139, 143-144, 147, 153, 158, 160, 162, 164, 167, 169, 171-172, 174, 178, 186, 195, 210, 214, 241-242
St. Petersburg, Russia 33
stagecoach 168
State Historical Society of Missouri 20, 22, 119, 129
state penitentiary 101
Ste. Genevieve 79, 87, 240, 241
steamboats 50, 85, 113, 135, 157, 168, 169, 172, 186, 197
  Cincinnati 79, 239-240
  Kansas 143
  Mandan 240
  New Jersey 87, 241
  Pocahontas 98, 242
  St. Ange 141-142, 24
  Smyrna 240
Stephens, Joseph L. 169
Stewart, Sir William Drummond 88, 111
Strassburg 190
Stretz, Frank 118
Stuttgart 13, 26, 81-82, 88, 138, 176, 215, 240, 243
Sublette, William L. 79, 88-90
Sudan (Nubia) 87, 172
Sutter, Colonel 96
Swabian Alb 95
swamps 67, 195, 229
Switzerland 14, 76, 123, 149, 150, 187

Tabeau Creek 67, 73
tales of a traveler 157

Tampico 241
Target shooting 76
Tasmania 214
telegraph 137, 169
Tennessee 44, 53, 55, 113
Teton Dakota (Sioux) shirt 93
Tetons 205
Texas 96, 97, 166, 193, 213
Theresienwiese 82
Thespian Hall 131, 135
Thuringia 119
Thurn und Taxis, Sophie Princess of 82, 96, 237, 240
Tierra del Fiego 214
Tierra del Fuego 213
tobacco 50, 52, 104, 196
Todd, C. W. 129
Tracy, Joshua 130, 132
travel incognito 214
Treasure in the River 21
Treaty of Cordoba 238
Trieste 88
Truby (Boonville photographer) 117
Turks 83
Turner Hall 15, 135
Twain, Mark 26
Tyrol 76

Umlauf 92
Union Town 199
University of Jena 120
University of Leipzig 119
University of Missouri 12, 15, 20, 51, 137
University of Tuebingen 88
Uruguay River 213
Utah 166, 167, 205-206
Utah Indians 207

Venezuela 164
viceroy of Egypt 87
Victoria, Queen of Great Britain 157
Vienna 88, 214
Viles, Jonas 51
Vine Clad City 117, 135

261

Virginia 44, 53, 113, 128, 131
Virginia Hotel 125
Vollrath, George 118

Wakarussi, River 198
War of 1812 44
Washington D.C. 166, 193
Weber, Wilhelm 163
Weimar 120
Wellington, Mo. 242
Wesley, John] 188
Wesleyans, German 191
West Indies 26
Western Emigrant 125, 129
Westminster College 131
Weston, Mo. 198
Westphalia, King of 35, 238
Westphalian meats 196
Westport, Mo. 90, 109
wetlands 234
Weyland, Louis 118
Whigs 129, 166, 193
Whipple, Capt. A.W. 97
Wied-Neuwied, Maximilian, Prince of 25, 89, 180
Wilmot Proviso 165
Wind River Mountains 91, 181, 205
wine (wine making and vineyards; see also Catawba grapes) 135-136, 197-198
Wisconsin 190
Woods, Dr. Kerry 236
Wooldridge 57, 224
Workman, David 52
World War II 26, 216
Wuerttemberg (numerous entries, see especially 31-40, 237-238, 240)
Wuerttemberg, Charlotte, Queen of 33, 237, 241
Wuerttemberg, Duke Maximilian of 215
Wuerttemberg, Friedrich, King of 32, 35, 38-39, 237
Wuerttemberg, Katharine Princess of 238
Wuerttemberg, king of, kingdom of 82, 158, 237-238, 240
Wuerttemberg State Archives (Hauptstaatsarchiv) 138, 174
Wuerttemberg, Wilhelm Eugen, Duke of 26
Wuerzburg 115
Wyan, Jacob 131

Yankee tricksters 188
Yellowstone River 142
Yellowstone Expedition 50
Yellowstone National Park 91
Young, Brigham 206

Zichlinsky, von 96, 98, 109, 110, 111, 161, 186
Zierlein 84
zoological observations (Duke Paul) 60, 182-184, 199-202

262

PRINCE HANS VON SACHSEN-ALTENBURG, a native of Germany, has spent many years living, studying and working in the United States as well as traveling extensively throughout the United States, Europe, the Far East and Russia. He has completed degrees in archaeology, sociology, anthropology, business, and languages.

Because his own family history is rooted in the central European kingdoms that later became Germany he developed an early interest in the lives and travels of a number of 19th century European aristocrats, especially Duke Paul of Wuerttemberg who made three extensive trips up the Mississippi and Missouri River valleys in the 1820s, 30s and 50s. In addition to the present volume, Prince Hans has plans to publish a complete biography of Duke Paul and his travels. He is also presently working on a book related to the expeditions of Stephen Watts Kearney.

ROBERT L. DYER is a native Missourian who has spent most of his life delving into the history and folklore of the Missouri River. He has a Masters degree in English and taught for a number of years at the University of Missouri-Columbia. For the last 15 years he has been part of the Missouri Arts Alliance's artist-in-education program and Young Audiences Inc. presenting school assemblies, workshops and residencies in public schools throughout the state.

He is a songwriter, free lance writer, publisher, and poet whose books include *Jesse James and the Civil War in Missouri*, *Oracle of the Turtle*, *Boonville: An Illustrated History*, and *The Big Canoe Songbook*. His recordings include *Songteller* (original songs relating to the Missouri River country), and two collections of Civil War songs from the Trans-Mississippi West, *Johnny Whistletrigger* and *Rebel in the Woods*, with noted Midwestern folk performers Cathy Barton and Dave Para.